97. 歹 chip 408
98. 瓦 tile 739
99. 牙 tooth 671
100. 车 car 416
101. 戈 lance 30
102. 止 toe 246
103. 日 sun 179
104. 曰 say 110
105. 中 middle 150
106. 贝 cowrie 140
107. 见 see 266
108. 父 father 264
109. 气 breath 64
110. 牛 cow 340
111. 手 hand 27
112. 毛 fur 114
113. 攵 knock 316
114. 片 slice 422
115. 斤 ax 342
116. 爪 (⺥) claws 306 (447)
117. 尺 foot (length) 949
118. 月 moon/meat 104
119. 殳 club 234
120. 欠 yawn 244
121. 风 wind 819
122. 氏 clan 276
123. 比 compare 660
124. 肀 "top of 肀" 109
125. 水 water 473

— 5 —

126. 立 stand 144
127. 疒 sick 604
128. 穴 cave 454
129. 衤 (side-) gown 290 (cp.161)
130. 夫 "top of 春" 811
131. 玉 jade 74
132. 示 sign 899
133. 去 go 556
134. 艹 "top of 劳" p. 221a
135. 甘 sweet 195
136. 石 rock 749
137. 龙 dragon p. 241a
138. 戊 halberd 517
139. 灬 "top of 常" 482
140. 业 business 714
141. 目 eye 129
142. 田 field 10
143. 由 from 799
144. 申 stretch 804

145. 皿 net 175
146. 皿 dish 138
147. 钅 (side-) gold 117 (cp. 209)
148. 矢 arrow 82
149. 禾 grain 81
150. 白 white 282
151. 瓜 melon p. 243b
152. 鸟 bird p. 215a
153. 皮 skin 747
154. 癶 back 796
155. 矛 spear p. 226a
156. 疋 bolt 326

— 6 —

157. 羊 (⺶,⺷) sheep 156
158. 犬 roll, p. 232b
159. 米 rice 126
160. 齐 line-up p. 217b
161. 衣 gown 152
162. 市 (亦) also 751
163. 耳 ear 256
164. 臣 bureaucrat p. 216b
165. 𢦏 "top of 栽" 470
166. 西 (覀) cover (west) 162
167. 束 thorn p. 229b
168. 亚 inferior p. 236b
169. 而 beard 986
170. 页 head 371
171. 至 reach 514
172. 光 light 839
173. 虍 tiger 772
174. 虫 bug 731
175. 缶 crock p. 234b
176. 耒 plow p. 219a
177. 舌 tongue 426
178. 竹 (⺮) bamboo 65
179. 臼 mortar 280
180. 自 small nose 619
181. 血 blood 1010
182. 舟 boat 583
183. 羽 wings 869
184. 艮 (⻗) stubborn 51

— 7 —

185. 言 words 57
186. 辛 bitter 70
187. 辰 early 851
188. 麦 wheat p. 246
189. 走 walk 227
190. 赤 red p. 216b

191. 豆 flask 797
192. 束 bundle 745
193. 酉 wine 474
194. 豕 pig 502
195. 里 village 145
196. 足 foot 247
197. 采 cull 620
198. 豸 snake p. 216b
199. 谷 valley 489
200. 身 torso 236
201. 角 horn 996

— 8 —

202. 青 green 249
203. 𠦝 "side of 朝" p. 227a
204. 雨 rain 368
205. 非 wrong 742
206. 齿 teeth 374
207. 黾 toad p. 239b
208. 隹 dove 59
209. 金 gold 218
210. 鱼 fish 653

— 9 —

211. 音 tone 445
212. 革 hide 486
213. 是 be 327
214. 骨 bone p. 227b
215. 香 scent p. 217b
216. 鬼 ghost 385
217. 食 food 413

— 10 —

218. 高 tall 99
219. 鬲 cauldron, p. 216b
220. 髟 hair 1032

— 11 —

221. 麻 hemp p. 226a
222. 鹿 deer p. 217a

— 12 —

223. 黑 black 357

"leftovers"
pp. 272–73

Reading & Writing
CHINESE
Simplified Character Edition

A Comprehensive Guide to the Chinese Writing System

Third Edition

William McNaughton

TUTTLE PUBLISHING
Tokyo • Rutland, Vermont • Singapore

Published by Tuttle Publishing, an imprint of Periplus Editions (HK) Ltd., with editorial offices at 364 Innovation Drive, North Clarendon, VT 05759 and 130 Joo Seng Road, #06-01/03, Singapore 368357.

Original edition © 1979 Charles E. Tuttle Publishing Company, Inc.
Revised edition © 1999 Charles E. Tuttle Publishing Company, Inc.
Third Edition (Simplified Character Edition) © 2005 Periplus Editions (HK) Ltd.

LCC Card No. 2005923053
ISBN 0-8048-3509-8

Printed in Singapore

Distributed by:

North America, Latin America & Europe
Tuttle Publishing
364 Innovation Drive
North Clarendon, VT 05759-9436
Tel: (802) 773 8930; Fax: (802) 773 6993
info@tuttlepublishing.com
www.tuttlepublishing.com

Japan
Tuttle Publishing
Yaekari Building, 3rd Floor
5-4-12 Osaki, Shinagawa-ku
Tokyo 141-0032
Tel: (03) 5437 0171; Fax: (03) 5437 0755
tuttle-sales@gol.com

Asia Pacific
Berkeley Books Pte. Ltd.
130 Joo Seng Road, #06-01/03
Singapore 368357
Tel: (65) 6280 1330; Fax: (65) 6280 6290
inquiries@periplus.com.sg
www.periplus.com

09 08 07 06 05
9 8 7 6 5 4 3 2

TUTTLE PUBLISHING® is a registered trademark of Tuttle Publishing.

TABLE OF CONTENTS

PREFACE

This new edition of *Reading and Writing Chinese* uses the modern "simplified forms" which resulted from "script reform" after the Revolution of 1949. (The traditional forms, however, receive collateral presentation as variations of the modern simplified forms. The modern simplified forms are standard in the People's Republic of China and in Singapore; the traditional forms are standard in Taiwan and Hong Kong.)

In the last 50 years, three developments in modern China have made it much easier for one to learn to read and write the Chinese language with a reasonable fluency:
- the simplification of the Chinese writing system in the early 1950s;
- the publication of a list of the 2,000 most useful characters to learn first, for adult education, also in the early 1950s; and
- the recent establishment of a "standard vocabulary of the Chinese language and graded outline of Chinese characters," with a related TOEFL-like test for proficiency in Chinese (*Zhongguo Hanyu Shuiping Kaoshi* or HSK).

This third edition exploits all three of these developments, with the aim of enabling the foreign student of Chinese to acquire, quickly and painlessly (perhaps even pleasurably), a large vocabulary of Chinese written characters and of character combinations.

Using *Reading and Writing Chinese* with a good Chinese language teacher or in classes for spoken Chinese and written Chinese with a focus on Chinese culture or on other interests (business, politics, history, literature, etc.), it is now possible for the average student to achieve this large vocabulary in a period of time that would not have been possible before the Chinese government's massive efforts at adult education and (more recently) at education of foreign students in Chinese. (Refer to pages vii–viii for a discussion of *Hanyu Shuiping Cihui Yu Hanzi Dengji Dagang* [HSCHDD; Standard Vocabulary of the Chinese Language and Graded Outline of Chinese Characters].)

In the preparation of this new edition of *Reading and Writing Chinese*, the same pedagogical method has been used to present the material as was used in earlier editions.

1. The student studies the most useful characters (as determined, for this new edition, by *Hanyu Shuiping Cihui Yu Hanzi Dengji Dagang* [HSCHDD]).
2. The characters are presented in the order in which they are likely to be most useful; the most frequently seen characters appear before the less frequently seen ones.
3. In learning the characters, the student will also learn the elements of the writing system— the 226 radicals, and the "phonetics" (sound components) which he/she will find most useful in the study of the HSCHDD lists.

4. Each entry for a character is given in units of information based on developments in "programmed instruction," and these units have been arranged in order of growing difficulty.
5. Help is given to students in mastering the problem of "look-alike" characters: through juxtaposition and cross-reference, the author has tried to clarify the main causes of the problem, look-alike radicals and look-alike characters.

The new edition's content and organization are based on the analysis and vocabulary presented in HSCHDD (Beijing: Beijing Yuyanxue Chubanshe, 1995 [1992]). The earlier editions of *Reading and Writing Chinese* depended heavily on work done at Yale to prepare teaching materials and were based largely on George A. Kennedy, ed., *Minimum Vocabularies of Written Chinese* (New Haven: Far Eastern Publications, 1954), which, in turn, makes use of the 2,000-character list prepared in China in the early 1950s to facilitate adult education.

Hanyu Shuiping Cihui Yu Hanzi Dengji Dagang is tied to the *Zhongguo Hanyu Shuiping Kaoshi,* or *Chinese Proficiency Test* (HSK). HSK aims to measure the level of proficiency in Chinese attained by those, especially foreigners and overseas Chinese, who do not have a native speaker's background and education. An HSK certificate can indicate the holder's preparedness to study at a Chinese university or his/her level of Chinese proficiency to potential employers. It is, in other words, the contemporary Chinese equivalent of the TOEFL test in English. The graded organization in the printed HSCHDD copy, based on statistical studies and experts' judgment about *the most useful vocabulary items* for non-native-speaker students to learn at each stage of their studies, is of great value and is of greater contemporary relevance than is *Minimum Vocabularies of Written Chinese.*

Hanyu Shuiping Cihui Yu Hanzi Dengji Dagang is focused more on "words" (ci 词) than on zi (字, single characters), although all of the characters (zi) needed to write the words of the basic vocabulary of words (ci) are included in graded lists (at the back of HSCHDD). The lists of "ci" include all of their component zi (single characters) which may, by themselves, stand for a word of the language. The ci are mostly two-character expressions, but there may be some items comprising three or even four characters (zi).

The study plan implied by HSCHDD is as follows:

In years one and two of study, it is contemplated that a vocabulary of 5,253 words (ci), including the 2,205 zi needed to write those 5,253 words, will be learned. This vocabulary is broken down into three lists:

- List A: 1,033 ci ("most frequently used words", needing 800 zi),
- List B: 2,018 ci ("frequently used words", needing 804 additional zi), and
- List C: 2,202 ci ("words the frequency of use of which is next below words in category B", needing 590 additional zi plus 11 zi in a "supplement").

Note that a large number of the 5,253 vocabulary items (ci) are identical to items in the list of 2,205 zi. For example, the first list (of 1,033 ci) is comprised of 459 single-character items and of 574 items of two- or more characters—i.e., 44% zi and 56% ci.

In years 3 and 4 of study of HSCHDD, it is contemplated that a vocabulary of 3,569 words, including the 700 additional zi needed to write those words, will be learned —"1,500 vocabulary items in each of the last two years of study," according to the "prefatory article" (*daixu*). The words in this list D are characterized as "other words in common use."

This new Tuttle guide to the Chinese writing system presents all of the characters (zi) in the A, B, and C lists, introducing students to the 2,205 single characters (zi) needed to write the 5,253 (ci) words. In addition, as many of the words (ci) as is possible are introduced as sub-items within the frames of each character (zi), modified by the principle of not introducing a character in a sub-item until it has been introduced as a main item. The new edition also —which HSCHDD does not—introduces students to "elements of the writing system" (e.g., "radicals" (*bùshŏu*) and productive phonetics). This will make it easier for foreign students to use *Reading and Writing Chinese*, in their progress toward acquiring a large enough vocabulary to be competent in the Chinese written language.

Also, grouping characters into "phonetic series" (i.e., several characters having the same phonetic element) gives the following benefits:

• makes it easier for students to learn several characters by connecting them through a common element (the phonetic);

• helps students to distinguish between look-alike characters; and

• helps students grasp the logic of the writing system.

The organization of characters into phonetic series is one of the features of earlier editions which has been strengthened in the new version.

For the three HSCHDD lists used to prepare the new *Reading and Writing Chinese* (*RWC*), the relation to earlier editions of *Reading and Writing Chinese* is as follows:

— List "A," 800 characters (zi), of which 25 are not in earlier editions of *RWC*;

— List "B," 804 characters, of which 144 are not in earlier editions of *RWC*; and

— List "C" (including the 11-character supplement), 601 characters, of which 290 are not in earlier editions of *RWC*.

This means that 459 new characters have been added to this new edition. From the characters included in earlier editions of *Reading and Writing Chinese*, a few dozen, maybe, have been deleted as being irrelevant to mastery of the HSCHDD lists. One of the features of this and previous editions of *Reading and Writing Chinese* is that ci are regularly introduced throughout the book—and, in fact, about 25% more ci than zi are introduced (2,500 ci as against 2,000 zi). This means that it has been fairly easy to adapt the format and method of *Reading and Writing Chinese* to present the lists in HSCHDD, including ci.

This new edition preserves, as far as possible, a successful and popular feature of earlier editions—introducing first the characters which the student would meet early in his studies of other kinds of textbooks in Chinese—readers, conversation books, etc. Since the first publication of *Reading and Writing Chinese* in 1979, a vast number of elementary and intermediate textbooks have been published—especially in the People's Republic of China—so that it is now impossible to follow rigorously any such scheme as was possible in 1979 when the Yale series of textbooks was a virtual monopoly. For this new edition the effort to deal with this has been made in two ways.

Firstly, the editor has used his judgment about the characters foreign students in the 21st century are most likely to meet early in their studies (the list of such characters is not that much different from what it was at the time earlier editions were prepared). Secondly, every character (zi) and every word (ci) have been marked as "A" or "B" or "C" on their first appearance in the new edition of *Reading and Writing Chinese*, following the "A" list, the "B" list, or the "C" list of first-year and second-year study materials in the HSCHDD. That way, the student can follow his/her preference, using the arrangement of characters into phonetic series to pick up a larger number of characters fast; or (alternatively) learning at first only the "A" character with its radicals and phonetic (if any), taking note of related characters, and moving on, to return later and learn the "B" character(s) in the phonetic series, and finally coming back later still, to learn the "C" character or characters.

While the editor certainly does not want to discourage ambitious students who would follow the first method of study, he recommends the alternative method, as follows:
- that students learn at first only the characters on the "A" list, taking note of related characters;
- return later and learn the characters on the "B" list, and finally
- come back later still and learn the "C" characters.

Using this method, students should learn all of the radicals as they are introduced. The editor recommends this method because of the pace of learning inherent in it. In a Western university curriculum, where the student studies several subjects at the same time in a 16-week semester, the student can learn seven new characters (zi) a night (35 new characters a week). By the end of the first year of study, he/she should know all of the "A" characters (up through the tenth character in column "a" of Part II, p. 227) as well as their radicals and phonetics; and he/she should also know 270 characters of the "B" list and their radicals and phonetics. By the end of his/her third semester of study, the student should have learned all of the "A" and "B" characters and their radicals and phonetics.

By the end of his/her second year of study, the student should have learned all of the characters of the "A," "B," and "C" lists—and will have kept pace, as far as the learning of characters (zi) is concerned, with the study plan implied by HSCHDD.

The study plan implied by HSCHDD, however—at least with reference to the rate at which the student is expected to learn ci—seems to assume that the student will be studying Chinese in an intensive course—in Beijing, perhaps; as sole, or almost sole, subject of study; and for more than the 28 to 32 weeks of the usual Western university academic year. All this means, in the long run, is that the student studying in a Western university may want to spread out over eight semesters (rather than four) the time and cerebral energy devoted to the study of *Reading and Writing Chinese* and use the "space" so created in his study week to learn all of the ci on the various HSCHDD lists (as well, of course, as the 700 new zi on List "D" and its supplement).

William McNaughton

STUDENT'S GUIDE

The Writing System

The Chinese writing system is based on two hundred or so basic elements, referred to as "radicals" in the Western world (in China as *bùshǒu* (部首), or "section headings," with reference to the way in which they are used to arrange, or to index, dictionaries).

I say "two hundred or so" because the pre-modern system (prevailing from the early 18th century to the early 20th century) contained 214 radicals, but post-1949 systems have varied around that number. For example, the system of *Han-Ying Cidian* or *The Chinese-English Dictionary* (probably the most widely used Chinese-English dictionary in the world) depends on a system of 226 radicals plus a supplementary category. It is the radical system of this dictionary which is presented in this revised edition of *Reading and Writing Chinese*.

Lexicographers use the radicals to organize dictionaries or indexes to dictionaries which are arranged phonetically. They begin with one-stroke radicals, and end with the radical or radicals having the largest number of strokes (17 strokes in pre-modern dictionaries, 13 strokes in *Han-Ying Cidian* plus 11 characters called "leftovers"). The dictionary-makers take every character which is not a radical, decide which radical in it is logically the most important, and then classify the character under that radical in the dictionary or index. Under each radical, the characters are then arranged, from the fewest strokes to the most strokes (not counting the strokes in the radical).

Every time a new character was created to represent some word of the spoken language, the character was formed according to one of six principles, giving six different classes of characters: 1) pictures, 2) symbols, 3) sound-loans, 4) sound-meaning compounds, 5) meaning-meaning compounds, and 6) reclarified compounds. Hence by extension, we can say that six—and only six—kinds of characters exist.

If we understand these six principles, we will be able to see *why* every new character we study means what it does. Instead of seeming to be a capricious aggregation of strokes, the character will reflect a logical system for representing words and concepts. And each new more-complicated character—the compounds— will be a combination of familiar elements.

Let us look at each of the six kinds of Chinese characters.

1. *Pictures.* Some Chinese characters are pictures of things. The character for "person/ human being" is a simple stick drawing of a human being: 人. The character for "child" or "baby" is a drawing of an infant with open fontanel: 兒. Sometimes the modern character is a very stylized picture of what it represents. We then have to look into the history of the character before we can see the resemblance clearly.

The character for "moon" 月 used to look like this: 𝄐 ; the character for "eye" 目 like this: 👁 .

2. *Symbols.* Some Chinese characters are symbols—some more, some less arbitrary—for the concept to which they refer. Some examples of symbols are: 上 "above," 下 "below," 一 "one," 二 "two," 三 "three."

3. *Sound-loans.* Some Chinese characters stand for a word which is, or once was, pronounced the same as another word but with a different meaning, like "feet" and "feat" in English. This type of character, a picture or symbol for one of two homonyms, was borrowed to represent the companion homonym, too; the context was relied on to make the meaning clear. For example, the words for "scorpion" and "10,000" were once homonyms. The character 萬 (modern simplified form, less representational: 万) originally meant "scorpion" but was borrowed for "10,000" since there was little danger of confusing the two meanings in a context. You can probably see that it would have been inconvenient to write "10,000" in the same symbolic notation used to write the numbers "one," "two," and "three."

4. *Sound-meaning compounds.* Sometimes one part of a Chinese character gives a hint about the meaning, while another part gives a hint about the pronunciation. For example, the character 包, "to wrap," is pronounced *bāo.* (The pronunciation of the romanization and the tone markings used here are explained on pages xxii–xxiv.) If this character is combined with the character 鱼 "fish," the result is a new character 鲍 "salted fish," pronounced *bào.* The "fish" component suggests the meaning, and the "wrap" component (*bāo*) suggests the sound.

5. *Meaning-meaning compounds.* Sometimes two characters are put together to form a new character whose meaning derives from some logic in the juxtaposition of the two component characters. The character 女 "woman" beside the character 子 "child" forms 好, a character that means "to love" or "to be lovable, to be likable, to be good." Although the logic in such a juxtaposition is usually not obvious enough to allow you to figure out the meaning of a new character, it is usually a great help when trying to remember a character which you have seen only once.

6. *Reclarified compounds.* At various times in the history of the written language, a scribe had wanted to better "control" the meaning of a character he was using, for various reasons. The reasons could be: because the character—due to sound-loan, perhaps—had come to stand for a number of different words, or perhaps it represented a word with a number of different meanings. The scribe could add to the existing character either to clarify the word to which it referred, or to pinpoint the meaning intended in the particular context. For example, the character for "scorpion" 萬 [Point 3 above] was later reclarified when it was used to represent "scorpion" (rather than "10,000") by adding the "bug" radical 虫 to produce the

new character 蠆 that always meant "scorpion" (or, metonymically, "scorpion's sting/tail") and never "10,000." The character 廷 *tíng* stood for "court"—whether it was the king's court or the court in someone's front yard. Eventually someone added the "lean-to" radical 广, which is a picture of a roof and a wall, to distinguish the king's court (廷 *tíng*) from the ordinary subject's front yard (庭 *tíng*). Some of these reclarified compounds will, in their new guise, be simple sound-meaning compounds, and some of them—if the reclarified character itself was already a sound-meaning compound—will be sound-meaning compounds with one component to suggest the sound and two components to suggest the meaning.*

Explanatory Notes

The following is an annotated character entry from this edition:

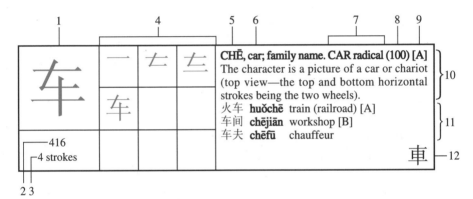

KEY:

1. the character
2. character serial number
3. stroke count
4. stroke-order diagram
5. pronunciation and tone
6. character definition
7. radical information
8. radical number
9. *Hanyu Shuiping Cihui*... list (see the Preface)
10. character explanation
11. character combinations with pronunciation, meaning, and *HSC* list
12. traditional character

---

* Bernhard Karlgren identifies dozens of such characters in *Analytic Dictionary of Chinese and Sino-Japanese* (Paris: Librairie Orientaliste Paul Geuthner, 1923). Chao Yuen Ren treats reclarified compounds as a sub-class of sound-meaning compounds: see *Mandarin Primer* (Cambridge University Press, 1961), pp. 61–63. Traditionally, the sixth of the six principles was something called *zhuǎnzhù* (转注), and whether or not this had anything to do with reclarified compounds is uncertain, since there is a great deal of dispute about the correct interpretation and reference of *zhuǎnzhù*.

Understanding the Entries

The student should pay special attention, at the beginning of his/her studies, to the information given in #6 above, "character definition." It is, of course, essential to know what a character "means." In *Reading and Writing Chinese*, this information is given in the form of an English definition or "gloss." Because there are significant differences between the grammatical systems of Chinese (a member of the "Sino-Tibetan" language family), and of English (a member of the "Indo-European" language family), problems can arise with these definitions. Let us consider this point a little further.

Chao Yuen Ren, in his grammar of Chinese (*A Grammar of Spoken Chinese*, Berkeley: University of California Press, 1968) recognizes as below the basic categories of words ("word-classes," "parts of speech") in Chinese; the basic word-classes of English are as set out in the right-hand column.

Chinese Word-classes (acc. Chao)	English Word-classes
verbs (including adjectives)	verbs
	adjectives
nouns	nouns
proper names	
place words	
time-words	
determinatives	
measure-words	
localizers (suffixes that convert non-place words to place words)	
pronouns	pronouns
other substitutes	
adverbs	adverbs
prepositions	prepositions
conjunctions	conjunctions
particles	
interjections	interjections

Anyone trying, then, to give English definitions for Chinese words (or the characters which stand for them) faces the problem of "mapping" a system of 15 elements onto a system of eight elements. The editor of *Reading and Writing Chinese*, in preparing the definitions, has given the student as much help as he could with this problem. English verbs are used to translate Chinese verbs, English nouns to translate Chinese nouns, etc. Where grammatical categories do not match, explanations and paraphrases are given (especially for Chinese measure-words, localizers, and particles). *Reading and Writing Chinese*, however, is a guide to the Chinese writing system, not a comprehensive grammar (Chao's grammar runs to 847 pages). As is stated in the Preface, the student should be using *Reading and Writing Chinese* in tandem with classroom work or with a tutor. The apparent anomalies created by such "mapping" will be resolved as the student's mind becomes more and more comfortable with the differences between the two grammatical systems. The achievement of that kind of comfort is, of course, one of the pleasures of studying a foreign language.

Most of the punctuation marks used in the characters' explanatory blocks are grammatically logical. However, I have also adopted a few rules of my own to help the reader/student. Semicolons are used to distinguish meaning "groups." Semicolons are also used after a character's romanized reading when a character's usage rather than the meaning is given. In addition to their use with slang terms, or for clarity, quotation marks are used around character-compound definitions that are contextually proper in English but which cannot be derived from the characters themselves. For example, the Chinese use a character for "red" 红 and the character for "tea" 茶 to write what in English is called "black tea." Since the more literal definition "red tea" would be meaningless, I have used quotation marks in the definition of the compound, as follows:

红茶 hóngchá "black" tea

Written versus Printed Forms

Problems of character identification may result from the fact that typeset forms sometimes differ from the handwritten forms that are usually learned first. Always compare a character which appears in a compound, with its written counterpart as you work through this book. The typeset list below provides the most common of these variant forms. Numbers refer to the serial number of characters in the first half of this book (characters 1–1,067); page numbers are for characters in the second half.

艹	16	示	166	直	403
忄	19	入	204	眞	404
辶	90	靑	249	歉	Pt. 2, p. 239
八	124	令	369	卽	Pt. 2, p. 244

DICTIONARIES

Chinese dictionaries—whether they are Chinese–Chinese dictionaries or Chinese–English dictionaries—may be organized according to the radical system, or they may be organized phonetically (from "A" to "Z," like a Western dictionary) according to the standard romanized spelling (*Hanyu Pinyin*) of the Beijing pronunciation (*Putonghua*, "Mandarin") of the character. The order of entries follows the English alphabetical order, starting with "A" and ending with "Z." Such phonetic organization works fine until you encounter a character you don't know how to pronounce—a common experience for foreign students (but it also happens with Chinese readers). So all dictionaries organized phonetically, as just described, also have an index—an index organized by some modern adaptation of the traditional radical system. There is no universally accepted adaptation, however, so different dictionaries use slightly different radical systems. But all such systems are derived from the traditional radical system, all of them overlap to a great degree, and all follow quite closely the logic of the traditional system.

CHARACTER COMBINATIONS

Individual characters themselves—each of which, in general, represents a single syllable of the spoken language—may occur in combination with other characters to denote Chinese words and expressions of two or more syllables. For example, a common expression for "woman" in the spoken language is the two syllable *nǚrén,* written with the characters for "woman" 女 *nǚ* and "person" 人 *rén.* Many of these common combinations are given in this book so that you will get used to seeing the characters within important expressions and words. Learning the combination in which a character occurs can be a valuable aid to understanding that character. Moreover, since the characters used in these combinations are restricted to those that have already been presented in the text, these combinations provide review as well as usage examples.

Some examples are also given of a favorite stylistic device in Chinese speech and writing—four-character set expressions (成语). Learning these four-character set expressions will be useful for the student in the same way as learning two-character combinations, and it will also prepare the student to deal with them when he/she encounters them or similar four-character expressions—written or spoken. Finally, practice with two-character combinations and four-character set expressions will tend to break down the illusion, which the writing system so insistently encourages, that Chinese is a monosyllabic language. To some extent it may be so, but the disyllable is an extremely important unit in modern Chinese, and the four-character expression is also important in anything above the level of "survival Chinese."

PHONETIC SERIES

When a certain character has been used to give the sound in a number of sound-meaning compounds, a group of characters emerges, each of which has a different meaning but contains the same sound-component. The different meanings are established, of course, by using a different meaning-component in each character. Such a group of characters is called a "phonetic series," and students have often found that learning becomes more rapid when they study such character groups. In *Reading and Writing Chinese* we have therefore introduced common characters as part of a phonetic series if the characters belong to a phonetic series. For example, the character "wrap" 包 *bāo*, mentioned above, is the sound-component for a number of common characters that appear in this book: 抱, 饱, 泡, 炮, 袍, 跑. The meaning is determined by the other part of the character: "扌 hand," "饣 food," "氵 water," "火 fire," "衤 gown," and "足 foot," to give meanings: "to embrace," "to be full" (after eating), "to soak," "artillery," "long gown," and "to run," respectively.

THE CHINESE WRITING SYSTEM AS CULTURAL ARTIFACT

There are, more or less, 13 dialects of the Chinese language—spoken languages which differ from one another as much as English, German, and Dutch differ from one another, or as French, Spanish, Italian, and Portuguese differ. The remarkable thing about the Chinese writing system, including the simplified form of it which is studied in this book, is that a literate native speaker of one dialect can communicate with another person of a different native dialect by simply writing down his thoughts. The other party will immediately understand—although if the two tried to speak in their native dialects, neither would understand the other. That is, with the Chinese writing system, you can simultaneously write down a message in 13 different languages!* There has never been anything else like it in human history.

Some foreign students, initially vexed when they realize that the Chinese writing system is somewhat more complicated than their own, think that the Chinese should switch to an alphabetical one. To do so, however, would eliminate the increment of universal intelligibility which exists in China. Furthermore, while it does take some months longer for a Chinese child to master the writing system than it does for an American or French child, say, to master their own writing systems, in the long run there is little difference. Japan, whose writing system is based on the Chinese system, has one of the highest literacy rates in the world (illiteracy in Japan is about one-fifth that of the United States). And James Traub notes that only slightly more than four per cent of Taiwanese fifth graders and slightly more than 10 per cent of Japanese scored as low as the average American fifth grader on a battery of reading tests.**

The foreign student should also consider that the logic of the Chinese writing system, as sketched on pages xi–xiii above, has stimulated a number of Western thinkers, from Leibniz in his work on the Calculus to Eisenstein on montage.

---

* True regionalisms and some dialectal slang are not reached by the writing system, but the relative unimportance and the ephemeral nature of slang and regionalisms make this a trivial exception.
** James Traub, "It's Elementary," *New Yorker,* 17 July 1995, 78 (74–79).

A project was floated after World War II to have traffic signs all over the world prepared in Chinese "ideograms." Although the proposal was derided by Yale's widely respected Sinologist, George A. Kennedy, who called it "deranged," something like this has actually happened—with modern pictures, symbols, and especially "meaning-meaning compounds" now to be seen on traffic signs and other public notices around the world: school crossing...men working...slippery when wet...steep hill ahead...slow-moving vehicles, keep right...no smoking...no eating or drinking on the subway...do not play boom boxes on the beach...danger of falling rocks...watch out for deer...low-flying aircraft ahead...emergency fire exit, this way...the list goes on.

There is a complex ideogram on the bus-boats in Venice which clearly says, in just four elements, "sit down or you will block the captain's view and make it difficult for him to navigate the boat safely!" The city fathers in one Italian town have put up signs on a main street, with the silhouette of a woman smoking and leaning up against a lamp-post, crossed out by the "no/not" symbol, a diagonal stroke from lower right to upper left corner. The meaning is clear enough: "no solicitation." Many computer icons, too, are a modern form of ideography, universally intelligible to computer users around the world, whatever their native language. In fact, these international systems of modern ideograms have even begun to develop "sound-meaning compounds." The driver passing through a French village (for example) may see at the far end of the village a sign with the village's name in the phonetic Roman alphabet (the sound component) crossed out by the "no/not" symbol, a diagonal stroke from lower right to upper left corner (the meaning component): "you are leaving Mirepoix."

Study Methods

Each radical introduced in this book is assigned a number in parentheses. This number is the radical number and indicates where the radical occurs within the sequence of 226 radicals. Every effort you make to memorize the number, at least for radicals having two, three, four, five, or six strokes, will pay off in time saved after you start to use dictionaries. Just as it is a great time-saver with Western-language dictionaries to know where "F" occurs in the alphabet (and whether it occurs before or after "M," for example), these numbers serve the same purpose in Chinese.

You are also advised, when first learning a character, to be conscious of all the radicals that appear in it. Say aloud the radicals while writing a new character. For example, say "mouth-down-one-cowrie" while writing 贵, "be expensive, be precious" (character 163); or "word-torso-thumb" when writing 谢 "thanks, to thank" (character 239). Such incantations may be of considerable help in recalling characters to memory three or four days after first encountering them.

You should read the explanation of the sources of new characters, but you need not formally study these explanations unless (as sometimes happens) you become fascinated by the Chinese written character itself. In that case you may want to learn all the explanations given and even to carry your own studies further afield into the various books which present such explanations in greater (and sometimes fanciful) detail. A reference which can be useful for such study is Bernhard Karlgren, *Analytic Dictionary of Chinese and Sino-Japanese* (see note above, p. xiii), referred to in *Reading and Writing Chinese* as "*AD.*"*

You can easily use *Reading and Writing Chinese* as a programmed textbook. Cover the character with a blank piece of paper placed along the vertical line that separates the character from the box containing its pronunciation and meaning, then try to write out the character, and immediately after doing so, pull the answer sheet away and compare the character you have written with the character in the book. If you have written the character incorrectly, take note of the error or errors and write the character correctly before proceeding to the next one. After working to the bottom of a page in this way, reverse the procedure and try to write down the pronunciation and meaning while looking only at the character. Immediately check your work against the pronunciation and meaning that appear in the text.

How to Write the Characters

The Chinese learn to write the characters by using an easy and effective method. The essential ingredient of this method is the fixed order in which the strokes of a character are written. Although Chinese people occasionally disagree among themselves about minor details, the method has been developed and perfected through centuries of experience. Follow the stroke-order diagrams presented in this book in order to acquire the correct habits early, and remember to keep your characters uniform in size.

---

* Other such references are: L. Weiger. *Chinese Characters: Their Origins, Etymology, History, Classification, and Signification* (New York: Paragon/Dover, 1965 [1927, 1915]). Some of Weiger's statements and analyses must be taken with a grain of salt, but the person who fancies this sort of thing may enjoy the book. There is also Chang Hsuan, *The Etymologies of 3000 Chinese Characters in Common Usage* (Hong Kong: Hong Kong UP, 1968). This is a very useful compendium of Chinese sources of the past 1,900 years—but, being all in Chinese, it is not for the beginning foreign student. It is, however, very well indexed, and the foreign student with some knowledge of Chinese can use it— especially if he/she learns a few key lexicographic terms: "象形" *xiàngxíng* "picture;" 声 *shēng* "phonetic, sound component;" 从 *cóng* "from" or "is composed of...;" and 会意 *huìyì*, "meaning-meaning compound."

The rules below explain the method in general.

1. Top to bottom:

一	二	三	
⼕	田	罒	累
丶	亠	言	言

三 →
累 →
言 →

2. Left to right:

他 →
谁 →
啊 →

亻	𠂉	仲	他
讠	讠	诈	谁
口	阝	啊	啊

3. Upper left corner to lower right corner:

矢 →
隹 →
您 →

丿	宀	午	矢
丿	亻	侔	隹
亻	你	您	您

4. Outside to inside:

田 →
冈 →
国 →

丨	冂	用	田
丨	冂	冈	冈
丨	冂	国	国

5. When two or more strokes cross, horizontal strokes before perpendicular strokes:

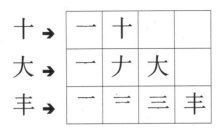

6. Slanting stroke to the left before slanting stroke to the right:

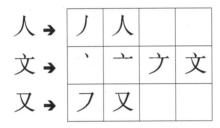

7. Center stroke before symmetrical wings:

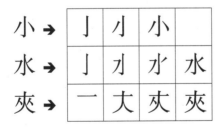

The Pronunciation of Chinese

The system used in *Reading and Writing Chinese* to write romanized Chinese is the Hanyu Pinyin system which is standard in mainland China and is now used almost universally, too, in printed materials (newspapers, magazines, books, textbooks), and so on—*used, that is, whenever the writer wants, for some reason, to give a word or words in Roman letters.* The student should remember that Chinese is written with the characters, not with the Roman alphabet.

HANYU PINYIN

Spoken Chinese, represented by pinyin (romanized) text , has the following vowels, consonants and combinations:

1. The following letters are pronounced like their English equivalents: *f*, *k*, *l*, *m*, *n*, *p*, *s* (except in "sh"), *t*, *w*, and *y*:

2. The following letters are pronounced like the English sounds indicated: *a* (except as described in 8, below), as in *father*; *i*, as in *machine* (except when appearing immediately after *u*—see end of this paragraph—or when appearing immediately after *c*, *ch*, *r*, *s*, *sh*, *z*, or *zh*: see 9, below; *o* as in *worn*; *ai* in *aisle*; and *ui*, *wei* in *weight*

3. The following combinations are pronounced like the English sounds indicated: *ao* like *ow* in *how*; *ou* like *o* in *so*; and *e* (except *e* after *i* or *y*: see point 8, below), like *o* in *done*.

4. The following letters are pronounced as explained: *b*, like *p* in *spy*; *d*, like *t* in *sty*; *g* like *k* in *sky*; that is, like English *p*, *t*, or *k* but with less aspiration (compare with point 1, above);

5. The following letters are pronounced as described: *h*, with more friction than English *h*; *u* (but not *ü*, and also not when followed by another vowel or pair of vowels, or when preceded by *j*, *q*, or by *i* or *y*), like *oo* in *moon* but with the lips rounded and the tongue back; *u* preceded by *i* or *y*, like *o* in *so*; *u* preceded by *j*, *q*, or *x*, round the lips to say *oo* as in *moon* but try to pronounce instead *i* as in *machine* (compare with *ü* in point 8, below); *z*, like *ds* in *cads*; and *c*, like *ts* in *it's* hot.

6. The following letters and combinations are pronounced as described: *sh* as in *shred*, tongue very far back; *ch*, tongue flat against roof of mouth, very far back; *zh*, like *ch* just described but with less breath; and *r*, tongue flat against roof of mouth, far back—like a *j* and *r* pronounced together.

7. The following letters are pronounced as described: *j*, like English *j* but with tongue tip forward where teeth meet; *q*, like *j* just described with more breath; and *x*, tongue tip against back of lower teeth (like a lisping English *s*).

8. The following letters are pronounced as described: *e* after *i* or *y*, as in *yet*; *ü*, round the lips to say *oo* as in *moon* but try to pronounce instead *i* as in *machine*; *ü* plus *e*, like *ü* just described plus English *e* in *yet*; *a* after *i* or *y*, and before *n* but not before *ng*), like *e* in *yet*; and *a* after *ü* and before *n*, like *e* in *yet*.

9. When *i* comes immediately after *c*, *r*, *s*, or *z*, it indicates that the mouth and tongue are held in place where the consonant is pronounced without a vowel (but with a tone; see next section; we can say that 'the consonant becomes its own vowel;' that is, *si* is just a hiss, *zi* is just a buzz, and *ri* is a kind of purr; when *i* comes immediately

after *ch* or *zh*, the resulting syllables *chi* and *zhi* are pronounced as explained in point 6, above, but they slide toward the *r* sound and get a tone—rather like the first syllable of <u>Ch</u>urchill and *gerbil*, respectively; and when *i* comes immediately after *sh*, the resulting syllable *sh* sounds like English <u>sh</u>irr but with the *sh* described above, and with a tone.

10. The letter *u* when followed by another vowel or pair of vowels is pronounced like English *w*; the combination *iu* at the end of syllables is pronounced like the American greeting *Yo!*; and *yi* is pronounced like the first syllable of <u>east</u>.

To use this system of writing Chinese (*Putonghua,* "Mandarin") with Roman letters, the student should know about three further features: word-division, the occasional use of apostrophes, and the placement of tone-marks (see below) over vowels when the syllable has more than one vowel-letter (*a, e, i, o, u,* and *ü*) in it. Chinese is written in the 'real world' with Chinese characters, not with Roman letters, so the system of romanization has not been 'worn smooth' by those great creators and molders of language, the folk. Many details, therefore, have not been worked out; the division into words is one of them. For example, should the expression for "overseas Chinese," composed of *Huá* (Chinese) + *qiáo* (person or people living abroad), be written *Huá qiáo* or *Huáqiáo*? I recommend that the student follow the advice I used to give to my students at City University of Hong Kong: look it up in a good dictionary, like *Han-Ying Cidian!* (It's *Huáqiáo*, one word.) Apostrophes are occasionally used (rarely) between syllables where a romanized expression might be misread at first: for example, 反而 "on the contrary," is usually romanized as *fǎn'ér*. As to the correct placement of tone-marks when a syllable has two or more vowel-letters in it, the situation is fairly simple, and practice and observation will help a great deal. The letters *a* and *e* always get the tone-mark in combinations, and *o* always gets the tone-mark except when the combination is *ao* or *iao*, in which case the *a* gets it. When the *i* and *u* appear together—as in *iu* or *ui*— whichever one comes *second* gets the tone-mark.

TONE

In addition to its vowels and consonants, a syllable in modern Chinese has its characteristic "tone." The tone (or tones, for words of more than one syllable) of a word is very important because it allows our ears to discriminate between words that have the same vowels and consonants. Tones result from changes in pitch which the speaker produces with the vocal chords while pronouncing the syllable. The difficulty of learning these tones has been much exaggerated. In fact, the system of tones in *Putonghua* ("Mandarin," the standard, and most commonly studied, spoken language of China, based on the dialect of the capital, Beijing) is actually one of the simplest of all Chinese dialects.

In *Putonghua* there are four tones (or five, if we count the neutral/'zero' tone: see below). These tones are indicated in Hanyu Pinyin by the tone marks ū, ú, ǔ, and ù, like the accents in French (see above on what to do when a syllable has more than one vowel). Thus, *mā* is *m* + *a* (as described above) pronounced in the first tone, *má* is *m* + *a* pronounced in the second tone, and so on. The way in which the speaker uses the vocal chords to change the pitch can be written on a musical staff, as below. Note that it is only the contour of the pitch which determines the tone; thus, a man's normal first tone will be a bit lower than a woman's. Pitch will normally be somewhere near the center of the speaking voice and will vary according to the individual and to his or her mood.*

The description of tones given here is the simplest and is the one most often presented in texts. It is intended to enable the student to pronounce words in isolation. In normal speech the tone may disappear from a syllable, and the syllable will be pronounced in a "neutral" or "zero" tone. In such cases in this book, the tone-marks have been omitted. In the case of two third tones in succession, native speakers automatically change the first of them into a second tone: *hěn hǎo* becomes *hén hǎo*. We have indicated such changes in this book if the expression is a very common one.

---

*The musical diagram is from Chao Yuen Ren, *A Grammar of Spoken Chinese*, p. 26. A few common words change their tone frequently, depending on the tone of the following word, and in these cases we have indicated the tone appropriate to each expression. Problems of words in discourse are, however, more properly the subject for a textbook in modern spoken Chinese, which you are urged to consult for more specific information.

1,067 BASIC CHARACTERS

and

Elements of the Writing System

一 1 1 stroke	一			**YĪ (YÍ, YÌ), one. ONE radical (2) [A]** 一 "one," 二 "two" (5, p. 2), and 三 "three"(6, p. 2) are probably the three simplest symbol characters in the language. As a radical this form is often called "the horizontal stroke." 一 is pronounced **yí** before a word in the fourth tone, and **yì** before words in the first, second, or third tones.
丿 2 1 stroke	丿			**PIĚ, left-falling stroke. LEFT radical (4)**
女 3 3 strokes	乡	乡	女	**NǓ, woman. WOMAN radical (73) [A]** 女 is a picture—a rough stick drawing of a woman (with legs modestly crossed, say commentators). It occurs as an independent character and means "woman" or, occasionally, "daughter."
人 4 2 strokes	丿	人		**RÉN, human being, person. The "person" radical (old style: "man" radical) (23) [A]** **Rén** is a picture—a rough stick drawing of a human being. It occurs as an independent character. Learn to distinguish **rén** from 入 **rù**, "enter" (204, p. 41)—although both are now the same radical. 女人 **nǚrén** woman, female [B]

				ÈR, two. TWO radical (11) [A]
5 2 strokes				
				SĀN, three [A]
6 3 strokes				
				SHÍ, ten. TEN radical (12) [A] The "ten" radical is simply an arbitrary symbol for the number "ten." 十一　shíyī　eleven; October 1, National Day (People's Republic of China) 十二　shíèr　twelve 二十　èrshí　twenty 二十一　èrshíyī　twenty-one 三十　sānshí thirty
7 2 strokes				
				JIŌNG, borders. BORDERS radical (19) Jiōng, "borders," is not in use as an independent character. It is, however, the radical under which about 10 common characters are classified in modern dictionaries or in the indexes to modern dictionaries arranged phonetically, so the student should learn it. Distinguish "gate" (25, p. 6).
8 2 strokes				
				WÉI, to surround. SURROUND radical (59) Dictionaries sometimes gloss this character as "the old form of 圍" ("to go around; circumference," 968, p. 194). 囗 is the radical of over 20 modern characters and should be learned.
9 3 strokes				

田	│	⊓	冂	**TIÁN, field; a family name. FIELD radical (142) [B]**
	田	田		The "field" radical is a picture of the typical Chinese (and East Asian) field—a large field divided by raised paths into small paddies.
10 5 strokes				

力	⁊	力		**LÌ, strength. STRENGTH radical (28) [A]**
				The student should distinguish "strength" from the "knife" radical 刀 (131, p. 27)
				人力 **rénlì** manpower, labor power [C]
11 2 strokes				

男	│	⊓	冂	**NÁN, male [A]**
	田	田	男	According to the classic dictionary *Shuō wén jiě zì*, 男 is a meaning-meaning compound: "it's the *males* who use their strength 力 in the fields 田."
12 7 strokes	男			男人 **nánrén** man, male [B] 男女 **nánnǔ** men and women

│	│			**SHÙ, downstroke. DOWN radical (3)**
				Anciently, the "down" radical was pronounced "gǔn," but now everybody reads it as "shù," meaning "the vertical stroke." Not in use now as an independent character, it is the radical of six common modern characters.
13 1 stroke				

亻	⁄	亻		**RÉN, man. SIDE-MAN radical (21)**
				Traditional dictionaries classify this form as a special case of the "human being, person" radical (4, p. 1), but this form, in its functions in the writing system, seems definitely to mean "male human being." See, for example, 24, p. 5. Not independent, but an important radical.
14 2 strokes				

3

乙	乙			**YǏ, twist; the second "heavenly stem". TWIST radical (7). Used to enumerate headings in an outline, like "B"—second letter of the Western alphabet.** The form 乙 and the form ∟ are variant forms of this radical. In early texts it means "fish guts" and may have been a picture. On "heavenly stems," see *Lin Yutang's Dictionary* 1451f.
15 1 stroke				
廿	一	十	卅	**No pronunciation. GRASS radical (50)**
16 3 strokes				
艺	一	十	卅	**YÌ, skill; art [A]**
	艺	艺		
17 4 strokes				藝
亿	丿	亻	亿	**YÌ, a hundred million [A]**
18 3 strokes				億
忄	丿	丷	忄	**XĪN, heart. SIDE-HEART radical (41)** This does not occur as an independent character; the independent form of "heart" is 87, p. 18. Serious students of Chinese culture should note that "heart" is often given a double gloss: "heart-mind," as if they were one thing.
19 3 strokes				

忆	'	ハ	忄	**YÌ, to remember [B]**
	忆			
20 4 strokes				憶

⼀	⼀			**No pronunciation. Radical (5) "Back-turned stroke."** ⼀ is the radical in six or so common modern characters. In two of these, it appears with a slanted horizontal part and a longer vertical part, as in the next character.
21 1 stroke				

也	ㄱ	卄	也	**YĚ, also [A]** The history of 也 is very complicated, involving the confusion of at least three different characters. The radical is ⼀ (21, above).
22 3 strokes				

她	く	女	女	**TĀ, she, her [A]** This character is a sound-meaning compound. The "woman" radical suggests the meaning, and 也 (22, above) once suggested the sound—although it is not now such a good phonetic. Compare with 24, below.
	女ㄅ	女ㄅ	她	
23 6 strokes				

他	ノ	亻	亻ㄱ	**TĀ, he, him [A]** 他 is a sound-meaning compound. The "man" radical suggests the meaning, the right half, 也 (22, above) at one time suggested the sound. Note the logic of the writing system: the "man" radical occurs in the character for "he, him," the "woman" radical in the character for "she, her."
	亻卄	他		
24 5 strokes				

5

	、	⼀	门	**MÉN, gate. GATE radical (46) [A]**
门				A picture. Its resemblance to a gate may not be clear, but the traditional form (see lower righthand corner of this frame) clearly resembles the swinging saloon doors in old Westerns. It occurs as an independent character and means "gate, door, entrance." Distinguish from "borders"(8, p. 2). 門
25 3 strokes				

	⼃	亻	亻	**MÉN, pluralizing suffix for pronouns and for certain nouns [A]**
们	价	们		Mén is used with nouns and pronouns referring to people: the "side-man" radical for meaning; mén (25, above) for sound. 她们 **tāmén** they, them (feminine) [A] 他们 **tāmén** they, them (masculine) [A] 們
26 5 strokes				

	一	二	三	**SHǑU, hand. HAND radical (111) [A]**
手	手			Shǒu often occurs as an independent character meaning "hand;" it may also occur as a part of characters. The form 扌 (see 28, below) was considered a variant of 27 here, but it is now a separate radical (55) and may be called "sidehand" to distinguish it.
27 4 strokes				

	一	丁	扌	**SHǑU, hand. SIDE-HAND radical (55)**
扌				Traditionally, this form was considered a variant of the "hand" radical (27, above), but in modern dictionaries, it is classified as a separate radical. The form here (扌) does not appear as an independent character. Distinguish from "thumb" 寸 (237, p. 48) and from "then" 才 (689).
28 3 strokes				

	一	弋	弋	**YÌ, dart. DART radical (56)**
弋				The "dart" radical is a picture. *Han-Ying Cidian* defines it as "a retrievable arrow with string attached" and calls it "bookish." Compare the "lance" radical (30, p. 7) and learn to distinguish "lance" from "dart."
29 3 strokes				

戈	一	七	戈	**GĒ, lance. LANCE radical (101)**
	戈			The "lance" radical is a picture. Note that "lance" has one more stroke than "dart", at the bottom. In museums you can see that the old weapon called "**gē**" had a blade like this at the lower end. The weapon is also sometimes called a "dagger-ax."
30 4 strokes				

我	一	二	手	**WŎ, I, me [A]**
	扎	扎	我	The student should learn to distinguish 我 **wǒ** from 找 **zhǎo** "look for" (32, below). **Wǒ** *is* "hand" + "lance;" **zhǎo** is "side-hand" plus "lance."
31 7 strokes	我			我们 **wǒmen** we, us [A]

找	一	寸	扌	**ZHĂO, to look for; to visit; to give change [A]**
	扩	扡	找	The student should distinguish **zhǎo** from **wǒ** 我 (31, above).
32 7 strokes	找			

亠	丶	亠		**TÓU, lid. LID radical (9)**
				Originally, **tóu** had a more general meaning: "above; a thing that goes on top of something else, covering." It may be easier to remember as "lid" because it looks like a lid. Distinguish the "crown" radical ⌐ (36, p. 8), and the "roof" radical ⌐ (40, p. 9). Not used independently, **tóu** is the radical in over 20 common characters.
33 2 strokes				

土	一	十	土	**TŬ, earth. EARTH radical (49) [B]**
				This appears to be a picture of a cross stuck into the earth ("The axis mundi!" say some scholars). It occurs as an independent character and means "earth, soil." Distinguish from the character 士 **shì**, "knight, scholar" (35) although they are the same modern radical.
34 3 strokes				土人 **tǔrén** a native, an aborigine

7

土	一	十	土	**SHÌ, knight, scholar; KNIGHT form of the EARTH radical (34, above) [B]** A **shì** took ten (十) things and organized them into one (一) for his lord. 人士 **rénshì** personage, notable person [C] 士女 **shìnǚ** young men and women, "guys and dolls" 女士 **nǚshì** polite address for women, especially professionals; Ms. [B]
35 3 strokes				

冖	㇒	冖		**MÌ, crown. CROWN radical (18)** **Mì** had a general meaning of "to cover, a cover"—crown by metonymy (and as a useful mnemonic). Not used independently now, it appears at the top of characters. Distinguish from the "roof" radical 宀 (40, p. 9) and from the "lid" radical 亠 (33, p. 7).
36 2 strokes				

小	亅	小	小	**XIĂO, be small, be little. SMALL radical (79) [A]** Variant: ⺌. Originally, this radical was three dots to suggest "small." Two of the dots remain, but the center dot has been replaced by a downstroke with a little hook on the end, made by an elegant movement of the wrist with a brush (ballpoint pens won't do it).
37 3 strokes				

尔	㇒	宀	勹	**ĚR, you, your; -ly, -like; that (opposite to "this") [C]** This character has a complicated history. It came to mean "you" by sound-loan. Bookish.
	尔	尔		
38 5 strokes			爾	

你	㇒	亻	亻	**NǏ, you [A]** **Nǐ** and **ěr** (38, above) most likely stood for cognate words meaning "you." **Nǐ** is **ěr** reclarified with the "man" radical. 你们 **nǐmen** you (plural) [A]
	你	你	你	
39 7 strokes	你			

	`	`/ \`	`⌐→`	**MIÁN, roof. ROOF radical (45)**
`宀→`				The character is a picture. The top stroke may represent a chimney. The student will want to distinguish "roof" from "lid" ⌐ (33, p. 7) and from "crown" ⌐ (36). Not an independent character, **mián** is the radical of over 50 common modern characters.
40 **3 strokes**				

	`ノ`	`匕`		**BǏ, ladle. LADLE radical (39)**
`匕`				The character is a picture.
41 **2 strokes**				

	`	`/ \`	`⌐→`	**TĀ, it [A]**
`它`	`宀`	`它`		Karlgren sees this as originally a pictograph meaning "cobra" (*Analytic Dictionary* 1011), later corrupted into "roof" over "ladle," and as coming by sound-loan to mean "the other, another, *it*."
42 **5 strokes**				它们 **tāmen** they, them (not human beings) [A]

	`→`	`了`		**LE; a particle: after verbs or sentences;** *le* basically means "changed status" or "completed action;" **LIǍO, to finish, to conclude; to understand [A]**
`了`				Students who want a fuller account of this busy little particle should consult the index to Chao Yuen Ren, *A Grammar of Spoken Chinese* (1968) (26 references). 瞭 (for liǎo)
43 **2 strokes**				

	`→`	`了`	`子`	**ZǏ, child; first of the twelve "earthly branches" (used in enumerations and to name two-hour periods of the day). CHILD radical (74) [A]**
`子`				子 is a picture. In older forms, it quite clearly resembles a child. 子 occurs often independently and as a suffix to many nouns. "Earthly branches:" see *Lin Yutang's Dictionary* 1451f.
44 **3 strokes**				

9

| 好 45 6 strokes | ⼃ | ⼅ | ⼥ | **HǍO, be good, be well; HÀO, to consider good; to like, to love [A]** 好 combines meanings. "Woman" beside "child" suggests "goodness, well-being, something desirable." 好人 **hǎorén** good person; healthy person; a "good guy" who tries to get along with everybody, often sacrificing principle to do so. |
| | 女 | 奵 | 好 | |

| 厶 46 2 strokes | ⼂ | 厶 | | **SĪ, be selfish, be private. COCOON radical (37)** The radical was originally a picture of a tightly wound silk cocoon. Note that it appears in several characters related to silk (47 and 48, below). Dictionaries often note that this is the original form of 私, "private, selfish" (Pt. 2, p. 216a) |

| 幺 47 3 strokes | ⼄ | ⼆ | 幺 | **YĀO, coil; be immature, be tender, be little. COIL radical (76)** The "coil" radical was originally a picture of a coil of silk thread. Learn to distinguish "coil" from the "cocoon" radical 厶 (46, above), from the "silk" radical 纟 (48, below). |

| 纟 48 3 strokes | ⼂ | 纟 | 纟 | **SĪ, silk. SILK radical (77)** In seven common modern characters, the "silk" radical appears in its more complex, traditional form (see below, this frame). Lèi (49, below) is one example. This happens when the "silk" radical is at the bottom, rather than at the side, of the character. It's done, no doubt, for aesthetic reasons. 糸 |

累 49 11 strokes	丨	冂	冃	**LÈI, be tired; LĚI, pile up; be repeated [A]** In ancient China, the men's main work was in the fields; the women's main work was sericulture (silk-farming). 累 may be a meaning-meaning compound to suggest everybody's work, whence "be tired."
	田	田	罗	好累 **hǎolèi** be very tired
	累	累	累	

10

彳 50 3 strokes	ノ	㇒	彳	CHÌ, step. STEP radical (62) Note that the "step" radical includes the "sideman" (14, p. 3), to which a stroke has been added—supposedly to suggest movement, a step taken. The "step" radical occurs often in characters for action or movement.
艮 51 6 strokes	㇆	㇕	㇌	GÈN, be stubborn; be blunt; be tough, leathery (of food or people). STUBBORN radical (184) In early texts, 艮 is clearly a picture of a man with a big, staring eye—an obstinate type, an insolent fellow. Now the spoken word gèn is dialect—used in certain localities, but not part of modern standard Chinese. Distinguish from 良 (412, p. 83)
	𠃌	𠃌	艮	
很 52 9 strokes	ノ	㇒	彳	HĚN, very [A] This character is a sound-loan for hěn, "very." Originally, it stood for a word that meant "to act stubborn, to resist"—a word that probably was cognate with gèn (51, above). The "stubborn" radical was reclarified with the "step" radical, and sometime later the character was borrowed for hěn, "very."
	彳	彳	彳	
	很	很	很	
口 53 3 strokes	∣	ㄇ	口	KǑU, mouth; a measure for human beings. MOUTH radical (58) [A] 口 is a picture. It also occurs as an independent character and means "mouth." 人口　　**rénkǒu**　population [B] 口子　　**kǒuzi**　(noun) hole, opening, cut, rip 三口人　**sānkǒu rén**　three people
灬 54 4 strokes	㇔	丷	灬	HUǑ, fire. FIRE-DOTS radical (80) This is a picture of a fire burning on the ground. It occurs only as a part of characters. There is also a "fire" radical (see 295, p. 60). Traditionally, "fire-dots" appeared in many characters for creatures which generate heat—"horse," "bird," "fish," "bear," "swallow (bird)," "crow," etc.—and for cooking processes.
	灬			

马	ㄱ	马	马	**MǍ, horse; a family name. HORSE radical (75) [A]** A picture: the traditional form below is more representational. In modern times, fire-dots is abbreviated to a single horizontal stroke. As Neitzsche said, "Nowadays, everybody's in a big hurry."
55 3 strokes				小马 **xiǎomǎ** pony 马力 **mǎlì** horsepower [D] 馬

吗	丨	冂	口	**MA; a particle [A]:** at the end of a sentence, it makes the sentence into a question; it may also appear within a sentence after the subject or topic to mark it off: "X 吗 ma: As for X, ..."
	叮	吗	吗	吗 is a sound-meaning compound, with the "mouth" radical warning, as it often does, that the other part is phonetic, not semantic.
56 6 strokes				嗎

言	丶	亠	二	**YÁN, word, words; family name. WORDS radical (185) [A]** Notice the "mouth" in "words." The other lines
	三	言	言	may be words pouring from the mouth, or "motion lines" to suggest the mouth moving. **Yán** often occurs as an independent character
57 7 strokes	言			and means "words, speech."

讠	丶	讠	**YÁN, word, words. SIDEWORDS radical (10)** This character is the modern abbreviation for 57, above. The "words" radical (57) is the radical in about four modern characters, "sidewords" in dozens of characters.
58 2 strokes			

隹	丿	亻	个	**ZHUĪ, dove. DOVE radical (208)** Dictionaries often define **zhuī** as a "short-tailed bird." In some ancient texts, it specifically
	疒	乍	乍	means "dove." The older forms of the character were clearly a picture of a bird. This character does not exist as an independent
59 8 strokes	隹	隹		character.

12

谁	`	讠	讠	**SHÉI, who? whom? Also SHUÍ [A]** This character is probably a sound-meaning compound. **Zhuī** (59, p. 12) is supposed to suggest the sound.
	讠	讠	讠	
60 10 strokes	讠	谁	谁	誰

| 大 | 一 | 𠂇 | 大 | **DÀ, be big. BIG radical (52) [A]**
大 is a man with arms extended: "big." **dàxiǎo**, size. (Abstract nouns in Chinese are often antonyms combined, as if to say "the big and the small of it, the size;" **duōshǎo** "many/ few: how many" (see 380, p. 77); **qīngzhòng** "light/ heavy: weight" (Pt. 2, p. 218a); **kuānzhǎi** "broad/ narrow: width" (950), etc.) |
| 61
3 strokes | | | | |

夫	一	二	𠂇	**FŪ, husband, "big man" [A]** 大夫　　**dàifu**　medical doctor (note change of pronunciation for "大" **dà →** **dài**) [A] 夫人　　**fūren**　Mrs.; Madam [A] 马夫人　**Mǎ fūren** Mrs. Ma, Madam Ma
	夫			
62 4 strokes				

天	一	二	于	**TIĀN, heaven, God, day, natural. HEAVEN radical (90); see 66, p. 14 [A]** 天 is said to be a picture of an anthropomorphic deity. The form 夭 **yāo** "be gentle, tender," historically distinct from 天, is now, *as radical*, considered a variant of 天.
	天			
63 4 strokes				天天　**tiāntiān** every day 天子　**tiānzǐ**　the emperor

气	丿	𠂉	气	**QÌ, breath, vapors, exhalation, animus, energy, soul. BREATH radical (109) [A]** The character is a picture of breath passing off in waves.
	气			
64 4 strokes				氣

13

竹	ノ	⺊	⺮
	⺯	⺮	竹
65 6 strokes			

ZHÚ, bamboo. BAMBOO radical (178) [B]
This character is a good picture of the slender, drooping leaves of the bamboo. The form is modified (slightly) when this radical appears as a part of characters (see 66, below).
竹子 **zhúzi** bamboo [B]
竹马 **zhúmǎ** stick used as a toy horse

笑	ノ	⺊	⺮
	⺮	⺮⺮	竺
66 10 strokes	竺	笋	笑

XIÀO, to laugh, smile; to ridicule [A]
One scholar says, "When bamboo takes the wind, it leans back gently like a man who laughs." That may be better as a mnemonic than as a philological explanation.
好笑 **hǎoxiào** be easy to laugh at, be funny, be ridiculous

儿	丿	儿	
67 2 strokes			

ÉR, child, son. R, suffix to nouns (rarely to verbs). SON radical (29) [A]
Anciently, this radical was recognized as the "legs" radical. Its use now, however, is primarily as the short form for 兒 "son, child," 兒 being a picture of a child with open fontanel.
儿子 **érzi** son [A]
儿女 **érnǚ** sons and daughters, children [C]
兒

尢	一	ナ	尢
68 3 strokes			

WĀNG, be lame; YÓU, still; a family name. LAME radical (53)
This is a picture of two legs, one shorter than the other to suggest lameness. The horizontal stroke serves to emphasize the unequal length of the two legs. In independent use only as a variant for 尤 (394, p. 79), whence the pronunciation **yóu**.
Distinguish from 大 (61, p. 13) and 无 (69).

无	一	二	于
	无		
69 4 strokes			

WÚ, to lack, not to have; not... (negator of verbs) [B]
Distinguish from 元 (89, p. 18). Variant: 無.
无人 **wúrén** unmanned; depopulated; self-service
无力 **wúlì** lack strength, feel weak; be incapable of . . .
无大无小 **wúdàwúxiǎo** regardless of size
無

辛	`	亠	亠	**XĪN**, be bitter, be toilsome; the eighth "heavenly stem" (used to enumerate items in an outline, like "H"—eighth letter of the Western alphabet); family name. BITTER radical (186) [A]
	立	立	立	
70 7 strokes	辛			For more on the "heavenly stems," see *Lin Yutang's Dictionary* 1451f. Distinguish from 幸 "be lucky" (next entry).
幸	一	十	土	**XÌNG**, lucky [A]
	吉	吉	幸	The student should learn to distinguish this character from the "bitter" character (70, above). "Lucky" has "earth" on top, "bitter" has "lid" on top.
71 8 strokes	幸	幸		
王	一	二	干	**WÁNG**, king, family name. KING radical (88) [B]
	王			The explanation of **wáng** is pretty philosophical (even Confucius endorses it). As one scholar says: "There are the three—Heaven, Earth, and Man: the mediator between them is the king."
72 4 strokes				
`	`			**ZHǓ**, dot. DOT radical (1)
73 1 stroke				
玉	一	二	干	**YÙ**, jade. JADE radical (131) [B]
	王	玉		Originally this character was a picture of three disks of jade (the horizontal strokes) strung together on a string (the vertical stroke). The dot may have been added to distinguish "jade" from "king" (72, above).
74 5 strokes				玉手 **yùshǒu** (bookish), a very white, beautiful hand

15

	、	二	二	**ZHǓ**, lord, host; principal; to indicate [A]
主				**Zhǔ** (73, p. 15) gives the sound; "king" suggests the meaning. This is the phonetic in several common characters (see 76, 78, 79 below).
	主	主		主人 **zhǔrén** host; landlord; master [B]
75 5 strokes				主力 **zhǔlì** main force (of a team, crew, army, factory shift, etc.) [C]
住	ノ	亻	亻	**ZHÙ**, to live, to stay; to stop; verb-ending [A]
				As verb-ending, 住 carries the idea of "stop, stump, stymie; be stopped/stumped/stymied." See Chao Yuen Ren's *Grammar*, 464-65. See also 问住 (255, p. 52) and 难住 (488).
	亻	仁	住	
76 7 strokes	住			
氵	、	冫	氵	**SHUǏ**, water. The "THREE-DOTS-WATER" radical (40).
				The other form of the "water" radical, which may occur independently, is 473, p. 95. This radical does not occur as an independent radical. It often appears as part of characters for liquids.
77 3 strokes				
注	、	冫	氵	**ZHÙ**, to comment on, to annotate; to concentrate on; note, commentary; to pour into; bet, stake; a measure for business transactions or for sums of money [A]
	氵	汢	泞	
78 8 strokes	汢	注		
驻	乛	马	马	**ZHÙ**, to stop; be stationed at, posted to [C]
	马	驴	驴	
79 8 strokes	驴	驻		駐

木 80 4 strokes	一 十 才 木	**MÙ, tree; be dull, stiff, "wooden" (metaphorically). TREE radical (94) [B]** The "tree" radical is a picture of a tree. As a radical, it often occurs in characters for objects made of wood. Distinguish it from 禾 "grain" (81, below), 米 "rice" (126, p. 26), and 采 "sift" (620, p. 125). 土木 **tǔmù** building and construction
禾 81 5 strokes	一 二 千 禾 禾	**HÉ, grain, especially rice. GRAIN radical (149) [D]** Note the similarity between "grain" and 木 "tree" (80, above). "Grain" has the left stroke across the top to represent the head of ripened grain. Distinguish "grain" from 采 "sift" (620, p. 125).
矢 82 5 strokes	ノ ㇒ 二 午 矢	**SHǏ, arrow; to vow. ARROW radical (148)** The character is a picture. The point of the arrow is at the top, and the feathers and notch are at the bottom. Distinguish from **shī** 失, "to misplace, lose; fail, be defeated" (83, below).
失 83 5 strokes	ノ ㇒ 二 失 失	**SHĪ, to misplace, lose, fail; be defeated [B]** Distinguish from 矢, "arrow," above.
矮 84 13 strokes	矢 矢 矢 矫 矫 矮 矮 矮 矮	**ǍI, be short (not tall) [A]** 矮 is composed of "arrow" 矢 + "grain" 禾 + "woman" 女 —all things which, within their classes, are generally shorter: arrows than spears, grain than trees, women than men. 矮子 **ǎizi** short person, dwarf 矮小 **ǎixiǎo** be diminutive, under-sized

亡	丶	亠	亡	**WÁNG, to flee, to hide; be gone; to die; be subjugated. FLEE radical (43) [C]** What is now "lid" (33, p. 7) was once 入 "enter" (124, p. 25) or 人 "person" (4, p. 1)—somebody entering a corner or nook to hide in it. Basic meaning, then, is "to flee, to hide." The other meanings are derived.
85 3 strokes				

忙	丿	⺆	忄	**MÁNG, be busy [A]** 忙 is supposed to be a sound-meaning compound. **Wáng** (85, above) supposedly suggests the sound, and "heart" suggests the meaning.
	忄	忙	忙	
86 6 strokes				

心	丿	心	心	**XĪN, heart. HEART radical (81) [A]** In the old form of 心, it is easy to see the picture of a heart. In this form, the "heart" radical occurs as an independent character and as an element at the bottom of characters. Compare with 19, p. 4. 小心 **xiǎo xīn** Be careful! [B] 无心 **wúxīn** not feel like it, not be in the mood for; unintentionally
	心			
87 4 strokes				

您	丿	亻	亻	**NÍN, you [A]** 您 is deferential, used to address elders and superiors. Note that the top of this character is 你 "you" (39, p. 8).
	你	你	你	
您	你	您	您	
88 11 strokes				

元	一	二	亍	**YUÁN, first; "dollar," Japanese "yen" [A]** The "legs" radical at the bottom represents a man: the "two" radical at the top represents his head. From "head" comes the idea of "primary:" thus, "first." 元 is also sometimes used to write 圓, "dollar," (Japanese) "yen" (826, p. 166). 一元 **yìyuán** one (Chinese) dollar
	元			
89 4 strokes				

辶	丶	辶	辶	**CHUÒ, to halt. HALT radical (47)** The character was a picture of a foot halted at a crossroads. The "halt" radical does not occur as an independent character but only as a part of characters.
90 **3 strokes**				

远	一	二	亍	**YUĂN, be far away; family name [A]** The "halt" radical is for meaning; **yuán** 元 for sound. Distinguish from 运 (93, below). 远大 **yuǎndà** be long-range [D]
	元	远	远	
91 **7 strokes**	远			遠

云	一	二	云	**YÚN, to say; a cloud; family name [A]** **Yún** originally was a picture and meant "cloud." It came to mean "to say" by sound-loan.
	云			
92 **4 strokes**				雲

运	一	二	云	**YÙN, to transport; fate, luck (A)** Distinguish from 远 (91, above).
	云	运	运	
93 **7 strokes**	运			運

阝	阝	阝		**FÙ, mound. "LEFT-EAR" radical (33)** **Fù** was a picture of steps leading down from the mound. In form, "mound" and "city" (766, p. 154) are identical, but because of their positioning as part of characters, **fù** is called the "left-ear" radical and "city" the "right-ear" radical. Neither radical has anything to do, semantically, with organs of hearing.
94 **2 strokes**				

院 95 9 strokes	了	阝	阝`
	阝`	阝宀	阝宀
	阝宀	阝宀	院

YUÀN, public building; courtyard [A]
Yuán (89, p. 18) is used here to give the sound.

园 96 7 strokes	丨	冂	冂
	冃	戸	园
	园		

YUÁN, garden, park [A]
This is another character in which 元 gives the sound.

園

| 不 97 4 strokes | 一 | 丆 | 不 |
| | 不 | | |

BÙ, a negative prefix for verbs and adverbs; NOT radical (95) [A]
Bù is bú before a word in the 4th tone.

不好 **bùhǎo** It's not very good; No good!
不很 **bùhěn** not very…
很不 **hěn bù** very un-…
不忙 **bùmáng** There's no hurry; take your time; easy does it

| 太 98 4 strokes | 一 | 丆 | 大 |
| | 太 | | |

TÀI, extremely [A]

太忙 **tài máng** be too busy
太太 **tàitai** married lady, wife [B]
田太太 **Tián tàitai** Mrs. Tian
太子 **tàizi** prince, crown prince

高 99 10 strokes	丶	亠	广
	亠	古	声
	高	高	高

GĀO, be tall; to tower; family name. TALL radical (218) [A]
Karlgren says "picture of a high building, a tower with roof and windows" (*Analytic Dictionary* 308).

高大 **gāodà** be big and tall, be tall [B]
高小 **gāoxiǎo** higher primary school
高矮 **gāoǎi** height (see frame 61 on abstract nouns in Chinese)

20

搞	一	丁	扌	**GĂO, to do, to make; to manage, to get; to purge [A]**
	扩	扩	护	
100 13 strokes	护	搞	搞	

| 又 | 乛 | 又 | | **YÒU, again. RIGHT-HAND radical (35) [A]**
A drawing (compare "left hand," 221, p. 45). 又 means "again" by sound-loan.
又不 **yòu bù** not at all ...
又高又大 **yòu gāo yòu dà** be both tall and big.
又矮又小 **yòu ǎi yòu xiǎo** be both short and small. |
| **101**
2 strokes | | | | |

敲	亠	亡	高	**QIĀO, to rap on; to blackmail; (colloquial) to swindle, cheat [B]** The right-hand part, 攴, was a radical in the traditional system; it meant "to knock, to hit." In 敲 it gives the meaning. **Gāo** (99, p. 20) suggests the sound.
	高	高'	高卜	
102 14 strokes	敲	敲		

稿	一	二	千	**GĂO, stalk (of grain); draft, sketch; manuscript [C]** 稿子 **gǎozi** draft; manuscript; plan, outline [D]
	千	禾	秆	
103 15 strokes	秆	稿	稿	

月	丿	月	月	**YUÈ, moon, month. MOON/MEAT radical (118) [A]** 月 is a picture of the moon. As an independent character, it means "moon." But as a result of modern simplifications, two traditional radicals—"moon" and "meat"—which were identical in form have become one radical. "Meat" as an independent character is 肉 (1013, p. 203).
	月			
104 4 strokes				

21

膏	亠	言	言	**GĀO, ointment; fat; grease; be oily, rich, sleek [C]**
	亭	膏	膏	The "moon/meat" radical—with the signification here of "meat"—gives the meaning. 高 **gāo** (99, p. 20) gives the sound.
105 14 strokes	膏	膏	膏	

可	一	丁	丁	**KĚ, may, can; to suit; certainly [A]** The origin of this character is unclear.
	可	可		可笑 **kěxiào** be laughable [C] 可口 **kěkǒu** to "suit your mouth," to taste good [D] 不可 **bùkě** should not 可心 **kěxīn** be satisfying, pleasing 可可 **kěkě** cocoa
106 5 strokes				

阿	阝	阝	阝	**Ā, prefix for people's names [B]** This character originally meant "slope." "Mound" (94, p. 19) suggested the meaning, and **kě** (106, above) suggested the sound. As a prefix, it is used by sound-loan.
	阿	阿	阿	阿门 **amén** Amen (in prayer) 阿高 **A-Gao** (Old) Gao (our friend or acquaintance, Mr. Gao)
107 7 strokes	阿			

啊	丨	刂	口	**Ā; a sentence-final particle—for questions, exclamations, commands, warnings, reminders, emphatic pauses, enumerations, direct address, and impatient statements. [A]** Sound-loan, reclarified with "mouth."
	叮	呀	呀	好累啊 **hǎo lèi a** (I'm) really tired!* 小心啊 **xiǎo xīn a** Be careful!
108 10 strokes	啊	啊	啊	

聿	乛	⺕	⺕	**No pronunciation; radical (124), "top of 聿 yù."**
	聿			聿 **yù** was a picture of a hand holding the Chinese writing brush. 聿 **yù**, once the "brush" radical, is no longer a radical.
109 4 strokes				

*Perhaps more correctly, for euphonic reasons, 好累呀 **hǎo lèi ya**. For 呀, see 672, below.

日 110 4 strokes	｜	冂	日
	日		

YUĒ, to say. SAY radical (104) [D]
Yuē has a stroke inside the mouth, perhaps to suggest the tongue moving. Learn to tell "say" 曰 from 日 "sun" (179, p. 36). In "say" (but never in "sun") the inner stroke is usually incomplete (stops short of the right vertical stroke). Also, "say" is shorter and fatter than "sun."

书 111 4 strokes	㇇	乛	书
	书		

SHŪ, book; letter; document; to write [A]
Shū used to be brush over yuē, "say" (see frame, bottom right). Now, it's pretty abstract.
手书 shǒu shū to write in your own hand; a personal letter
天书 tiān shū a book from outer space— abstruse or illegible writing

書

卩 112 2 strokes	㇆	卩	

JIÉ, seal (as in "seal ring"). SEAL radical (32)
The student should learn to tell the "seal" radical from the "right-ear" radical (191, p. 39). Like the "right-ear" radical, jié appears always at the right-hand side of characters (with one exception, where jié appears top-center).

报 113 7 strokes	一	十	扌
	扌ᐟ	护	报
	报		

BÀO, to announce, report; newspaper; to requite [A]
The old form of bào meant "requite" because it was a picture of a man kneeling, in manacles, with a hand to mete out punishment. Other meanings by sound-loan.
小报 xiǎobào tabloid

報

毛 114 4 strokes	一	二	三
	毛		

MÁO, hair, fur, feathers; wool; mildew; semifinished; gross (not net); a measure for dimes; family name. FUR radical (112) [A]
Máo is a picture of an animal's pelt. Distinguish from 手 "hand" (27, p. 6).

笔 115 10 strokes	丿	亇	𠂆	**BǏ, brush, writing instrument [A]** 笔 appears nicely to combine meanings, for the traditional Chinese writing brush is made of hair + bamboo. 毛笔 **máobǐ** writing brush [C] 笔心 **bǐxīn** pencil-lead; refill for ball-point pen
	𥫗	𥫗𥫗	𥫗	
	筆	筆	笔	筆

玩 116 8 strokes	一	二	干	**WÁN, to play, to amuse oneself [A]** A sound-meaning compound. 元 **yuán** (89, p. 18) suggests the sound. The "king" is undoubtedly a survival of the time when "king" 王 was an alternative form of the "jade" radical 玉 —toys being often made of jade. 玩笑 **wánxiào** a joke [C]
	王	王	王	
	玡	玩		

| 钅 117 5 strokes | 丿 | 卜 | 𠂉 | **JĪN, gold, metals; family name. SIDE-GOLD radical (147)** The radical in over 200 characters, this form does not occur independently (see 218, p. 44, for the independent form of "gold, metals"). Often in characters for various metals or metallic objects. |
| | 𠂉 | 钅 | | 金 |

| 山 118 3 strokes | 丨 | 山 | 山 | **SHĀN, mountain. MOUNTAIN radical (60) [A]** 山 is a picture. In old forms, it is clearly three peaks sticking up. 山 often occurs independently as a character and means "mountain" or "hill." 山口 **shānkǒu** mountain pass |

| 冈 119 4 strokes | 丨 | 冂 | 冈 | **GĀNG, ridge [D]** In the traditional form (see below, this frame), the "X" inside of 冈 had "mountain" as part of it. That has been lost in the modern simplified form. 山冈 **shāngāng** low hill, hillock [D] |
| | 冈 | | | 岡 |

钢	ノ	╭	╒	**GĀNG, steel; GÀNG, to sharpen, whet [A]**
	╘	钅	钊	This is a sound-meaning compound: 钅 "side-gold" ("metals") for meaning, **gāng** (119, p. 24) for sound.
120 9 strokes	钔	钢	钢	钢笔 **gāngbǐ** (modern) pen [A] 鋼

刚	ㅣ	冂	刀	**GĀNG, just now; exactly; only; to be firm, be hard [B]**
	冈	刚	刚	刚才 **gāngcái** just now [A] 刚刚 **gānggāng** be exactly…; just now [B] 刚好 **gānghǎo** Perfect!
121 6 strokes				剛

岗	⼁	⼳	⼳	**GĀNG, ridge; mound or hill; sentry [C]**
	广	屵	岗	
122 7 strokes	岗			崗

纲	ㄥ	ㄠ	纟	**GĀNG, main rope of a net; essential principle; discipline; authority [C]**
	纠	纫	纲	The "silk" radical helps with the meaning.
123 7 strokes	纲			綱

八	ノ	八		**BĀ, eight. EIGHT radical (24) [A]**
				There are a number of common modern characters in which this radical appears in the form ⺍, so the student should learn both forms. The form here is the independent form.
124 2 strokes				王八 **wángbā** tortoise; (vulgar, abusive) cuckold

铅	丿	𠂉	𠂉	**QIĀN, lead (the metal) [A]** 铅笔 **qiānbǐ** pencil [A]
	钅	钅	钌	
125 10 strokes	钌	钌	铅	鉛

米	丶	ヽノ	⸌⸍	**MǏ, rice; a family name. RICE radical (159) [A]** 米 was originally a picture of rice growing in a paddy, with the horizontal stroke to represent the water that stands in paddies. Distinguish from 采 "sift" (620, p. 125), from 禾 "grain" (81, p. 17), and from 木 "tree" (80 p. 17). See next two items for **mǐ** as phonetic.
	半	米	米	
126 6 strokes				

迷	丶	ヽノ	⸌⸍	**MÍ, to get lost; to get dirt in your eye; to develop an (unreasonable) passion for; fan, "bug" [B]**
	半	米	米	
127 9 strokes	米	迷	迷	

谜	丶	讠	讠'	**MÍ, riddle [C]**
	讠⸍	讠半	谜	
128 11 strokes	谜	谜	谜	謎

目	｜	冂	冃	**MÙ, eye. EYE radical (141) [A]** This character is a picture. Learn to distinguish the "eye" radical from the "small nose" radical 自 (619, p. 124). 书目 **shūmù** booklist, catalog of book titles 目中无人 **mùzhōngwúrén** be supercilious, haughty; consider no one worth your time
	目	目		
129 5 strokes				

26

眯	l	ll	目	**MĪ**, narrow your eyes; (dialect), take a nap; **MÍ**, get into a person's eyes (as, dust, dirt) [C]
	目	目	目′	
130 11 strokes	目′	眇	眯	眯

| 刀 | ㄅ | 刀 | | **DĀO**, knife. KNIFE radical (27) [A]
 The form ㄅ, seen in some combinations, is also classified as radical (27).
 刀 is a picture. Distinguish it from 力 "strength" (11, p. 3).
 刀子 **dāozi** knife [B]
 刀口 **dāokǒu** knife edge; a crucial point; incision |
| 131
 2 strokes | | | | |

分	ノ	八	分	**FĒN**, to divide; a fraction; a very small part; **FÈN**, a component; a share, one's lot [A] The "eight" is a picture of something being cut in two by the knife. 分 is phonetic in several items, where it may give the rhyme (**-en**, **-an**, **-in**), not a homonym. 分手 **fēnshǒu** to part with somebody 分心 **fēnxīn** to distract somebody
	分			
132 4 strokes				

份	ノ	亻	亻′	**FÈN**, share, portion; a measure for portions [B] Compare with 分 (132, above)
	价	份	份	
133 6 strokes				

粉	丶	丷	丷	**FĚN**, dust, powder [B] Face powder used to be made of rice. **Fěn** is a sound-meaning compound: "rice" for meaning, **fēn** (132, above) to suggest the sound.
	半	米	米	
134 10 strokes	米丶	粉	粉	

纷	↙	↙	↙	**FĒN, be tangled, be confusing; be profuse [B]**
	↙	↙	纷	The "silk" radical may help with the meaning. Fēn (132, p. 27) gives the sound.
135 **7 strokes**	纷			纷纷 **fēnfēn** one after another; be numerous and confused 纷

吩	∣	⺆	⺕	**FĒN, first syllable of** 吩咐 **fēnfu, to give somebody an order (instruction), to tell somebody to do something [B]**
	吥	吩	吩	For 咐, see 908, p. 182.
136 **7 strokes**	吩			

盼	∣	⺆	月	**PÀN, to hope for; to look [B]**
	目	目	盼	The "eye" radical helps with the meaning here. 分 (132, p. 27) gives, if imperfectly, the sound.
137 **9 strokes**	盼	盼	盼	

皿	∣	⺆	⺆	**MĬN, dish. DISH radical (146)**
	皿	皿		Distinguish from the "blood" radical 血 (1010, p. 203).
138 **5 strokes**				

盆	ノ	八	分	**PÉN, pot, basin, container [B]**
	分	分	盆	
139 **9 strokes**	盆	盆	盆	

28

| 贝 140 4 strokes | 丨 | 冂 | 贝 | **BÈI, a cowrie; a family name. COWRIE radical (106) [D]** A cowrie is a small, yellowish-white shell "with a fine gloss, used by various peoples as money" (*Century Dictionary*). Cowries used to be money in ancient China. The "cowrie" radical appears in characters for value, money, business transactions, etc. 貝 |
| | 贝 | | | |

贫 141 8 strokes	丿	八	分	**PÍN, be poor, insufficient [C]** 贫 looks like a meaning-meaning compound: "to divide" + "the cowries" (money) = "to be poor."
	分	分	谷	
	贫	贫		貧

扮 142 7 strokes	一	丁	扌	**BÀN, to act (in a play); disguise yourself as; make a face [B]**
	扌	扒	扮	
	扮			

氛 143 8 strokes	丿	广	气	**FĒN, atmosphere [C]** This character has 分 **fēn** (132) for sound and 气 "breath, vapors" for meaning. 气氛 **qìfēn** ambience
	气	气	气	
	氛	氛		雰

| 立 144 5 strokes | 丶 | 亠 | 亠 | **LÌ, to stand; to cause to stand, to set up; to be standing: be upright, vertical; to exist, to live; immediate (right away, instant). STAND radical (126) [A]** 立言 **lìyán** (old expression), write up your ideas; get a reputation through your writing |
| | 立 | 立 | | |

29

里	丨	冂	日	**LǏ**, village; li, a unit of distance (⅓ of an English mile); lining; inside, in. VILLAGE radical (195) [A]
	日	甲	単	A meaning-meaning compound: "land" + "fields" = "village." Other meanings by sound-loan. Its meaning "inside, in" gives 里 the function of turning some nouns and pronouns
145 7 strokes	里			into place-words. Consult a grammar (e.g., Chao 620-24).* 裏／裡

理	一	二	干	**LǏ**, grain (e.g., of wood); principle; reason, logic, truth; (by metonymy) natural science; to set in order; to speak to; to pay attention to [A]
	王	刲	玑	理 originally meant "veins in jade" and was a sound-meaning compound.
146 11 strokes	珇	珒	理	

厘	一	厂	厂	**LÍ**, a fraction, a smallest part; 0.33 millimetre; 0.05 gram; 0.667 square meters; a mill, one thousandth of a (Chinese) dollar (yuán); a unit of monthly interest—0.01%; a unit of annual interest—1% [B]
	斤	𠂤	盾	
147 9 strokes	厍	厙	厘	釐

哩	丨	冂	口	**LǏ, LI, see below (B)**
	叮	叮	吅	The mouth 口 at the side warns, as often, that the character is to be read for its sound value alone. 哩 **lī** is used to write such imitative vernacular expressions as 哩哩 啦啦 **līlīlālā**, "off and on, scattered," and (as **li**) at the end
148 10.strokes	呷	唖	哩	of an obvious statement ("..., of course") or after items in a list of examples. 啦: see Pt. 2, p. 219a.

童	丶	亠	六	**TÓNG**, child; children; a family name [B]
	立	立	音	童女 **tóngnǔ** maiden, virgin 童心 **tóngxīn** childlike innocence of an old man; playfulness of a young man
149 12 strokes	音	童	童	

*The meanings "lining; inside, in," and the related grammatical function, are a different word than "village." They attach to this character because 里 is now also used as a sound-loan for a word that, before the script reform, was written with the "gown" radical: 裏 or 裡.

中	｜	冂	口	ZHŌNG, middle; Chinese; ZHÒNG, hit the middle, fit perfectly; be hit or affected by; MIDDLE radical (105) [A]
	中			The downstroke through the center of the rectangle suggests "middle."
150 4 strokes				中心 **zhōngxīn** center, core [B] 中立 **zhōnglì** "standing in the middle," i.e., neutrality [D]

钟	ノ	𠂉	𠂉	ZHŌNG, clock; a family name [A]
	𠂉	钅	钅	The "gold" radical here signifies some object made of metal, and the "middle" radical gives the sound: a sound-meaning compound.
151 9 strokes	钅	钅	钟	十分钟 **shífēn zhōng** ten minutes 鐘

衣	、	亠	亠	YĪ, gown. GOWN radical (161) [A]
	衤	衤	衣	This character is a picture. The gown's sleeves and skirt can be seen clearly in older forms. As a part of characters, this radical often (not always) means that that character refers to an article of clothing.
152 6 strokes				毛衣 **máoyī** (wool) sweater [B] 大衣 **dàyī** overcoat

圭	一	二	丰	No pronunciation. Radical (89) "Top of 青" (see 249, p. 50).
	圭			See also the next character.
153 4 strokes				

表	一	二	丰	BIǍO, to show; be on the surface, be external; list, form; meter, gauge; watch (timepiece) [A]
	圭	丰	耒	**Biǎo** once meant "overcoat" and came to its other meanings by sound-loan—unless "overcoat" and "to show" are cognate words (the overcoat: the external coat).
154 8 strokes	耒	表		手表 **shǒubiǎo** wristwatch [B] (watch only) 錶

国		⊓	⊓	**GUÓ, nation [A]**
	⊐	⊞	国	中国 **Zhōngguó** China, the "Middle Kingdom" 国王 **guówáng** king [B] 中立国 **zhōnglì guó** a neutral nation
155 8 strokes	国	国		國

羊	`	`'	`''	**YÁNG, sheep, goat; a family name. SHEEP radical (157) [A]**
	兰	兰	羊	**Yáng** is a picture. The "eight" radical at the top gives the horns. Other forms in which this radical may appear, as part of characters, are 羊 and 羊.
156 6 strokes				小羊 **xiǎoyáng** lamb 山羊 **shānyáng** mountain goat

美	`	`'	`''	**MĚI, be beautiful [B]**
	兰	羊	羊	This character is supposed to be a meaning-meaning compound; one dictionary says, "If the sheep is big, it will be beautiful." Plumpness in women has often been considered beautiful.
157 9 strokes	美	美	美	美国 **Měiguó** America, the U.S.A. 美好 **měihǎo** be fine, happy, glorious [B]

夕	ノ	ク	夕	**XĪ, dusk. DUSK radical (64) [D]**
				The character is a drawing of the moon, to suggest "dusk." Learn to tell " dusk" from the "chip" radical 歹 (408, p. 82).
158 3 strokes				

卜		卜		**BŬ, to divine. DIVINE radical (16) [B]**
				In the Shang Dynasty (1751–1122 B.C.), the kings divined by scratching messages on tortoise shells. A professional diviner applied heat to the shell until it cracked, then read the cracks to divine. The "divine" radical is supposed to represent the divination cracks in the shell.
159 2 strokes				

外 160 5 strokes	丿	夕	夕	**WÀI, outside; relatives of one's mother, sisters, or daughters [A]**
	列	外		Karlgren says, "…'Moon' [dusk] and 'divine'… Moon may be phonetic…and the oracle crack appeared on the outside… of the shell when the inside was singed" (*GSR* 322). 外国 **wàiguó** foreign country [A] 外表 **wàibiǎo** surface, appearance [D]

看 161 9 strokes	一	二	三	**KÀN, to look at; KĀN, to look after, take care of [A]**
	手	手	看	A meaning-meaning compound: "hand" over "eye" to suggest "to look at." Note that the "hand" radical is slightly altered. Distinguish "look at" from 着 (586, p. 118).
	看	看	看	看中 **kànzhòng** to select, choose 看门 **kānmén** to act as doorkeeper

西 162 6 strokes	一	丨	冂	**XĪ, west. COVER radical (166) [A]**
	丙	西	西	Xī came to be the "cover" radical when, because of similarities in form, script-reformers put it together with a traditional "cover" radical As a radical, it appears at the top of characters. It is a picture of a bird in a nest and originally meant "to nest." "West" by sound-loan. Distinguish from 酉 the "wine" radical (474, p. 95).

贵 163 9 strokes	丨	⼌	⼐	**GUÌ, be expensive, precious [A]**
	虫	虫	串	Guì is a sound-meaning compound. The top part, no longer used as an independent character, gave the sound, and "cowrie" suggests the meaning.
	串	贵	贵	可贵 **kěguì** be valuable, deserve commendation [D] 贵人 **guìrén** government VIP 貴

更 164 7 strokes	一	丆	冂	**GÈNG, still more; GĒNG, to change; a "watch" (two-hour period of the night) [A]**
	同	百	更	The modern character is too much changed to make the explanation helpful. 更好 **gènghǎo** be better; even more
	更			

便 **165** 9 strokes	ノ イ 信	イ 伝 伊	仁 佰 便	**BIÀN, be convenient; PIÁN, the first syllable of *piányi*, be inexpensive [A]** 小便 **xiǎobiàn** to piss, a piss [C] 大便 **dàbiàn** to shit, defecation [C] 便衣 **biànyī** street clothes, "civvies;" plainclothesman
礻 **166** 4 strokes	丶 礻	ラ	礻	**No pronunciation. "SIDE-SIGN" radical (87)** Pre script reform, this was a variant of the "sign" radical (899, p. 180). Consistent with the reformist principle "what you see is what you get," it is now a separate radical. "Sign" in the sense of "signs from heaven" as well as "to exhibit, show." Distinguish from 衤, "side-gown" (290, p. 59).
且 **167** 5 strokes	丨 月	冂 且	月	**QIĚ, further [A]** The character is a drawing of an ancestral tablet. Originally it stood for a word meaning "ancestor" or "grandfather." Now it is used by sound-loan. It appears as the sound element in a number of characters (see below), where it has the value **zu** or **cu**.
祖 **168** 9 strokes	丶 礻 祀	ラ 礼 祖	礻 初 祖	**ZŬ, grandfather; ancestor; family name [A]** 祖国 **zŭguó** fatherland [A] 祖父 **zŭfù** ancestor [C]
租 **169** 10 strokes	一 千 和	二 禾 租	千 利 租	**ZŪ, rent, to rent [A]; hire, lease** Rent traditionally was land rent and was paid in grain; hence the "grain" radical in this character.

34

组	╯	⸝	⸜	**ZǓ, to organize; a unit of organization, such as a section or department [A]**
	纟	纠	纠	且 is the sound element here, for **zǔ**. "Silk" is for meaning (although exactly why is not obvious).
170 **8 strokes**	纠	组		

粗	⸍	⸍⸝	⸝⸜	**CŪ, be coarse (not fine) [B]**
	半	半	米	且 works as phonetic here, for **cū**. The "rice" radical works for the meaning. 粗心 **cūxīn** be careless, thoughtless 粗人 **cūrén** rough/uncouth person
171 **11 strokes**	籼	粗	粗	

阻	⸜	阝	阝	**ZǓ, to block, to obstruct [C]**
	阝	阴	阴	The "mound" radical ("left ear," (94, p. 19)) is intended to help with the meaning. 且 gives the sound **zu** here. 阻力 **zǔlì** obstruction; (physics) resistance, drag [C]
172 **7 strokes**	阻			

宜	⸍	⸍⸌	宀	**YÍ, be appropriate [A]**
	宀	宁	宜	The character is a picture of "the sacred pole of the altar of the soil, behung with ... meat" (Karlgren, *Grammata Serica Recensa* 21). It meant "sacrifice to the earth god." It is used for "be appropriate" by sound-loan.
173 **8 strokes**	宜	宜		便宜 **piányi** be inexpensive [A]

要	一	厂	襾	**YÀO, to want, to ask for; be "wanted," be important, essential [A]**
	襾	襾	西	要人 **yàorén** important person (usually a government official) 要不 **yàobù** otherwise, or else, or [C] 要好 **yàohǎo** be on good terms, be friends;
174 **9 strokes**	要	要	要	be eager to improve yourself [C]

皿	丨	冂	冂	**WĂNG, net. NET radical (145)** 罒 is not seen as an independent character. It appears as a radical in about 20 modern characters, always at the top.
175 **5 strokes**	罒	皿		

头	丶	丷	丷	**TÓU, the head; a suffix used to form nouns and noun-phrases; a bulb (of garlic); a measure-word for certain animals [A]** The "big" radical (61, p. 13) in **tóu** should be thought of as the drawing of a man and the two dots as an indicator: "the top part," i.e. "head."
176 **5 strokes**	头	头		木头 **mùtou** wood [B]　　　**頭**

买	乛	乛	乛	**MĂI, to buy [A]** Why these elements—a stroke above "head"— should mean **măi**, "to buy" is not clear. The pre-reform character (see below) had an eye watching the cowries (money), making a pretty good meaning-meaning compound.
177 **6 strokes**	买	买	买	**買**

卖	一	十	士	**MÀI, to sell [A]** In the pre-reform character, the "ten" radical at the top was 士 **shì** "knight" (see 35, p. 8)—perhaps a supervisor or assistant working with the seller to make sure the seller got it right.
178 **8 strokes**	去	卖	壶	买卖 **măimai** business [B] 卖国 **màiguó** be a traitor [D] **賣**
	卖	卖		

日	丨	冂	日	**RÌ, sun. SUN radical (103) [A]** **Rì** is a picture. Distinguish "sun" from "say" 曰. See 110, p. 23. 日子 **rìzi**　day, date; period of time; life, livelihood [A] 日元 **rìyuán** Japanese yen (unit of money). (日 here is short for 日本 **Rìben**, Japan. 本: see 308. [B])
179 **4 strokes**	日			日报 **rìbào**　daily newspaper [C]

36

业	一	十	土	No pronunciation; radical of "old" (see next) and three other characters. OLD radical (92)
	业			This seems to be an abbreviated form of 181, below, which is explained as a picture of an old man with long hair and a cane (analyzable as "earth-left-ladle").
180 4 strokes				Three of this radical's compounds have to do with age or seniority.

老	一	十	土	**LǍO, be old.** [A] 老二 **lǎoèr** second son or daughter [A] 老人 **lǎorén** old person; "old folks"—grand- parents (or old parents)[B] 老小 **lǎoxiǎo** young and old, family 老太太 **lǎotàitai** old lady, my ma [B] 老头儿 **lǎotóur** old coot [B] 老头子 **lǎotóuzi** old fart, (colloquial) my "old man" (= husband)
181 6 strokes	业	考	老	

者	一	十	土	**ZHĚ, a suffix to verbs: verb +** *zhe* **means "a person who... ." Compare with English suffix "-er."** [A]
	业	才	者	者 gives the sound in several characters (see the following few items).
182 8 strokes	者	者		老者 **lǎozhě** an old guy, old guys 大者小者 **dàzhě xiǎozhě** the big and the little, big guys and little guys

犭	ノ	犭	犭	**QUǍN, dog. SIDE-DOG radical (69)** As a radical, 犭 appears at the side of cha- racters (about 60 characters). 犬 (638, p. 128) also means "dog" (they were the same radical before script reform). 犭 appears often in char- acters for medium-size animals (pig, wolf, monkey, otter, cat—even lion) and for such qualities as ferocity, cruelty, courage, impetuosity.
183 3 strokes				

猪	ノ	犭	犭	**ZHŪ, pig** [A] The "side-dog" radical helps with the meaning; 者 (182, above) is there for the sound.
	犭	犭	犭	
184 11 strokes	犷	猪	猪	猪

煮	一	十	土	**ZHǓ, to boil, cook up [B]** "Fire-dots" for meaning, 者 (182, p. 37) for sound.
	耂	者	者	
185 12 strokes	者	者	煮	煑

著	一	艹	艹	**ZHÙ, to spread out, to display, be displayed; to author [B]** 著者 **zhùzhě** writer, author
	艹	芏	芝	
186 11 strokes	著	著	著	

暑	丨	冂	日	**SHǓ, summer, summer heat [B]** The "sun" radical 日 gives the meaning. 者 (182) may help with the sound.
	日	早	昇	
187 12 strokes	异	暑	暑	

绪	㇀	纟	纟	**XÙ, end of a thread; clue; to be together; succession; dynasty; profession [B]** "Silk" 纟 is there for the meaning.
	纟	纟	纠	
188 11 strokes	纱	绪	绪	緒

堵	一	十	土	**DǓ, to stop up; to stifle, be stifled; (bookish) wall; (often metaphorically: "a wall of spectators" [meaning many]); a measure for walls [B]** The "earth" radical 土 is the meaning part of this compound.
	圡	坴	坺	
189 11 strokes	堵	堵	堵	

署	丨	冖	冖	**SHǓ, an office, a government office; to arrange a piece of work; to handle as a deputy; to put your signature to [C]**
	冖	罒	罒	Karlgren sees "net" 罒 as the meaning component and 者 **zhě** (182, p. 37) as the sound component in this character.
190 **13 strokes**	罗	署	署	

阝	乛	阝		**YÌ, city. "RIGHT-EAR" radical (34)** Learn to tell this radical from the "mound" radical (94, p. 19). In form, "mound" and "city" are identical, but because of where they appear as part of characters, "mound" is called the "left-ear" radical and "city" the "right-ear" radical. Neither character means "ear."
191 **2 strokes**				

都	一	十	土	**DŌU, all; DŪ, metropolis, capital [A]** In the sense of "metropolis," this character is a sound-meaning compound; "city" gives the meaning, and **zhě** (182, p. 37) once gave the sound. In the sense of "all," it is used by sound-loan.
	耂	耂	者	
192 **10 strokes**	者	都	都	

廾	一	ナ	廾	**GǑNG, clasped hands. CLASP radical (51)** **Gǒng** is a picture of two clasped hands. Not now in use as an independent character. Distinguish from ⺿, the "grass" radical (16, p. 4) and from 廿 (194, below)
193 **3 strokes**				

廿	一	十	廿	**NIÀN, twenty. TWENTY radical (93)** This character is formed of two "ten" radicals written together. Sometimes written ⺿. This character is normally read aloud simply as 二十 **èrshí**—"twenty."
	廿			
194 **4 strokes**				

甘	一	十	廿	**GĀN, to taste sweet; a family name. SWEET radical (135) [C]**
	廿	甘		
195 **5 strokes**				

或	一	一	一	**HUÒ, perhaps; or [A]**
	口	豆	式	Originally, this character meant "nation." As "nation," it combined meanings: "lance" (for the army) + "mouth" (for a language) + "earth." ("Earth" got corrupted into the "one" radical.) Compare with the traditional form of 国 (155, p. 32). 或 = "perhaps" and "or" by sound-loan.
196 **8 strokes**	或	或		

匚	一	匚		**FĀNG, basket. BASKET radical [15]**
				The "basket" radical is a picture. The basket appears to be turned on its side, with the open top to the right. Not in modern use as an independent character.
197 **2 strokes**				

匹	一	匚	匚	**PǏ, mate; one half of a pair [B]**
	匹			一匹马 **yìpǐ mǎ** a horse, one horse
				匹夫 **pǐfū** ordinary man; "dummy," stupid fellow
198 **4 strokes**				

四	丨	冂	冂	**SÌ, four [A]**
	四	四		This is an arbitrary symbol. Memorize it.
				四书 **sìshū** "The Four Books," the "core classics" of Confucianism
199 **5 strokes**				

五	一	丁	开	**WǓ, five [A]**
	五			
200 4 strokes				

六	㇔	亠	宀 /	**LIÙ, six [A]** 六书 **liùshū** the six categories of Chinese characters (see pp. xi–xiii, above)
	六			
201 4 strokes				

| 七 | 一 | 七 | | **QĪ, seven [A]** The student will want to distinguish 七 from the "ladle" radical 匕 (41, p. 9). 七夕 **qīxī** the seventh night of the seventh lunar month—the one night of the year, according to myth, that the legendary lovers "The Cowboy" and "The Weaver Girl" get to spend together. |
| 202 2 strokes | | | | |

| 九 | 丿 | 九 | | **JIǓ, nine [A]** 九天 **jiǔtiān** "Ninth Heaven," the highest of heavens (the Western world has "seventh heaven") |
| 203 2 strokes | | | | |

| 入 | 丿 | 入 | | **RÙ, to enter [B]** Distinguish "enter" from "person" 人 (4, p. 1). As independent characters, they have different pronunciations and meanings—but as radicals they are grouped as one in modern dictionaries. 入口 **rùkǒu** entrance [D] 入手 **rùshǒu** put your hand in, get started, make a beginning [D] |
| 204 2 strokes | | | | |

41

什	ノ	亻	仁	**SHÉN**; the first syllable of *shénme* what? [A] **SHÍ**, miscellaneous; ten
	什			什 is ubiquitous as **shén**; as **shí**, rarely seen.
205 4 strokes				甚

么	ノ	厶	么	**ME**; the second syllable of *shénme* (*shémme*), what? [A]
				什么 **shénme** what? [A]
206 3 strokes				麼

桌	⌐	⊢	⼘	**ZHUŌ**, table [A]
	占	卣	卣	The "tree" radical at the bottom gives a clue that this character stands for a word referring to some object made of wood. The signficance of "to divine" and "sun," however, is not clear.
207 10 strokes	直	卓	桌	桌子 **zhuōzi** table [A] 书桌 **shūzhuō** writing desk

奇	一	ナ	大	**QÍ**, be weird [B]
	去	杏	杏	**Qí** is said to be a meaning-meaning compound, but it is not clear why "big" + "be able" should mean "be weird."
				好奇 **hàoqí** be curious, be interested in oddities or just many things [C]
208 8 strokes	奇	奇		好奇心 **hàoqíxīn** curiosity (state of mind, not a thing)

椅	一	十	才	**YĬ**, chair [A]
	木	杧	栌	**Yǐ** is supposed to be a sound-meaning compound: **qí** (208, above) for sound, "tree" for meaning (= something made of wood).
209 12 strokes	栌	栌	椅	椅子 **yǐzi** chair [A]

				DŌNG, east [A]
东	一	亡	存	Originally a picture of a bundle; used for "east" by sound-loan. Later scholars said the tradi-
	东	东		tional form (see below) was "the sun tangled in the branches of a tree, hence 'east'." In *Han-Ying Cidian*, 东 is one of 11 "left-over" characters, not classified under a radical.
210 5 strokes				東

				JIĀN, be thin
戋	一	二	弋	Jiān originally meant "be fierce, be cruel" and was a meaning-meaning compound: two lances to suggest ferocity. It means "be thin" by sound-loan.
	戋	戋		
211 5 strokes				戔

				QIÁN, money; a family name [A]
钱	丿	𠂆	钅	The "side-gold" radical (117, p. 24) gives the meaning, and **jiān** (211, above) suggests the sound.
	钅	钅	钅	九分钱 **jiǔfēn qián** 9 cents 金钱 **jīn qián** money [D]
212 10 strokes	钅	钱	钱	錢

				QIǍN, be shallow, superficial; be mild [A]
浅	`	⺀	氵	This would appear to be a sound-meaning compound, like **qián** "money" (212, above), but the meaning of "thin" may also be involved in the sound-element 戋: "thin water." Compare with 212, above.
	氵	浐	浅	
213 8 strokes	浅	浅		淺

				GÈ; a "measure," used to enumerate nouns in the construction "number + *gè* + noun;" be individual [A]
个	丿	人	个	三个 **sāngè** three . . . 个人 **gèrén** each person; oneself (B) 个子 **gèzi** stature (B) 个儿 **gèr** stature; each one (C) 个个 **gègè** all of 'em
214 3 strokes				個

43

文 215 4 strokes	`	亠	方	**WÉN**, pattern; language, literature, culture; civil (opposed to military); a family name. PATTERN radical (84) [A] This was a picture: a man with patterns worked onto his shirt. Distinguish "hand over" 交 (520, p. 105). 中文 **zhōngwén** the Chinese language [A] 文言 **wényán** classical Chinese (compare with 白话 "spoken language" in 427) [D]
	文			

这 216 7 strokes	`	亠	方	**ZHÈI, ZHÈ, this [A]** Zhèi normally appears in the construction "zhèi + 'measure'" or "zhèi + 'measure' + noun" (compare with 214, p. 43). 这个 **zhèige** this, this one [A] 这么 **zhème** so, thus, in this case, to this extent or degree [A] 这里 **zhèlǐ** here [A] 这儿 **zhèr** here [A] 這
	文	这	这	
	这			

那 217 6 strokes	刁	ヨ	彐	**NÀ, NÈI, NÈ, that (opposite to "this") [A]** 那 normally appears in the construction " 那 + 'measure'" or " 那 + 'measure' + noun" (compare with 214 and 216). 那个 **nàge** that, that one [A] 那么 **nàme** that being so, in that case, in that way; to that extent [A] 那里 **nàlǐ** there [A] 那儿 **nàr** there [A]
	用	那	那	

金 218 8 strokes	丿	人	亼	**JĪN**, gold, metals; family name. GOLD radical (209) [B] 金 occurs as an independent character and means "gold" or "metals." As a radical, it appears in four or five modern characters. "Side-gold" (117) is the radical in over 200 characters. 五金 **wǔjīn** the five metals (gold, silver, copper, iron, and tin); metals generally
	全	全	余	
	金	金		

合 219 6 strokes	丿	人	亼	**HÉ, to join, to bring together [A]** The root meaning of **hé** is "to join or close," like the two panels of a double door. The topmost three strokes at one time meant "to come together," early dictionaries say. "A meaning-meaning compound: to close, like the mouth." 合金 **héjīn** (combined metals, i.e.) alloy [C] 组合 **zǔhé** to form; combination [D]
	仐	合	合	

44

给 220 9 strokes	⟨stroke order diagrams⟩			**GĚI**, to give; to allow; for (someone) … ; **JĬ**, to supply [A] 给我书 **gěi wǒ shū** gives me books 给我看 **gěi wǒ kàn** let me look 给我买 **gěi wǒ mǎi** buys for me 给予 **jǐyǔ** to render, display 給
广 221 2 strokes	⟨stroke order diagrams⟩			**No pronunciation. "Top-of 左 ZUǑ" radical (14)** This is a picture of a left hand. Compare with the right-hand radical (101, p. 21). Not in current use as an independent character. As a modern radical this form is called "top of 左 zuǒ," "left" (668, p. 134).
有 222 6 strokes	⟨stroke order diagrams⟩			**YǑU**, to have; there is, there are [A] The earliest forms show a hand taking hold of a piece of meat. 有力 **yǒulì** be energetic, strong [B] 有钱 **yǒuqián** be rich 有口无心 **yǒu kǒu wú xīn** speak sharply but without malice [D]
干 223 3 strokes	⟨stroke order diagrams⟩			**GĀN**, shield; have to do with; be dry, be dried; be empty; emptily, futilely; **GÀN**, trunk, main part; to do [A] **Gān** depicts a shield; other meanings by sound-loan. See next few items for 干 as phonetic with various meaning elements. 干吗 **gàn ma** (colloquial) What the h—! What's this all about? OR, What shall we do? [B]
汗 224 6 strokes	⟨stroke order diagrams⟩			**HÀN**, sweat [B] **Hàn** is a sound-meaning compound: "three-dots-water" for meaning, **gān** (223, above) for sound. 汗毛 **hànmáo** fine body-hair (human)

45

肝	)	刀	月
	月	肝	肝
225 7 strokes	肝		

GĀN, the liver [B]

The sound is given by 干 (223, p. 45). "Meat" helps with the meaning.

杆	一	十	才
	木	杆	杆
226 7 strokes	杆		

GĀN, pole; GĂN, a measure for rifles, pistols, and spears [B]

干 **gān** gives the sound; "tree" is here for the meaning.

桿

走	一	十	土
	丰	丰	走
227 7 strokes	走		

ZŎU, to walk. WALK radical (189) [A]

The character was originally a meaning-meaning compound: "man" + "foot." The modern character is corrupted.

她走了 **tā zǒu le** She's left, she's gone.

赶	一	十	土
	丰	丰	走
228 10 strokes	走	赶	赶

GĂN, to rush after, to rush at; to chase off; by the time that ... [B]

The "walk" radical helps, perhaps, with the meaning. 干 is, again, the sound element.

趕

厂	一	厂	
229 2 strokes			

CHĂNG, factory. SLOPE radical (13)

"Slope"—once a picture—has become "factory" through the process of simplification. Following popular usage, 厂 "slope" is sometimes now used for 广, "lean-to" (363, p. 73—radical 44). A modern look-alike radical is the form 厂 ("top of 盾, 398, p. 80—radical 22).

(for "factory") 廠

岸 230 8 strokes	'	ㅛ	山
	山	户	户
	岸	岸	

ÀN, high cliff, high riverbank [B]

"Mountain" and "slope" both appear to contribute to the meaning. 干 **gān** helps fix the sound—here, however, by giving the rhyme, not as a homonym or near-homonym (not an unusual function for a sound element).

旱 231 7 strokes	∣	⼌	日
	日	且	旦
	旱		

HÀN, drought; dry land [C]

The "sun" radical 日 helps fix the meaning. 干 is the sound element.

| ⺉ 232 2 strokes | ∣ | ⺉ | |
| | | | |

DĀO, knife. SIDE-KNIFE radical (17)

This form of the "knife" radical does not occur independently but only as a part of characters. Called "side-knife" to distinguish it from the independent form (131, p. 27).

| 刊 233 5 strokes | 一 | 二 | 干 |
| | 刊 | 刊 | |

KĀN, to carve, to engrave [C]

The "knife" ("side-knife") gives the meaning.

| 殳 234 4 strokes | ⼃ | 几 | 𠬝 |
| | 殳 | | |

SHŪ, club, to club. CLUB radical (119)

Shū is a picture: a right hand holds the club. Distinguish "club" from these characters: "branch" 支 (351, p. 71), "knock" 攵 (316, p. 64), "pattern" 文 (215, p. 44) and "follow, slow" 夊 (431, p. 87). **Shū**, "club," is not now in common use as an independent character.

没	`	`	氵
	沪	沪	汐
235 7 strokes	没		

MÒ, inundate; MÉI, negates *yǒu* (222, p. 45) and other verbs. [A]

没 functions by sound-loan as a negator of **yǒu** and other verbs.

没有 **méiyǒu** there isn't, there aren't; doesn't have; hasn't (done it) [A]

没买 **méimǎi** hasn't bought

没什么 **méishénme** it doesn't matter; never mind [B]

身	`	⼃	勹
	白	白	身
236 7 strokes	身		

SHĒN, torso. TORSO radical (200) [A]

Shēn is a picture of a person in which the torso is the most prominent part. It also means "self."

可身 **kěshēn** to fit well (clothes)

合身 **héshēn** to fit well (clothes)

身分 **shēnfèn** position, rank [C]

寸	一	寸	寸
237 3 strokes			

CÙN, thumb; inch. THUMB radical (54) [A]

The "thumb" radical is a picture of a hand, with the dot added to indicate the thumb. Learn to distinguish "thumb," "side-hand" 扌 (28, p. 6), and "then" 才 (689, p. 138).

射	`	⼃	勹
	白	白	身
238 10 strokes	身	身一	射

SHÈ, to shoot [B]

The character has been corrupted through time. Originally, the "torso" was a picture of an arrow on a bow, and the "thumb" was a hand drawing on a bow, whence "to shoot."

射门 **shèmén** to shoot (at the goal, in sports)

射手 **shèshǒu** marksman, sharpshooter

谢	`	讠	讠
	讠	讠	诮
239 12 strokes	诮	谢	谢

XIÈ, thanks; to thank; excuse oneself; a family name [A]

Xiè is a sound-meaning compound; the "side-word" radical gives the meaning, and **shè** suggests the sound.

谢谢 **xièxiè** Thank you. [A]

不谢 **búxiè** You're welcome

謝

吉 240 6 strokes	一	十	士	**JÍ, lucky; a family name (D)** An early dictionary says the character is a meaning-meaning compound: "scholar" (or "knight") + "mouth" = "lucky." 吉日 **jírì** A "lucky day" on the traditional calendar; a good day for taking action 吉他 **jítā** guitar
	吉	吉	吉	

桔 241 10 strokes	一	十	才	**JÚ, tangerine [A]** This is the popular form of a character written 橘 (see Pt. 2, p. 226a). In the expression 桔汁 (**zhī**), "orange juice," either character can mean "orange" (rather than "tangerine"). 汁 means "juice, gravy" [D].
	木	杧	村	
	村	桔	桔	

结 242 9 strokes	𠃋	𢆉	纟	**JIÉ, to tie together; knot; JIĒ, to bear fruit [A]** 结合 **jiéhé** to unite, to combine; to be married [B]
	纟	纠	结	
	结	结	结	結

喜 243 12 strokes	一	吉	声	**XǏ, to enjoy, to give enjoyment to [A]** The top part of this, what is now "knight-mouth-eight-one," used to be a picture of a drum. **Xǐ** was a meaning-meaning compound: "drum" + "mouth" = "to sing and play drums, to enjoy yourself." 喜人 **xǐrén** be satisfying 喜好 **xǐhào** to like, to love, be fond of
	吉	吉	喜	
	壴	喜	喜	

欠 244 4 strokes	丿	𠂉	勹	**QIÀN, yawn; to owe, to lack. YAWN radical (120) [B]** Note that the lower part of this character is the "person" radical. If it helps you to remember the character, think of the upper part as the person's hand covering the mouth while yawning. 欠钱 **qiànqián** owe money, be in debt
	欠			

49

欢	㇆	又	𡿨	**HUĀN, be pleased [A]**
	𡿨ノ	欢	欢	The "yawn" radical for meaning, perhaps as a mouth open to smile or laugh. "Right hand" replaces the old sound-element.
245 6 strokes				喜欢 **xǐhuān** to like [A] 欢喜 **huānxǐ** be joyful; be fond of [C] 欢笑 **huānxiào** laugh delightedly [D] 歡

止	丨	卜	止	**ZHǏ, to stop. TOE radical (102) [B]**
	止			The "toe" radical is a picture of a foot. From "foot" came derived meanings of actions of the foot: "to march; to halt." Only the meaning "to halt" has stayed with the character to modern times.
246 4 strokes				阻止 **zǔzhǐ** to prevent, obstruct [C] 不止三个 **bùzhǐ sānge** not stopping at three, not only three

足	丨	冂	口	**ZÚ, foot; be sufficient. FOOT radical (196) [A]**
	𤴓	𤴔	𧾷	A picture. The bottom part of "foot," in fact, is the "toe" radical (246, above). In 248, below, the "foot" radical appears as part of the character; note that in the form used in compounds, "toe" can be clearly seen.
247 7 strokes	足			十足 **shízú** sheer, total, absolute, utter [D]

跟	丨	口	무	**GĒN, heel; to follow, to go with; with [A]**
	足	趵	跟	Gēn is a sound-meaning compound: the "foot" radical gives the meaning; gèn (51, p. 11) gives the sound.
248 13 strokes	跟	跟	跟	

青	一	二	丰	**QĪNG, be green or blue. GREEN radical (202) [A]**
	丰	青	青	Note that the bottom half of "green" resembles "moon." Qīng by itself, however, is recognized as a radical. The character also occurs independently and means "green" and sometimes other "colors of nature," like azure or even greenish black or grey.
249 8 strokes	青	青		

请	`	讠	讠	**QĬNG, to invite; please. . . [A]**
				This character is a sound-meaning compound: "side-word" gives the meaning, and **qīng** (249, p. 50) gives the sound.
	讠	讠	讠	谁请 **shéi qǐng** Who's paying?
250 10 strokes	讠	请	请	請

情	ノ	丷	忄	**QÍNG, emotion; circumstances [A]**
				Sound (青) + meaning ("heart"). This is something related to the heart, pronounced **qíng**: emotion.
	忄	忄	忄	情报 **qíngbào** information; intelligence (as in "intelligence agency") [C]
251 11 strokes	情	情	情	情人 **qíngrén** sweetheart

清	`	﹁	氵	**QĪNG, be clear; to clear [A]**
				This is a sound-meaning compound: 青 **qīng** for sound, "3-dots water" for meaning (it can also be read as a meaning-meaning compound: "water" + "azure" = "clear.")
	氵	氵	氵	清楚 **qīngchu** be clear, distinct
252 11 strokes	清	清	清	

晴	｜	冂	日	**QÍNG, clear sky [A]**
				"Sun" 日 + "azure" 青 = clear sky. 青 **qīng** also helps, of course, with the sound.
	日	日	日	晴天 **qíngtiān** a fine day [C]
253 12 strokes	晴	晴	晴	

睛	｜	冂	月	**JĪNG, the pupil of the eye [A]**
				"Eye" 目 + "azure" 青 = pupil of the eye. 青 **qīng** also helps with the sound.
	目	目	目	
254 13 strokes	睛	睛	睛	

51

问	﹀	﹢	门	**WÈN, to ask (for information) [A]** "Mouth" for meaning; **mén** once gave the sound in this compound.
	问	问	问	问住 **wènzhu** to stump with a question (问 不住 cannot stump..., 问得住, can stump...)
255 6 strokes				请问 **qǐngwèn** Would you please tell me ... [A] 問

耳	一	丁	丁丁	**ĚR, ear. EAR radical (163) [B]** The "ear" radical is a picture.
	丌	耳	耳	耳目 **ěrmù** hearsay, "scuttlebutt," information; spy, informer, "fink" 木耳 **mùěr** edible tree fungus
256 6 strokes				

闻	﹀	﹢	门	**WÉN, to hear [A]** **Mén** (25, p. 6) functions here, as in 255, to suggest the sound **wen**. The meaning is given by the "ear" radical.
	门	闩	闻	闻人 **wénrén** a famous person
257 9 strokes	闻	闻	闻	耳闻 **ěrwén** to hear about, especially superficially (in contrast to seeing it yourself) 聞

闲	﹀	﹢	门	**XIÁN, leisure [B]** This looks like a meaning-meaning compound: "put a tree across your door or gate so you won't be disturbed."
	闩	闭	闲	
258 7 strokes	闲			閑

间	﹀	﹢	门	**JIÀN, space; be separated from; to separate,** "drive a wedge between," sow discord; **JIĀN between; a measure-word for rooms [A]**
	问	问	间	中间 **zhōngjiān** between, among; the middle, center [A]
259 7 strokes	间		·	田间 **tiánjiān** farm, field [D] 人间 **rénjiān** world of human affairs [C] 間

另				LÌNG, separately [B]
260 5 strokes	丨	冂	口	另外 lìngwài in addition [B]
	弓	另		

别				BIÉ, to separate, to part; *Don't ... !* [A]
261 7 strokes	丨	冂	口	别人 biérén other people [A]
	弓	另	别	分别 fēnbié to part (from one another); sort out, differentiate; difference [B]
	别			个别 gèbié specific; very few; be exceptional [B]
				别买 biémǎi Don't buy it!

朋				PÉNG, friend [A]
262 8 strokes	丿	刀	月	The character originally stood for a fabulous bird and was a picture of the wings of that bird. It means "friend" by sound-loan.
	月	刖	朋	
	朋	朋		

友				YǑU, friend [A]
263 4 strokes	一	丆	方	友 combines meanings: "left hand" + "right hand" = "friend." The character suggests the gesture of parting: clasp your own hands in front of you and bow over them. Shaking hands Western style is, of course, right hand with right hand. Distinguish 友 from 反 (418, p. 84).
	友			朋友 péngyǒu friend

父				FÙ, father. FATHER radical (108) [A]
264 4 strokes	丶	八	分	祖父 zǔfù ancestors, forefathers [C]
	父			父老 fùlǎo elders (as in a district)

毋	ㄴ	ㄐ	母	**WÚ, don't!**
	毋			The character is supposed to be a picture of a woman in irons. The relation of that to its present meaning is unclear. Learn to distinguish "don't" from 母 **mǔ**, "mother" (268, below)
265 4 strokes				

见	丨	冂	刀	**JIÀN, to see, to perceive. SEE radical (107) [A]**
	见			The legs at the bottom of "see" represent a person; traditionally, the top part was a big eye to suggest "see" (see below, this frame). 远见 **yuǎnjiàn** foresight; vision
266 4 strokes				見

亲	丶	亠	亠	**QĪN, relatives; to hold dear; in person; QÌNG, relatives by marriage [A]**
	立	立	立	Sound-loan. 亲 —"hazel tree"—was the sound-element in the old character. 父亲 **fùqīn** father [A] 六亲 **liùqīn** the six (most important) relatives: father, mother, elder
267 9 strokes	辛	亲	亲	brothers, younger brothers, wife, children 親

母	ㄴ	ㄐ	口	**MǓ, mother [A]**
	母	母		**Mǔ** is a picture of a woman with two dots to emphasize the breasts. Learn to distinguish "mother" from "don't" 毋 (265, above). 母亲 **mǔqīn** mother [A] 父母 **fùmǔ** parents; mother and father
268 5 strokes				

哥	一	丆	丏	**GĒ, elder brother [A]** 哥哥 **gēge** older brother [A] 大哥 **dàgē** oldest brother; used to address politely a man about your own age [C] 表哥 **biǎogē** older male cousin such that the two of you are children or grandchildren of a brother and a sister, or of two sisters
	丏	丏	可	
269 10 strokes	哥	哥	哥	

弓	ㄱ	ㄱ	弓	**GŌNG, bow (as in "bow and arrow"); to bend or arch, like a bow; family name. BOW radical (71) [C]**
270 **3 strokes**				The "bow" radical is a picture. 弓子 **gōngzi** bow (e.g., a violin bow) .

弔	ㄱ	ㄱ	弓	**DIÀO, to pity**
	弔			This character is said to be a picture of an arrow stayed on the bow, hence "to pity." In modern use, this character has been replaced by 吊, which Bernhard Karlgren calls "a vulgar corruption" (*Analytic Dictionary* 989).
271 **4 strokes**				

弟	丶	丷	丷ㄏ	**DÌ, younger brother; family name [A]**
	丷	弟	弟	弟弟 **dìdi** younger brother, younger male cousin [A] 二弟 **èrdì** second younger brother 小弟 **xiǎodì** kid brother 弟子 **dìzi** disciple, pupil
272 **7 strokes**	弟			

姐	ㄑ	女	女	**JIĚ, older sister [A]**
	妅	如	姐	The "woman" radical gives the meaning, 且 **qiě** (167, p. 34) helps with the sound. 姐姐 **jiějie** older sister [A] 小姐 **xiǎojiě** Miss [A] 大姐 **dàjiě** oldest sister; used to address politely a woman about your own age
273 **8 strokes**	姐	姐		

未	一	二	十	**WÈI, not yet; the "eighth early branch" (used in enumerations and to name two-hour periods of the day) [B]**
	未	未		Distinguish "not yet" 未 from 末 (Pt. 2, p. 217a) and from 禾 (Pt. 2, p. 273b). See *Lin Yutang's Dictionary* 1451f for an account of the "earthly branches."
274 **5 strokes**				未可 **wèikě** cannot, be unable to

妹	㇛	女	女	**MÈI, younger sister [A]** 妹妹 **mèimei** younger sister [A] 姐妹 **jiěmèi** sisters 妹夫 **mèifū** brother-in-law (precisely, younger sister's husband) 表妹 **biǎomèi** younger female cousin such that you two are children or grandchildren of a brother and a sister, or of two sisters
275 8 strokes	女	女=	奸	
	奸	妹		

氏	一	厂	臣	**SHÌ, clan. CLAN radical (122) [C]** The student may find it difficult to remember how to write radicals which, like the "clan" radical, do not make a clear picture of anything. But the number of such non-representational radicals is small, and a little work should resolve it. 田王氏 **Tián Wáng shì** Mrs. Tian (whose maiden name is Wang)
276 4 strokes	氏			

纸	㇜	幺	纟	**ZHǏ, paper [A]** A sound-meaning compound. "Silk" gives the meaning, **shì** (276, above) gives the sound. 报纸 **bàozhǐ** newspaper [B] 手纸 **shǒuzhǐ** toilet paper
277 7 strokes	纟	纟'	纸	
	纸			帋, 紙

长	ノ	一	上	**CHÁNG, be long; ZHǍNG, to grow; be senior [A]** The character was a picture of a man with a long beard (see below)—now pretty abstract or impressionistic. 长大 **zhǎngdà** to grow up 长子 **zhǎngzi** eldest son
278 4 strokes	长			長

张	㇆	㇆	弓	**ZHĀNG, to open out, to open up; a measure for objects coming in sheets; a family name [A]** 张弓 **zhāng gōng** draw a bow 三张纸 **sānzhāng zhǐ** three sheets of paper
279 7 strokes	弓'	弓⁻	张	
	张			張

56

	一	厂	冂	**HUÀ, to paint, a painting [A]**
画	开	冊	田	The "field" in this character may be intended to suggest outdoors, the countryside—landscape painting.
280	画	画		画报 **huàbào** illustrated magazine [B] 国画 **guóhuà** "national painting," i.e. traditional Chinese painting
8 strokes				一张画 **yìzhāng huà** a painting 畫

	´	厂	F	**JIÙ, mortar. MORTAR radical (179)**
臼	臼	臼	臼	Jiù is the drawing of a mortar (a vessel in which to grind things up). Distinguish **jiù** from 白 "white" (282, below), from 日 "sun" (179, p. 36) and from 曰 "say" (110, p. 23).
281				
6 strokes				

	'	l'	冖	**BÁI, be white; a family name. WHITE radical (150) [A]**
白	白	白		Distinguish **bái** from 臼 (281, above), 日 (179, p. 36) and 自 (619, p. 124).
				白天 **bái tiān** in the daytime [B] 白白 **báibái** vainly, to no purpose 白给 **bái gěi** to give free of charge
282				白人 **báirén** white guy, white girl
5 strokes				表白 **biǎo bái** to vindicate

	ノ	勹		**BĀO, to wrap. WRAP radical (26)**
勹				The character is a picture of a wrapper. As part of a character, the "wrap" radical usually appears wrapped around other radicals or parts of characters.
283				
2 strokes				

	ノ	勺	勺	**SHÁO, spoon; frying pan [B]**
勺				勺子 **sháozi** spoon [B] 木勺 **mùsháo** wooden ladle
284				
3 strokes				

的	′	⌐	白	DE; a suffix to nouns and pronouns: A 的 B means "A's B, the B of A;" a grammatical particle; Dì, bull's-eye [A]
	白	白	的	我的 **wǒde** my, mine 有的 **yǒude** some [A] 目的 **mùdì** aim, purpose [B]
285 8 strokes	的	的		(note: **dì** for this word)

包	′	⌐	勹	BĀO, to wrap; a family name [A] **Bāo** gives the sound (**bao** or **pao**) in a number of common characters (see below and the next two pages).
	勹	包		包子 **bāozi** steamed filled dumpling [B] 书包 **shūbāo** book-bag, satchel [B]
286 5 strokes				

跑	I	冂	口	PǍO, to run [A] The "foot" radical gives the meaning; **bāo** (286) suggests the sound.
	𧾷	𧾷	𧾷	跑马 **pǎomǎ** a horse-race; ride a horse
287 12 strokes	𧾷	跑	跑	

抱	一	丁	扌	BÀO, to hold in your arms, to hug; to have your first grandchild; to adopt a child; to cherish; to sit on eggs to hatch them; a measure for armfuls; (dialect) to consort with, to hang out with [A]
	扌	扚	扚	
288 8 strokes	抱	抱		

胞	ノ	丿	月	BĀO, be related by blood; afterbirth, placenta [C]
	月	𦙶	肑	胞弟 **bāodì** younger blood brother 胞衣 **bāoyī** afterbirth
289 9 strokes	胞	胞	胞	

衤	丶	㇇	衤	**YĪ, gown. SIDE-GOWN radical (129)** Called "side-gown" to distinguish it from radical 161, 衣 (152, p. 31). 衤 appears always at the side in characters of which it is a part. These characters generally have to do with clothing. Independently, 衣 rather than 衤 is used.
290 5 strokes	衤	衤		

袍	丶	㇇	衤	**PÁO, long gown or robe [C]** 长袍 **chángpáo** long gown
	衤	衤	衤	
291 10 strokes	袍	袍	袍	

泡	丶	冫	氵	**PÀO, to soak; to pester; be together; bubble; blister; light bulb; PĀO, be fluffy; to waste [C]**
	泡	泡	泡	
292 8 strokes	泡	泡		

饣	丿	𠂉	饣	**No pronunciation. SIDE-FOOD radical (68)** Traditionally, this radical was classified as a variant of 食 "food" (413, p. 83). As part of the script-reform, it came to be identified as a separate radical It retains its meaning of "food" and food-related things. "Food" is the radical in five characters; "side-food" in about 40.
293 3 strokes				

饱	丿	𠂉	饣	**BĂO, to be full, to have had enough to eat [A]** 吃饱了! **chībăo le** I'm full; I have enough.
	饣	饱	饱	
294 8 strokes	饱	饱		饱

59

火	ヽ	ヽヽ	少	**HUǑ, fire. FIRE radical (83) [A]** The character is a picture of flames rising. 火力 **huǒlì** (military) firepower [C] 火山 **huǒshān** volcano [D] 肝火 **gānhuǒ** be hot-tempered
	火			
295 4 strokes				

炮	ヽ	ノ	リ	**PÀO, cannon, artillery; a shot from a gun [B]**
	火	火	灼	
296 9 strokes	灼	灼	炮	

己	⼅	⼆	己	**JǏ, self; the sixth "heavenly stem" (used to enumerate headings in an outline, like "F"— sixth letter of the Western alphabet). SELF radical (72) [A]**
				Learn to tell "self" from **yǐ** "already" 已 (298, next) and from **sì** 巳 (299). See *Lin Yutang's Dictionary* 1451f for more on "heavenly stems."
297 3 strokes				

| 已 | ⼅ | ⼆ | 已 | **YǏ, already; to end, to cease [A]**
See the preceding item for characters with which **yǐ** is likely to be confused. |
| 298
3 strokes | | | | |

| 巳 | ⼅ | ⼆ | 巳 | **SÌ, the sixth "earthly branch" (巳 and 己 (297, above) are classified as radical (72) in *Han-Ying Cidian*).**
Sì is supposed originally to have been a drawing of a fetus, with a large head and curled up lower part. Distinguish **sì** from 297 and 298, above. Compare with 包 (286, p. 58). See *Lin Yutang's Dictionary* 1451f on the "earthly branches." |
| 299
3 strokes | | | | |

纪	㇟	㇃	㇃	**JÌ, write down; record; year; discipline; JǏ, to order; a family name [A]** 年纪 **niánjì** age (number of years) [A] 世纪 **shìjì** century [B] 纪要 **jìyào** summary; minutes of a meeting, etc [D]
	纟	纩	纪	

300
6 strokes

紀

记	丶	讠	讠㇀	**JÌ, to remember; to record; mark, sign [A]** 记者 **jìzhě** reporter [B] 记住 **jìzhu** to fix in the mind; to remember
	讠㇀	记		

301
5 strokes

記

巴	㇕	㇆㇀	㇕	**BĀ, open hand; palm; to stick to; to hope for [B]** 巴 once meant "boa"—as the dictionaries call it, "the elephant snake"—and it was a picture. It means "open hand" by sound-loan. In *Han-Ying Cidian*, 巴 is one of 11 "left-over" characters, not classified under a radical. See next few frames for its use as a sound component.
	巴			

302
4 strokes

吧	丨	冂	囗	**BA; a sentence-final particle; indicates supposition ("..., I guess") or suggestion ("Maybe you should..."); BĀ, snap! (onomatopoetic); to draw (suck) on (e.g., a tobacco pipe); bar (drinking place) [A]** 吧 is a sound-meaning compound. 好吧 **hǎo ba** Okay! Bravo! Fine!
	口㇕	口㇆㇀	口㇕	
	吧			

303
7 strokes

把	一	扌	扌	**BǍ, to grasp; a handful; to guard; a particle used to bring direct objects in front of the verb; a measure for things with handles (knives, teapots) or that you grasp (chairs, handfuls of rice, bunches of flowers) [A]; BÀ, handle** 一把米 **yìbǎ mǐ** a handful of rice 一把勺 **yìbǎ sháo** a spoon
	扌㇕	扌㇆㇀	扌㇕	
	把			

304
7 strokes

61

爸	⺆	八	父	**BÀ, papa, father [A]** 爸爸 **bàba** papa, father [A]
	父	爷	爷	
305 8 strokes	爸	爸		

爪	⺀	厂	爪	**ZHǍO, claws. CLAWS radical (116)** See 447, p. 90, for the form of this radical which usually appears as a part of characters. The form 爪 is the independent form and appears as a radical in one common character (see next).
	爪			
306 4 strokes				

爬	⺀	厂	爪	**PÁ, to crawl, to creep; to climb [A]**
	爪	爬	爬	
307 8 strokes	爬	爬		

本	一	十	才	**BĚN, root; volume (book); capital (money); principal (money); a measure for books [A]** **Běn** is a tree with a horizontal stroke at the bottom to indicate the roots. 日本 **Rìběn** Japan 本人 **běnrén** I, myself; in person [C] 本钱 **běnqián** capital (money) [D] 一本书 **yìběn shū** a book, one book
	木	本		
308 5 strokes				

对	7	又	对	**DUÌ, to face; facing; to match; be correct [A]** 对了 **duìle** That's right! 对手 **duìshǒu** adversary, opponent [D] 对钟 **duì zhōng** to set a clock
	对	对		
309 5 strokes				對

兄	丨	冂	口	**XIŌNG, older brother [B]**
	尸	兄		兄弟 **xiōngdì** brothers [B] 胞兄 **bāoxiōng** older brother by blood 表兄 **biǎoxiōng** older male cousin on the mother's side
310 **5 strokes**				

兑	丶	丷	丷	**DUÌ, to hand over [C]**
	兯	兯	兌	兑给 **duìgěi** to pay to
311 **7 strokes**	兑			

税	一	二	千	**SHUÌ, tax [C]** The peasantry traditionally paid their taxes in grain, so "grain" + "to hand over" was a good meaning-meaning compound for "tax."
	千	禾	秒	租税 **zūshuì** land tax 报税 **bàoshuì** to make a customs declaration, to declare goods on which duty is owed
312 **12 strokes**	秒	秒	税	

说	丶	讠	讠	**SHUŌ, to speak; SHUÌ, try to persuade [A]; sometimes used for YUÈ 悦 "be happy, delighted."** This is a sound-meaning compound: the "side-word" radical for meaning, **duì** (311, above) for sound (only roughly, now).
	讠	讠	讠	说笑 **shuōxiào** to talk and laugh together, yuk it up
313 **9 strokes**	说	说	说	说一不二 **shuō yī bú èr** to mean what you say　　説

古	一	十	十	**GǓ, be ancient; a family name [B]** According to the usual explanation, **gǔ** is a meaning-meaning compound: "ten" + "mouth" suggests something that has been passed through ten generations of "mouths" (people); therefore, ancient.
	古	古		See next few items with 古 for sound. 古老 **gǔlǎo** be ancient, be age-old [B] 古玩 **gǔwán** antique, curio
314 **5 strokes**				

姑	﹀	女	女	**GŪ, unmarried girl; father's or husband's sister; temporarily; be lenient [A]**
	女	奴	奵	姑娘 **gūniang** girl; (colloquial) daughter [A]
315 8 strokes	姑	姑		姑母 **gūmǔ** married sister of your father, aunt 姑且 **gūqiě** tentatively; for the moment

攵	ノ	⺊	攵	**No pronunciation. KNOCK radical (113)**
	攵			Distinguish the "knock" radical from the "club" radical 殳 (234, p. 47), from "branch" 支 (351, p. 71), from the "pattern" radical 文 (215, p. 44), and (especially) from the "fol-
316 4 strokes				low/slow" radical 夂 (431, p. 87).

故	一	十	十	**GÙ, be ancient; to die; cause; intentionally [A]**
	古	古	古	古 for sound; the significance of "knock" is not clear.
317 9 strokes	故	故	故	故土 **gùtǔ** "the old country," one's native land

估	ノ	亻	亻	**GŪ, to appraise, to estimate [B]**
	什	佔	估	古 for sound.
318 7 strokes	估			估产 **gūchǎn** estimate the harvest/yield 估价 **gūjià** to appraise, evaluate

固	丨	冂	冃	**GÙ, be firm, solid, resolutely; originally, in the first place; a conjunction word [B]**
	冃	冃	固	
319 8 strokes	固	固		

苦	一	十	卝	**KŬ, be bitter [A]** A sound-meaning compound: 古 for sound, "grass" for meaning.
	芒	芒	芒	吃苦 **chīkŭ** to suffer, to endure hardship [C] 甘苦 **gānkŭ** "the sweet and the bitter," weal and woe
320 8 strokes	苦	苦		

枯	一	十	才	**KŬ, dried wood; be withered, be dried out [C]** 古 here suggests the sound; "tree" 木 suggests the meaning (although "tree" (for "wood") + "be ancient" could be taken as a meaning-meaning compound: old wood, therefore dried, withered, dried out).
	木	杧	杧	
321 9 strokes	枯	枯	枯	

辜	一	十	古	**GŪ, guilt; a crime; a family name [C]** **Gŭ** (314, p. 63) gives the sound. 辛 "bitter" (70, p. 15) helps with the meaning.
	古	克	克	
322 12 strokes	辜	辜	辜	

重	一	二	一	**ZHÒNG, be heavy; CHÓNG, do over again, to repeat by mistake [A]** Picture of a scale (weighing machine)?
	乍	盲	盲	重要 **zhòngyào** be important [A] 贵重 **guìzhòng** be valuable [D] 重了 **chóng le** be done twice, get repeated 买重了 **mǎichóng le** has/have bought an extra one (one too many)
323 9 strokes	重	重	重	

董	一	十	卝	**DŎNG, to correct, to supervise; a family name [D]** 古董 **gǔdǒng** an antique; an old duffer
	芒	苦	芎	
324 12 strokes	茜	苹	董	

65

懂	⟍	⟍	忄	**DǑNG, to understand [A]**
	忄	忄	忄	This character may stand for the same word as 324, above: "be correct (in the mind) about, to understand." Note that in form it is identical to 324, with the addition of the "heart" ("side-heart") radical (often glossed as "heart/ mind").
325 15 strokes	惜	懂	懂	看不懂 **kànbudǒng** be unable to read

疋	一	丁	下	**PǏ, bolt (of cloth). BOLT radical (156)**
	疋	疋		
326 5 strokes				

是	⎸	冂	日	**SHÌ, to be, am, is, are; be right. BE radical (213) [A]**
	日	且	旱	可是 **kěshì** but [A] 要是 **yàoshì** if [A]; if only 不是 **búshì** "No!;" a fault [C] 是的 **shìde** "Yes!," "That's right!" [C]
327 9 strokes	旱	是	是	

先	⟍	⟀	屮	**XIĀN, to precede; late (deceased) [A]**
	生	先	先	先父 **xiānfù** my late father 先夫 **xiānfū** my late husband 先天 **xiāntiān** innate, inborn
328 6 strokes				

生	⟍	⟀	仁	**SHĒNG, to bear (give birth to) [A]**
	牛	生		先生 **xiānshēng** "Mr;" teacher [A] 生日 **shēngrì** birthday [A] 生长 **shēngzhǎng** to grow; grow up, be brought up [B] 生人 **shēngrén** a stranger [D] 女生 **nǚshēng** female student 生手 **shēngshǒu** green horn; be new to something
329 5 strokes				

李	一	十	才	**Lǐ, plum tree; a family name [B]** 李子 **lǐzi** plum 李先生 **Lǐ Xiānshēng** Mr. Li
	木	杢	李	
330 7 strokes	李			

亥	丶	亠	亠	**HÀI, the twelfth "earthly branch" (used in enumerations and to name two-hour periods of the day).** 亥, originally a picture of a wild boar, is still similar in form to the "pig" radical 豕 (502, p. 101). See *Lin Yutang's Dictionary* 1451f on the "earthly branches." **Hài** gives the sound in some common characters (usually **hai**, sometimes **gai**).
	亥	亥	亥	
331 6 strokes				

孩	㇇	了	子	**HÁI, child [A]** The "child" radical gives the meaning; **hài** (331, above) gives the sound. 孩童　**háitóng** children 孩子　**háizi**　child [A] 小孩儿 **xiǎoháir** (colloquial) child [A]
	孑	孖	孖	
332 9 strokes	孩	孩	孩	

咳	丨	冂	口	**HĀI, exclamation: "Depressing!" or "Regrettable!" or "Astonishing!;" KÉ, cough, to cough; first syllable in** *késòu,* **"cough" (see next) [A]**
	口丶	口亠	口亠	
333 9 strokes	咳	咳	咳	

嗽	口	口	口	**SÒU, cough [A]** 咳嗽 **késòu** cough, to cough [A]
	口	𠯢	嗽	
334 14 strokes	嗽	嗽	嗽	

学	`	``	``/	**XUÉ, to study, to learn [A]** The "child" radical is, of course, the student. The top part used to be a picture of one hand guiding another to write.
	``/	``/	``/	学生 **xuéshēng** student [A] 大学 **dàxué** university [A] 学问 **xuéwèn** learning,
335 8 strokes	学	学		scholarship [B]　　　學

姓	く	女	女	**XÌNG, surname; to be surnamed. . . [A]** 姓氏 **xìngshì** surname 您贵姓 **nín guì xìng** What is your name? (polite)
	女	女	如	我姓李 **wǒ xìng Lǐ** My (sur)name is Li.
336 8 strokes	姓	姓		

名	ノ	ク	夕	**MÍNG, name [A]** 姓名 **xìngmíng** full name [B] 有名 **yǒumíng** be famous [A]
	夕	名	名	
337 6 strokes				

字	`	``	宀	**ZÌ, written character [A]** 名字 **míngzi** name (given name) [A] 字母 **zìmǔ** alphabet; letter [A] 别字 **biézì** mispronounced or wrongly written character [C]
	宁	宁	字	
338 6 strokes				

叫	⎮	冂	口	**JIÀO, to call; to be called; to order a person to do something [A]** 马叫 **mǎ jiào** the horse neighs 叫苦 **jiàokǔ** to complain, whine, "piss and moan" 叫什么 **jiào shénme** What's it called (named)?
	叫	叫		
339 5 strokes				叫

牛	ノ	ﾉ一	仁	**NIÚ, cow. COW radical (110) [A]** This character is a picture. In older forms, it is easy to see a cow with horns drawn from the front. Learn to distinguish "cow" from **wǔ** "noon" 午 (687, p. 138).
340 4 strokes	牛			

告	ノ	ﾉ一	牛	**GÀO, to inform [A]** The original meaning of this character was "muzzle for cows." The character combines meanings: "cow" + "mouth" suggests the device. By sound-loan, it means "inform." 报告 **bàogào** to report; a report [B] 告别 **gàobié** to leave, to part or depart from; to say goodbye to [B]
341 7 strokes	生	告	告	
	告			

斤	一	厂	斤	**JĪN, ax. AX radical (115) [A]** The "ax" radical is a picture. The character now stands also for a measure of weight, a *jin* or "catty," which equals about 1.5 pounds.
342 4 strokes	斤			

斥	一	厂	斤	**CHÌ, to scold [C]**
343 5 strokes	斤	斥		

诉	、	讠	讠	**SÙ, SÒNG, to inform [A]** 告诉 **gàosù** to inform [A] 诉说 **sùshuō** to tell, to relate
344 7 strokes	讦	讦	诉	
	诉			訴

69

知	ノ	├	⌐	**ZHĪ, to know [A]**
				The early lexicographers agree that this combines meanings: "arrow" (82, p. 17) + "mouth" (53) "because if you *know*, your mouth is far-reaching and accurate like an arrow."
	午	矢	矢|	知心 **zhīxīn** to understand each other
345 **8 strokes**	知|	知		先知 **xiānzhī** a person having foresight; prophet, soothsayer

首	⟍	⟍⟍	⸝⸝	**SHǑU, chief; the head [A]**
				"Chief" was originally a picture of a head with horns or some big headdress. Distinguish from
	⸝⸝	产	首	面 "face" (675, p. 136).
				首都 **shǒudū** capital city [A]
				首先 **shǒuxiān** be the first; in the first place, above all [C]
346 **9 strokes**	首	首	首	首要 **shǒuyào** be very important [D]
				首长 **shǒuzhǎng** senior officer [D]

道	⟍⟍	⸝⸝	⸝⸝	**DÀO, road; to say; the Way [A]**
				知道 **zhīdào** to know [A]
	首	首	首	道谢 **dàoxiè** to thank
				道喜 **dàoxǐ** to congratulate
				道士 **dàoshì** Taoist (Daoist) priest
				道学 **dàoxué** neo-Confucian
347 **12 strokes**	首	道	道	道理 **dàolǐ** reason, logical basis; doctrine [A]

此	|	├	⊢	**CǏ, this [B]**
				The form of the character can be analyzed as "toe" + "ladle," but the meaning cannot be explained on that basis. Just memorize it.
	止	止丿	此	此外 **cǐwài** furthermore, in addition [B]
348 **6 strokes**				

些	|	├	⊢	**XIĒ, few [A]**
				大些 **dàxiē** be a bit larger
				好些 **hǎoxiē** quite a few [B]
	止	止丿	此	这一些书 **zhè yìxiē shū** this lot of books
349 **8 strokes**	些	些		

位	ノ	イ	イ´	**WÈI**, position, standpoint; seat; a polite measure for persons [A]
	仁	伫	位	位子 **wèizi** seat 学位 **xuéwèi** academic degree [C] 三位小姐 **sānwèi xiǎojie** three young ladies
350 7 strokes	位			

支	一	十	方	**ZHĪ**, branch (of a tree); to prop up; to draw (money) [A] The student will need to distinguish 支 from "club" 殳 (234, p. 47), "knock" 攵 (316), "pattern" 文 (215, p. 44) and "follow/slow" 夊 (431, p. 87).
351 4 strokes	支			干支 **gānzhī** stems and branches (an old system of enumeration: see *Lin Yutang's Dictionary* 1451ff for details)

枝	一	十	才	**ZHĪ**, branch (of a tree); a measure for pens, pencils, pieces of chalk, etc. [C] This appears to be the preceding character, reclarified with the "tree" radical.
	木	杧	杧	枝子 **zhīzi** tree branch 一枝笔 **yìzhī bǐ** a pen
352 8 strokes	枋	枝		

技	一	扌	扌	**JÌ**, skill [A]; expertise or specialised training 技术 **jìshù** technology; skill
	扩	扩	抟	
353 7 strokes	技			

千	一	二	千	**QIĀN**, a thousand; a family name (rare) [A] 千古 **qiāngǔ** be eternal, of the ages 千里 **qiān lǐ** many miles; long journey 千里马 **qiānlǐ mǎ** a superb horse, a horse that can run many miles
354 3 strokes				

央	⎸	⎵	凸	**YĀNG, center [B]** 中央 **zhōngyāng** center, central [B]
	央	央		
355 5 strokes				

英	一	十	艹	**YĪNG, be bold; flower (bookish); a family name [A]** The original meaning was "flower, to flower;" "grass" above gave the meaning, and **yāng** (355, above) suggested the sound. "Bold" is by sound-loan.
	艹	艿	苬	
356 8 strokes	英	英		英国 **Yīngguó** England 英里 **yīnglǐ** English mile

黑	⎸	⎵	冂	**HĒI, black. BLACK radical (223) [A]** **Hēi** is said to be a picture of a man painted up with war paint and decorated with tattooing.
	冈	四	甲	黑心 **hēixīn** a "black heart," an evil mind 黑白不分 **hēi bái bù fēn** cannot distinguish
357 12 strokes	里	黑	黑	between right and wrong

占	⎸	⼘	上	**ZHĀN, to divine; ZHÀN, seize; constitute [A]** 占 combines meanings: the "divine" radical (159, p. 32) + "mouth" = "to explain (orally) the divination cracks." Other meanings by sound-loan. 占 gives the sound in several characters.
	占	占		
358 5 strokes				(**zhàn** only) 佔

站	丶	丷	亠	**ZHÀN, (taxi-, bus-) stand, to stand [A]** The "stand" radical gives the meaning; **zhān** (358, above) gives the sound.
	立	立	立丨	站长 **zhànzhǎng** stationmaster
359 10 strokes	立卜	立卜	站	

粘	丶	丷	⸝⸜	**ZHĀN, to paste, to glue; NIÁN, be sticky [B]**
	半	半	米	粘 combines meanings: "rice" for meaning, 占 for sound.
360 11 strokes	籿	籿	粘	

战	丨	⼘	⼘	**ZHÀN, war; family name [B]** The "lance" radical gives the meaning in this sound-meaning compound.
	占	占	占	战士 **zhànshì** soldier [B] 战友 **zhànyǒu** comrade-in-arms [C]
361 9 strokes	战	战	战	戰

沾	丶	冫	氵	**ZHĀN, to moisten; to receive benefits; to be infected by [C]**
	氵丨	沾	沾	This is another sound-meaning compound with 占 as the sound-component.
362 8 strokes	沾	沾		

| 广 | 丶 | 亠 | 广 | **YǍN, lean-to. LEAN-TO radical (44) GUǍNG, be broad; family name [A]** 广 is a picture. Distinguish it from 厂 "slope" (229, p. 46) and from 疒 the "sick" radical (605, p. 122). Now 广 is most often seen as the short form of 廣 **guǎng**. |
| 363 3 strokes | | | | 广大 **guǎngdà** be vast, huge (for **guǎng**) 廣 |

店	丶	亠	广	**DIÀN, store; inn [A]** The "lean-to" radical 广 (see 363, above) perhaps gives a hint of the meaning here.
	广	庐	庐	书店 **shūdiàn** bookstore [B]
364 8 strokes	店	店		

73

钻 365 10 strokes	ノ	ᒻ	ᒻ
	钅	钅l	钅卜
	钅卜	钻	钻

ZUĀN, to drill; to go into, go through (as, a tunnel, a forest); to study intensely, to "pound" the books; **ZUÀN**, a drill; a diamond; a gemstone; to bore, to drill [B]

The "side-gold (metals)" radical helps with the meaning here.

鑽

贴 366 9 strokes	l	冂	贝
	贝	贝l	贝卜
	贝卜	贴	贴

TIĒ, to paste something on; to "stick to," i.e., stay close to; to pay; allowance [B]

The analysis of this character—"cowrie" + 占 **zhān**—doesn't help much with the meaning or the sound. Memorize it!

粘贴 **zhāntiē** stick on, paste

貼

点 367 9 strokes	ᒷ	ᒻ	l ᒻ
	占	占	卢
	点	点	点

DIĂN, dot , drop (of liquid); to drip; a bit; feature; to light [A]

点心 **diǎnxīn** snack, pastry, "dim sum" [A]
要点 **yàodiǎn** main points, essential point or points [C]
三点六 **sān diǎn liù** 3.6
(五)点钟 **(wǔ) diǎn zhōng** (5) o'clock [A]

點

雨 368 8 strokes	一	l	冂
	帀	雨	雨
	雨	雨	

YǓ, rain. RAIN radical (204) [A]

The "rain" radical is a picture of raindrops falling from clouds.

雨点 **yǔdiǎn** raindrops
雨衣 **yǔyī** raincoat [B]

令 369 5 strokes	ノ	人	人
	今	令	

LÌNG, to command; to make, to cause; a command; your (respectful); **LǏNG**, ream (of paper) [B]

Lìng gives the sound in several common characters (see following entries). Sometimes printed 令.

令兄 **lìng xiōng** (respectful) your older brother
一令纸 **yílǐng zhǐ** a ream of paper

零	一	二	干	**LÍNG, zero; tiny bit [A]**
	干	干	雫	The original meaning of this character was "drop" (e.g., of water), and it was a combination of "rain" for meaning and **lìng** (369, p. 74) for sound. The meaning "zero" may be an extension: "drop," "tiny bit," "virtually nothing," "nothing;" or it may be a case of sound-loan.
370 13 strokes	雫	零	零	

页	一	二	厂	**YÈ, head; leaf (of a book or notebook), page. HEAD radical (170) [A]** The character was a picture of a person's head.
	页	页	页	
371 6 strokes				頁

领	ノ	人	人	**LǏNG, to lead; neck, collar; main point [A]** 领土 **lǐngtǔ** territory [C] 领先 **lǐngxiān** to be in the lead, to lead [D] 领子 **lǐngzi** collar [D] 要领 **yàolǐng** main points
	今	令	令	
372 11 strokes	领	领	领	領

铃	ノ	ト	ヒ	**LÍNG, a small bell [B]** 门铃 **ménlíng** doorbell
	钅	钅	钅	
373 10 strokes	钅	铃	铃	鈴

齿	l	ト	止	**CHǏ, teeth. TEETH radical (206)** 止 **zhǐ** at the top helps with the sound. The rest of the character is a drawing of a mouth with the teeth in it (easier to see in the traditional form, below).
	止	步	步	
374 8 strokes	齿	齿		齒

75

齢	丨	卜	止	**LÍNG**, age, years; length of time, duration [B] 高齢 **gāolíng** be advanced in years
	止	歩	齿	
375 13 strokes	齿\	齿^	齢	齢

邻	丿	人	仒	**LÍN**, neighbor; be "neighboring," be near to, adjacent to [B]
	今	令	令彡	
376 7 strokes	邻			鄰

怜	丿	丷	忄	**LIÁN**, to pity [B] 怜爱 **lián'ài** to love tenderly
	忄	忄	忄	
377 8 strokes	怜	怜		憐

半	丶	丷	丷	**BÀN**, half [A] The vertical stroke bisects the "eight" radical and the two "one" radicals to suggest "half."
	半	半		半天　　**bàntiān**　　a long time [A] 一大半　**yí dà bàn**　majority (大半: C) 三点半　**sān diǎn bàn** 3:30 另一半　**lìng yībàn**　the other half (of a couple)
378 5 strokes				

多	丿	夕	多	**DUŌ**, be numerous [A] 多么 **duōme** how... (as in 多么好 **Duōme hǎo** How very good!) [A] 多半 **duōbàn** the greater part; for the most part, probably [C] 多谢 **duōxiè** Many thanks! 好多了 **hǎo duō le** Much better!
	多	多	多	
379 6 strokes				

| 少 | 丨 | 小 | 小 | **SHǍO, be few; SHÀO, be young [A]**
多少 **duōshǎo** How much? How many? [A]
少女 **shàonǚ** young girl [C]
少不了 **shǎobuliǎo** cannot do without; must have; be unavoidable
少了三个 **shǎo le sānge** to be three short |
| 380
4 strokes | 少 | | | |

| 句 | 丿 | 勹 | 勹 | **JÙ, sentence; verse-line; measure for sentences and verse-lines [A]**
句子 **jùzi** sentence [A] |
| 381
5 strokes | 句 | 句 | | |

够	勹	勹	句	**GÒU, be enough [A]** **Duō** "be numerous" (379, p. 76) suggests the meaning; **jù** (381) once suggested the sound. 够朋友 **gòu péngyǒu** be a friend indeed
	句	够	够	
382 11 strokes	够	够	够	

| 夬 | ⊃ | ⊐ | 尹 | **JUĒ, archer's thimble; GUÀI, to divide.**
The character may be a picture of a person (here = the "big" radical) drawing the bow or fitting the thimble before he or she draws. It functions to give the sound (**jue** or **kuai**) in about six modern characters. Rarely independent. |
| 383
4 strokes | 夬 | | | |

块	一	十	土	**KUÀI, lump, clod; a measure for dollars [A]** The "earth" radical gives the meaning; 383, above, gives the sound. 七块钱 **qīkuài qián** seven dollars 一块田 **yīkuài tián** a piece of land, a field
	圹	圫	坱	
384 7 strokes	块			塊

鬼 385 9 strokes	′	宀	冂
	甶	白	尹
	鬼	鬼	鬼

GUǏ, ghost. GHOST radical (216) [B]

Guǐ is said to be the picture of a ghost.

白鬼 **báiguǐ** Caucasian, Westerner (non-standard; derisory, sometimes considered offensive)

鬼点子 **guǐdiǎnzi** (dialect), dirty trick, evil plan

心里有鬼 **xīnlǐ yǒu guǐ** to have a guilty conscience

相 386 9 strokes	一	十	才
	木	机	机
	相	相	相

XIĀNG, mutually, each other; XIÀNG, face, appearance; to examine [A]

The original meaning was "to examine." 相 is supposed to show someone studying a tree or a piece of wood with his eye; a carpenter checking material.

相对 **xiāngduì** relative (not absolute) [C]; opposite to one another; face to face

想 387 13 strokes	十	木	机
	相	相	相
	想	想	想

XIǍNG, to think [A]

This character may stand for a word cognate to 386, above. The "heart" radical means "mind," as it often does, and 想 can be explained as "to examine in the mind, to think." The character is then a reclarified compound.

想要 **xiǎngyào** to feel like, to want to

理想 **lǐxiǎng** ideals; be ideal [B]

得 388 11 strokes	′	⁄	彳
	彳⁷	彳日	得
	得	得	得

DĚI, must; DÉ, to get; DE; a grammatical particle [A]

得了 **dé le** That does it! Enough!

贵得多 **guì de duō** be much more expensive

看得见 **kàndejiàn** be able to see

巴不得 **bābude** (colloquial) be eager to do something, really want to do something

| 共 389 6 strokes | 一 | 十 | 艹 |
| | 土 | 共 | 共 |

GÒNG, all together, collectively, joint [A]

Older forms have "clasp" (193, p. 39) twice.

一共 **yígòng** all together

中共 **Zhōng Gòng** Chinese Communists (an acronym for "Chinese Collective Production [= Communist] Party")

供	ノ	亻	仁	GŌNG, to supply; GÒNG, to offer in worship, offering; to testify, testimony [B] 供给 **gōngjǐ** to provide, to supply [B]
	什	俳	供	
390 8 strokes	供	供		

洪	丶	冫	氵	HÓNG, be big, be vast; a flood; a family name [C]
	汇	汁	洪	
391 9 strokes	泄	洪	洪	

巷	一	十	卄	XIÀNG, crooked side street, lane [C] 巷口 **xiàngkǒu** entrance/opening to a lane
	苎	尹	共	
392 9 strokes	恭	巷	巷	

港	氵	汇	汀	GǍNG, small stream; port; lagoon [B] 港口 **gǎngkǒu** port, harbor [C]
	汢	泄	洪	
393 12 strokes	洪	港	港	

尤	一	尢	尤	YÓU, still more; a family name [A] 尤其 **yóuqí** particularly 姓尤的 **xìng Yóu de** someone surnamed "Yóu" 尤毛氏 **YóuMáoshì** Mrs. Yóu (whose maiden name was Máo)
	尤			
394 4 strokes				

79

京	丶	亠	广	**JĪNG, capital (city) [B]** The character is a picture of a tall building (compare with 99, p. 20), and "tall building" was its original meaning. It soon came, by metonymy, to mean "tall buildings: capital." 京都 **Jīngdū** Kyoto 东京 **Dōngjīng** Tokyo
	亠	古	亨	
395 8 strokes	亨	京		

景	丨	冂	日	**JĬNG scenery, view; condition, situation [B]** 美景 **měijǐng** beautiful scenery; picturesque landscape
	冃	昮	昰	
396 12 strokes	暠	昮	景	

就	丶	古	亨	**JIÙ, then; only; to go to; to go with [A]** 就学 **jiù xué** go to school 就是 **jiùshì** be precisely…; namely…; That's right! [B] 就是说 **jiùshìshuō** in other words [C] 就有三个 **jiù yǒu sānge** to have only three
	亨	京	京	
397 12 strokes	尌	就	就	

厂	一	厂		**No pronunciation. Radical (22), "top of 盾"** (401, p. 81). **Distinguish from the "slope" radical (229, p. 46)** 厂 is the radical in only four common modern characters: 反 **fǎn** (418, p. 84), 后 **hòu** (402, p. 81), 质 **zhí** (Pt. 2, p. 234a), and 盾 **dùn** (401, p. 81).
398 2 strokes				

历	一	厂	厉	**LÌ, to pass through, to experience; calendar [A]** In rural China, the main routes of passage in many places are roads or paths on the dykes that crisscross the paddies —whence, perhaps, the "slope" radical. **Lì** (11, p. 3) is phonetic. Distinguish from 厉 (400, p. 81). 歷 (pass through); 曆 (calendar)
	历			
399 4 strokes				

厉 400 5 strokes	一 厂 厂 厅 厉	**LÌ, be harsh, be severe; family name [B]** Distinguish from 历 (399, p. 80). 厲
盾 401 9 strokes	一 厂 厂 厃 厈 盾 盾 盾 盾	**DÙN, shield [B]** An important function of **dùn** in modern China has been as part of 矛盾 **máodùn** "contradiction," which is, of course, an important concept-word in Hegelian and Marxist dialectic. For 矛, see Pt. 2, p. 226a. 矛盾 is an interesting word, glossable as "spear-shield," a good metonymy (or metaphor) for "contradiction."
后 402 6 strokes	一 厂 厂 斤 后 后	**HÒU, back, in back of [A]** 后天 **hòutiān** (on) the day after tomorrow [B] 後
直 403 8 strokes	一 十 亠 市 青 直 直	**ZHÍ, be straight; to keep on; be a certain length [A]** A meaning-meaning compound: ten (十) eyes (目) inspect the line (一) and find it to be straight. 直 gives the sound in several characters (see following). 一直 **yìzhí** so far; straight on [A] 直言 **zhíyán** to "talk straight," speak bluntly
真 404 10 strokes	一 十 亠 市 青 直 真	**ZHĒN, be real, be true; truly [A]** Of **zhēn**, the bottom part was originally a pedestal. 真 was analyzed: ten eyes check out something put in plain view, on a pedestal, so it must be real, genuine. 真是 **zhēnshì** Oh, that's bad. [C] 真相 **zhēnxiàng** true picture [D] 真好 **zhēn hǎo** Great!

81

值 405 10 strokes	ノ	イ	仁
	广	估	佔
	侸	值	值

ZHÍ, to be worth, to have a certain value [B]

值得 **zhíde** to be worth …; to be worth-while [B]

值钱 **zhíqián** be worth some money, be valuable

植 406 12 strokes	一	十	才
	朩	朾	栖
	梢	植	植

ZHÍ, plant (growing thing), to plant; to establish [B]

The "tree" radical helps with the meaning. 直 **zhí** is, of course, phonetic.

置 407 13 strokes	丨	冂	冖
	罒	罒	罒
	罜	罝	置

ZHÌ, to buy [B]

The significance of "net" at the top of this character (for it is "net," not another "eye")—is not clear. Perhaps it is metaphorical—to "net" something, to get it, to acquire it, to buy it. 直 **zhí** is phonetic.

| 歹 408 4 strokes | 一 | 厂 | 歹 |
| | 歹 | | |

DǍI, chip. CHIP radical (97)

This character is supposed to be a picture of bone-chips. Distinguish "chip" from "dusk" 夕 (158, p. 32).

殖 409 12 strokes	一	丆	歹
	歹	歼	殅
	殆	殖	殖

ZHÍ, to breed, to multiply [C]

In the language of modern China, 殖 is especially important in two expressions: 殖民 **zhímín** "to establish a colony, colonize" and 殖民地 **zhímíndì** "colony." (民 = 715; 地 = 516).

生殖 **shēngzhí** to breed, reproduce [D]

| 现 410 8 strokes | 一 二 干 / 王 玗 玥 / 玥 现 | **XIÀN, present, now [A]**
现钱 **xiànqián** ready money [D]
兑现 **duìxiàn** to cash a check; to fulfill a promise [D]

现 |

| 在 411 6 strokes | 一 ナ イ / 右 在 在 | **ZÀI, be at, in, on [A]**
现在 **xiànzài** now [A]
在我看 **zài wǒ kàn** as I see it
不在了 **bú zài le** to exist no more, to be dead |

| 良 412 7 strokes | 丶 勹 刍 / 刍 自 良 / 良 | **LIÁNG, be good, be well [B]**
The student should distinguish **liáng** from the "stubborn" radical 艮 (51, p. 11). **Liáng** has the dot at the top.
良好 **liánghǎo** be good, be well [B]
良心 **liángxīn** conscience
良友 **liángyǒu** good companion |

| 食 413 9 strokes | 丿 人 人 / 今 今 含 / 食 食 食 | **SHÍ, food; to eat. FOOD radical (217) [A]**
The "food" radical is a picture of a jar commonly used to hold food.
零食 **língshí** snack
日食 **rìshí** solar eclipse
月食 **yuèshí** lunar eclipse
食言 **shíyán** go back on your word, break a promise |

| 两 414 7 strokes | 一 丆 冂 / 丙 丙 两 / 两 | **LIǍNG, two; a tael (ancient unit of weight equaling 50 grams) [A]**
两手 **liǎngshǒu** trick, skill; dual aspects [D]
两块钱 **liǎngkuài qián** two dollars
两口子 **liǎng kǒuzi** husband and wife [D]
一两金字 **yìliǎng jīnzi** a tael of gold

两 |

俩	丿	亻	亻	**LIǍ, (colloquial) two; some, several [A]** 俩 is pronounced **liǎng** in the (not-too-common) term 伎俩 **jìliǎng** "trick, ruse." 你们俩 **nǐmen liǎ** the two of you 俩钱 **liǎqián** a little money (not much)
415 **9 strokes**	伃	伝	俩	
	俩	俩	俩	俩

车	一	𠂇	车	**CHĒ, car; family name. CAR radical (100) [A]** The character is a picture of a car or chariot (top view—the top and bottom horizontal strokes being the two wheels). 火车 **huǒchē** train (railroad) [A] 车间 **chējiān** workshop [B] 车夫 **chēfū** chauffeur
416 **4 strokes**	车			
				車

辆	一	𠂇	车	**LIÀNG, a measure for vehicles [A]** 三辆车子 **sānliàng chēzi** three (small) vehicles
	车	轩	轫	
417 **11 strokes**	辆	辆	辆	輛

反	一	厂	𠂆	**FǍN, to turn back; to rebel [A]** 反对 **fǎnduì** to oppose [A] 相反 **xiāngfǎn** be the opposite of [B] 反问 **fǎnwèn** respond to a question with a question; rhetorical question [C] 反射 **fǎnshè** reflex; reflection [D] 反目 **fǎnmù** to quarrel (especially of husband and wife)
418 **4 strokes**	反			

饭	丿	𠂊	饣	**FÀN, cooked rice, food [A]** Fàn is a sound-meaning compound. The "side-food" radical gives the meaning; fǎn (418, above) suggests the sound. 米饭 **mǐfàn** cooked rice [A] 要饭 **yàofàn** beg for food 煮饭 **zhǔfàn** to cook rice
	饣	饤	饭	
419 **7 strokes**	饭			飯

84

				FĂN, to return, go back to [C]
返	一	厂	厉	This is a sound-meaning compound: "halt" to suggest movement, motion, travel; 反 **fǎn** to give the sound.
	反	𠃊	返	
420 7 strokes	返			
				BĂN, board; printing plate; a measure for editions; be "wooden" (lifeless) [A]
板	一	十	木	The "tree" radical suggests the meaning. 反 is the phonetic (now not such a good one).
	木	杁	杤	
421 8 strokes	枥	板		闠
				PIÀN, slice, to slice, piece; an expanse; PIĀN, card. SLICE radical (114) [A]
片	丿	丿	广	
	片			
422 4 strokes				
				BĂN, printing block; edition [B]
版	丿	丿	片	Compare this to the character (421) above.
	片	𡧀	𡧁	
423 8 strokes	版	版		
				TÁNG, the name of the Tang (T'ang) dynasty; family name [D]
唐	丶	亠	广	The classic dictionary *Shuō wén jiě zì* says that **táng** originally meant "to talk big," that is, to boast rudely. The "mouth" radical, of course, helps with the meaning. Tang dynasty by sound-loan.
	庁	庁	庐	
424 10 strokes	庚	庚	唐	

85

糖	⼃⼂	⼝	半
	米	米⼴	粁
425 16 strokes	粐	粐	糖

TÁNG, sugar, candy [A]

The "rice" radical helps with the meaning; it often appears in characters for words that mean a powdery substance, grain, or granular foodstuffs. **Táng** (424, p. 85) is, of course, phonetic.

白糖 **báitáng**   white sugar, refined sugar
糖水 **tángshuǐ** syrup

舌	一	二	千
	千	舌	舌
426 6 strokes			

SHÉ, tongue. TONGUE radical (177) [B]

Shé is a picture of a tongue sticking out of a mouth.

学舌 **xuéshé** to learn "by tongue," that is, so that you can parrot the teacher's words without really understanding them; (colloquial) gossipy

---

话	⼂	讠	讠
	讠	讠	讠
427 8 strokes	话	话	

HUÀ, speech, language [A]

Huà combines meanings: "words" + "tongue" = "speech, language."

说话 **shuōhuà** to speak, talk
白话 **báihuà**   the ordinary spoken language, contrasted to "classical Chinese" 文言: see 215
中国话 **Zhōngguóhuà** the Chinese language   話

舍	ノ	人	𠆢
	亼	仐	仐
428 8 strokes	舍	舍	

SHÈ, home; SHĚ, to give up, to give charity [A]

Once a meaning-meaning compound, 舍 now = "man" + "tongue," which doesn't help much with the meaning "home."

舍得   **shèdé** be willing to part with [C]
舍不得 **shěbudé** be unwilling to part with [C]   (verbs only) 捨

事	一	⼀	亓
	曰	㕚	亖
429 8 strokes	㕚	事	

SHÌ, affair, event [A]

事 shows a hand holding a writing instrument. It meant "to hold office, to serve" and suggested the scribes—early rulers' most important servants.

事情 **shìqíng** affair, business [A]
故事 **gùshì**   story [A]
懂事 **dǒng shì** be sensible, wise [C]

歌 430 14 strokes	一	可	可	**GĒ, song [A]**
	可	哥	哥	The "yawn" radical (to suggest the open mouth) combines with gē 哥 (269, p. 54) in this sound-meaning compound.
	哥	哥欠	歌	歌迷 **gēmí** fan of vocalist 歌手 **gēshǒu** singer [D] 国歌 **guógē** national anthem 情歌 **qínggē** love song

| 夂 431 3 strokes | 丿 | 夕 | 夂 | **No pronunciation; FOLLOW/SLOW radical (65)**
This modern radical results from the combination of two old radicals, meaning "follow" and "slow." It looks sort of like a person taking a long stride. It is the radical in eight common modern characters, appearing in all cases except one at the top or side. |

各 432 6 strokes	丿	夕	夂	**GÈ, each; various [A]**
	夂	各	各	各别 **gèbié** be different, peculiar, eccentric [B] 各人 **gèrén** each person, everyone 各个 **gège** every one; one by one 各国 **gèguó** various nations 各位 **gèwèi** everybody (used in addressing an audience, to get people's attention); each person

客 433 9 strokes	丶	丷	宀	**KÈ, guest [A]**
	宀	夗	客	客人 **kèrén** guest [B] 请客 **qǐng kè** to give a party [B] 客车 **kèchē** passenger train; bus [D] 说客 **shuōkè** an (informal) emissary, an eloquent fellow sent to win others to your point of view
	客	客	客	

| 丆 434 2 strokes | 丿 | 丆 | | **No pronunciation. Radical (20), "Top of 每 měi"**
Měi 每 is 684, p. 137. |

| 乞 435 3 strokes | ⼃ | ⼇ | 乞 | **QǏ, to beg [D]** This character once was identical to the "breath" radical (64, p. 13) and meant "breath, vapors, exhalations." It was probably by sound-loan that it came to mean "to beg." 乞食 **qǐ shí** to beg for food |

| 吃 436 6 strokes | ⼁ | ⼝ | 口 | **CHĪ, to eat [A]** 吃饭 **chīfàn** to eat 吃力 **chīlì** to require strength and exertion; be arduous [C] 吃苦 **chīkǔ** to suffer [C] 吃的东西 **chīde dōngxi** food, things to eat 我吃饱了 **wǒ chībǎole** Thanks, I've had enough to eat |
| | 吀 | 吃 | 吃 | |

| 兴 437 6 strokes | ⼂ | ⼳ | ⺍ | **XÌNG, be happy; XĪNG, to begin; family name [A]** 高兴 **gāoxìng** be happy, be cheerful [A] |
| | 业 | 兴 | 兴 | 興 |

能 438 10 strokes	⼂	⼛	台	**NÉNG, be able to; be expert (in…); energy [A]** For the sense "energy," see 443, p. 89. 能够 **nénggòu** be able to [A] 能干 **nénggàn** be capable, be competent [B] 能力 **nénglì** ability [B] 能手 **néngshǒu** an expert [D]
	台	自	育	
	能	能	能	

曾 439 12 strokes	⼂	⺍	广	**CÉNG, already; ZĒNG, relationship between great-grandparents and great-grandchildren through the male line; a family name [B]**
	广	兯	兯	
	兯	兯	曾	(日 179)

88

尸	ㄱ	ㄱ	尸	**SHĪ, corpse. CORPSE radical (67) [D]**
				The character was originally a picture of a man lying down. The student should learn to distinguish the "corpse" radical from the "door" radical 戶 (504).
440 **3 strokes**				屍 (not a radical)

会	丿	人	스	**HUÌ, to know how to, be able to; to meet; a while; KUÀI, to calculate [A]**
	仝	会	会	会话 **huìhuà** conversation, dialog [A] 会客 **huì kè** to receive a guest [B] 会见 **huìjiàn** to meet with (e.g., a foreign visitor) [B] 学会 **xuéhuì** an academic society; to learn, to master [C]
441 **6 strokes**				一会子 **yí huìzi** a moment 會

以	ㄥ	レ	ㄇㄣ	**YǏ, using, taking; because of; used as an indicator before words showing time, position, direction, or quantity (see below, and also 459 and 463) [A]**
	以			可以 **kéyi** may, be permitted to [A] … 以外 **yǐwài** beyond…, outside of…, in addition to… [B]
442 **4 strokes**				… 以东 **yǐdōng** to the east of …

原	一	厂	厂	**YUÁN, origin; a plain [A]**
	厂	厍	盾	The character originally was "slope" + "white" + "water" and meant "spring" (i.e., a water-source). "Water" was corrupted into "small." 原先 **yuánxiān** at first, previously 原子 **yuánzi** atom
443 **10 strokes**	盾	原	原	原子能 **yuánzi néng** nuclear energy

愿	厂	厂	盾	**YUÀN, be willing [A]**
	厚	原	原	The modern form and traditional form (below) are sound-meaning compounds, but in the modern form the "heart" radical replaces the "head" radical. A shift in the understanding of willingness?
444 **14 strokes**	愿	愿	愿	心愿 **xīnyuàn** heart's desire [D] 情愿 **qíngyuàn** voluntarily 願

音	`	亠	宀	**YĪN, tone. TONE radical (211) [A]** The old form of the "tone" radical was a mouth blowing on a flute—a pretty good way to suggest "tone." The character has been corrupted into "stand" over "say."
	亣	立	产	
445 9 strokes	竒	音	音	口音 **kǒuyīn** voice; accent 他的口音很重 **tāde kǒuyīn hěn zhòng** He has a very thick accent.

意	`	亠	亠	**YÌ, idea, opinion, motive [A]** This character is sometimes explained as "the tone in the heart" = "idea, motive."
	产	音	音	愿意 **yuànyì** be willing [A] 意见 **yìjiàn** opinion [A] 注意 **zhùyì** pay attention [A]
446 13 strokes	意	意	意	故意 **gùyì** on purpose [B] 意外 **yìwài** be unforeseeable (literally, "beyond thought"); accident [B]

爫	一	㇀	𭕄	**No pronunciation. CLAWS radical (116)** This is the form of the "claws" radical that appears as a part of characters. For the independent form, see 306, p. 62. The form 爫 always appears at the top of characters.
	爫			
447 4 strokes				

受	一	㇀	𭕄	**SHÒU, to receive [B]** The "crown" radical is said to be an object being received from the "claws" (fingernails, hand) by the right hand.
	爫	爫	严	受累 **shòulèi** be hassled, be put to a lot of trouble; **shòulěi**, to get involved for someone else
448 8 strokes	受	受		受不了 **shòubuliǎo** be unable to bear 受气 **shòuqì** get pushed around

爱	一	㇀	𭕄	**ÀI, to love [A]** "Love" used to have the "heart" radical (87, p. 18) in it (see below), but that has been replaced by 友 **yǒu** "friend" (363, p. 53). Distinguish "to love" from 受 (448).
	爫	严	严	爱情 **àiqíng** love (man and woman's) [B] 爱人 **àirén** lover, wife, husband [A]
449 10 strokes	爭	受	爱	爱国 **àiguó** be patriotic 喜爱 **xǐ'ài** to be fond of, to love [B] 愛

仁 450 4 strokes	ノ 仁	亻	仁	**RÉN, humaneness, kindness [D]** 仁 and **rén** 人 "person; be human" may be cognates. The "two" (二) is often explained philosophically: "two" = "another, other." 仁 is one of the four starting points of social order in Confucianism, with commitment to the common good 义 (1020), respect for social and religious forms 礼 (591), and wisdom 智 (1023).
乍 451 5 strokes	ノ 乍	⺡ 乍	乍	**ZHÀ, suddenly** This character is not frequently seen independently, but it occurs as the sound element in several common characters—where it usually has the value **zha**. 乍看 **zhà kàn** at first sight 乍有乍没 **zhà yǒu zhà méi** Now it's here, now it's not (idiomatically: "now you see it, now you don't").
作 452 7 strokes	ノ 亻 作	亻 竹	亻 作	**ZUÒ, to do, to make [A]** Sometimes foreign students have trouble distinguishing this character in meaning from the homonymous 做 "make, produce, act as, be…" (See Pt. 2, p. 224a). 作者 **zuòzhě** writer, author [B] 合作 **hézuò** to cooperate [B] 作对 **zuò duì** to oppose
炸 453 9 strokes	丶 火 灯	⺀ 火 炸	丬 灶 炸	**ZHÀ, to set off, blast [C]**
穴 454 5 strokes	丶 宀	八 穴	宀	**XUÉ, cave; lair; acupuncture point; a family name. CAVE radical (128) [D]** 穴位 **xuéwèi** (Chinese medicine) acupuncture point

91

窄	`	⼋	宀
	宀	穴	穴
455 **10 strokes**	窄	窄	窄

ZHĂI, be narrow [B]

See 950, p. 191, for 窄 in a common combination, 宽窄 **kuānzhǎi** "the broad and the narrow," i.e., "width, breadth."

昌	⼁	⼌	日
	日	日	昌
456 **8 strokes**	昌	昌	

CHĀNG, sunlight, splendor; a family name [D]

This is a meaning-meaning compound: "sun" + "sun."

昌言 **chāngyán** (bookish) frank and open speech or remarks

唱	⼁	冂	口
	叮	叮	叮
457 **11 strokes**	叮日	唱	唱

CHÀNG, to sing; a family name [A]

The "mouth" gives the meaning; **chāng** (456, above) suggests the sound.

唱歌 **chànggē** to sing
合唱 **héchàng** a chorus (group of singers)
卖唱 **màichàng** to sing for a living

倡	⼃	亻	亻
	亻	伊	伊
458 **10 strokes**	佣	倡	倡

CHÀNG, to initiate, start off, advocate [B]

倡言 **chàngyán** (bookish) to propose

上	⼁	卜	上
459 **3 strokes**			

SHÀNG, up, upon, above; to come or go up [A]

…以上 **…yǐ shàng** more than…; …and more
上学 **shàngxué** go to school, be in school [A]
上衣 **shàng yī** jacket, outer garment [B]
上马 **shàngmǎ** to get on a horse; to start a project
上个月 **shànggè yuè** last month

| 写 460 5 strokes | 丶 | 宀 | 宀 | **XIĔ, to write [A]** 写字 **xiězì** to write 写作 **xiězuò** to write (e.g., a novel, a   poem) [C] 写生 **xiěshēng** (artist's expression) to draw   from life 寫 |
| | 写 | 写 | | |

思 461 9 strokes	丨	冂	日	**SĪ, to think, thought [A]** This character was originally "head" + "heart;" "head" was corrupted to "field." 思想 **sīxiǎng** thought [A] 意思 **yìsi** idea [A]
	田	田	田	
	思	思	思	

| 乡 462 3 strokes | 乚 | 纟 | 乡 | **XIĀNG, country (opposite to city) [B]*** 故乡 **gùxiāng** hometown, birthplace[B] 乡亲 **xiāngqīn** fellow villager; local people,   folks [D] 思乡 **sīxiāng** be homesick, suffer nostalgia 乡土 **xiāngtǔ** native soil; local 乡音 **xiāngyīn** local accent; accent of   your native place 鄉 |

| 下 463 3 strokes | 一 | 丁 | 下 | **XIÀ, below; to come or go down [A]** 上下 **shàngxià** high and low, old and young,   top to bottom [C] 乡下 **xiāngxià** in the country; rural …以下 **yǐxià** below…, under… 下个月 **xiàge yuè** next month 上山下乡 **shàngshān xiàxiāng** go work in the   back country (as educated youth did,   for socialist education) |

| 巾 464 3 strokes | 丨 | 冂 | 巾 | **JĪN, cloth. CLOTH radical (57) [B]** The character is a picture of a small piece of cloth—a kerchief, napkin, or towel—hanging down. 毛巾 **máojīn** towel [B] 手巾 **shǒujīn** small towel, face towel [D] 纸巾 **zhǐjīn** paper towel, napkin |

*In *Han-Ying Cidian,* 乡 is one of the 11 "left-over" characters, not classified under a radical.

冒	丨	冂	冂	**MÀO**, to cover the eyes; to rush blindly forward, act rashly; to try to "pull the wool over people's eyes," to fool or defraud them; to emit [B]
	曰	尸	冐	冒名 **mào míng** to use another's name
465 9 strokes	冐	冐	冒	冒雨 **mào yǔ** to brave the rain 冒气 **mào qì** to emit steam

帽	丨	冂	巾	**MÀO**, hat [A] The "cloth" radical gives the meaning; **mào** (465, above) gives the sound.
	巾冃	帄	帽	帽子 **màozi** hat, cap [A] 帽舌 **màoshé** peak of a cap; visor
466 12 strokes	帽	帽	帽	笔帽儿 **bǐ màor** cap of a pen

新	丶	亠	立	**XĪN**, be new [A] 新闻 **xīnwén** news [A]
	立	亲	亲	重新 **chóngxīn** again, anew; fresh [B]
467 13 strokes	新	新	新	(亲 267)

旧	丨	刂	卪	**JIÙ**, be old (things, not people) [A] The "sun" radical may give a hint as to the meaning of this character, the sun being our measurer of time's passing.
	旧	旧		旧日 **jiùrì** bygone days of yore 旧学 **jiùxué** old (Chinese) learning
468 5 strokes				(contrasted to Western learning) 旧金山 **Jiùjīnshān** San Francisco 舊

昇	⺊	⺕	巳	**YÌ**, be strange; be separate; regard as strange [B] 奇异 **qíyì** be weird, bizarre, alien
	巳	异	异	异己 **yìjǐ** dissident, person belonging to another party 异乡 **yìxiāng** alien land
469 6 strokes				日新月异 **rìxīn yuèyì** to change or develop every day 異

94

| 戈 470 6 strokes | 一 | 十 | 士 | No pronunciation. Radical (165). "Top of 栽 " (Pt. 2, p. 265b). |
| | 弌 | 戈 | 戈 | |

戴 471 17 strokes	士	吉	吉	DÀI, to wear (hats, glasses, gloves, etc.); to honor; a family name [A] 爱戴 **àidài** love and honor [D] 戴帽子 **dài màozi** to wear a hat
	幸	幸	壴	
	壴	戴	戴	

茶 472 9 strokes	一	十	艹	CHÁ, tea [A] 吃茶 **chīchá** drink tea 茶点 **chádiǎn** refreshments 泡茶 **pàochá** to make (steep) tea 茶话会 **cháhuàhuì** tea party, reception (also "茶会") [C]
	艼	艿	芖	
	芩	茶	茶	

| 水 473 4 strokes | 亅 | 刁 | 水 | SHUǏ, water; a family name. WATER radical (125) [A]
The character is a picture of a stream of running water. Its meaning is, of course, closely related to another radical you have already learned—"three-dots water" (77, p. 16)
水土 **shuǐtǔ** climatic conditions [D]
汗水 **hànshuǐ** sweat (especially a lot) |
| | 水 | | | |

酉 474 7 strokes	一	厂	冂	YǑU, wine; the tenth "earthly branch" (used in enumerations and to name two-hour periods of the day). WINE radical (193) A wine-jug; the horizontal stroke inside = liquid in it. Distinguish the "wine" radical from 西 "west"/ COVER radical (162). See *Lin Yutang's Dictionary* 1451f for an account of the "earthly branches."
	兀	酉	酉	
	酉			

95

酒 475 10 strokes	丶	冫	氵
	汀	汀	沔
	洒	洒	酒

JIǓ, wine, alcoholic beverage [A]

Jiǔ combines meanings: "water" (氵) + "wine" (酉) = "wine, alcoholic beverage (酒)."

酒会　**jiǔhuì** cocktail party [D]
酒鬼　**jiǔguǐ** an alcoholic, wino, lush
酒意　**jiǔyì**　mild high from drink; tipsy
　　　　feeling

取 476 8 strokes	一	厂	丌
	开	耳	耳
	取	取	

QǓ, to grab, take hold of [A]

The form, of course, is "right hand" (又) + "ear (耳)." The hand is supposed to be grabbing the ear, hence "to grab."

取得　**qǔdé**　to get, to obtain [A]
取笑　**qǔxiào** to make fun of, to tease

最 477 12 strokes	丨	冂	曰
	曰	旦	旱
	昺	最	最

ZUÌ, most [A]

最好　**zuìhǎo** the greatest; the best thing to do
　　　　is … [B]

尚 478 8 strokes	丨	丷	丷
	冖	尚	尚
	尚	尚	

SHÀNG, still (adverb); to esteem, to respect; a family name [D]

尚 gives, or once gave, the sound in a number of characters. See following items.

躺 479 15 strokes	丿	亻	勹
	勹	身	身
	身	躺	躺

TǍNG, to lie down [A]

The "torso" radical helps, perhaps, with the meaning. The character 尚 (preceding) once helped with the sound.

躺下　**tǎngxià** to lie down
躺椅　**tǎngyǐ**　a "lying-down" chair, i.e., a
　　　　chaise longue, deck chair

趟	一	十	土	**TÀNG**, a measure for trips or visits; column, row [B]
	丰	丰	走	
480 15 strokes	走	起	趟	

倘	丿	亻	亻	**TǍNG**, if [C] 倘或 **tǎnghuò** if; supposing that...; in case
	亻	俨	俨	
481 10 strokes	倘	倘	倘	

尚	丨	丷	丷	No pronunciation. Radical (139). "Top of 常" (see next character).
	丷	尚		
482 5 strokes				

常	丨	丷	丷	**CHÁNG**, often; as a rule; a family name [A] The significance of the "cloth" radical is unclear.
	尚	尚	尚	常常 **chángcháng** often [A] 异常 **yìcháng** be unusual, abnormal; extremely [B]
483 11 strokes	常	常	常	常见 **chángjiàn** be common, ordinary [D]

掌	丨	丷	丷	**ZHǍNG**, palm of the hand; to slap; hold in the palm of your hand; be in charge of; bottom of some animals' feet (e.g., ducks, bears); sole or heel of a shoe; a horseshoe [A]
	尚	尚	堂	The significance of the "hand" radical is obvious; 尚 (478, p. 96) helps with the sound.
484 12 strokes	堂	堂	掌	

賞	⼁	⼂	⼃⼁⼂	**SHǍNG, to reward; to enjoy [C]**
	𫼿	𫰡	𫰢	賞 has the same phonetic as several of the preceding characters— 尚. The radical "cowrie (money)," logically enough, also appears in this character for reward and enjoyment.
485 12 strokes	尚	賞	賞	賞

革	一	十	廾	**GÉ, hide (as in "cowhide"); a family name. HIDE radical (212) [B]**
	廾	芇	芇	The character is a picture of a hide split and spread out to dry.
486 9 strokes	苗	莒	革	

艰	𠃌	又	又⼁	**JIĀN, be difficult [B]**
	𫦊	𫦋	𫞉	In the traditional character, the element on the left—now the "right hand" radical—was a picture of a man with his hands tied behind his back, hence "to be in difficulty."
487 8 strokes	艰	艰		艱

难	又	𫝀	𫝁	**NÁN, be difficult [A]; NÀN, a tough time; disaster, adversity**
	𫝂	𫝃	𫝄	难住 **nánzhù** to stop with a difficulty, to stymie (难不住, cannot stymie...) 难看 **nánkàn** be ugly [B] 难受 **nánshòu** feel sick, feel pain, be unhappy [B]
488 10 strokes	𫝅	难	难	难道 **nándào** It couldn't be that ...[B] 難

谷	丿	八	分	**GǓ, valley; grain, corn; a family name. VALLEY radical (199) [C]**
	𫝆	谷	谷	The character is a picture of a valley. Its other meanings come from its use in modern times as a short form for another, semantically unrelated character.
489 7 strokes	谷			山谷 **shāngǔ** ravine [C] 谷子 **gǔzi** millet 穀 (not "valley")

98

容	`	八	宀
	宀	宓	突
490 10 strokes	容	容	容

RÓNG, to allow; face; a family name [A]

容忍 **róngrén** be tolerant, put up with people

笑容 **xiàoróng** a smile; smiling face [C]

勿	ノ	勹	勿
	勿		
491 4 strokes			

WÙ, must not; Don't! [D]

This is said to be a picture of an old warning flag—Stop!—from which the meaning "must not" derives.

易	丨	冂	日
	日	尸	昜
492 8 strokes	昜	易	

YÌ, to change; be easy; family name [A]

Yì originallly meant "chameleon" and was a picture of a chameleon. The meaning "to change" is an easy extension of "chameleon." The meaning "easy" is probably by sound-loan.

容易 **róngyì** be easy [A]

聪	耳	耳	耴
	耴	聦	聦
493 15 strokes	聪	聪	聪

CŌNG, be intelligent [B]

Cōng originally meant "be quick of hearing, be quick of apprehension," from which it easily came to mean "be quick to understand, be intelligent." The "ear" radical helps with the meaning.

(耳 256)

聰

明	丨	冂	日
	日	刖	明
494 8 strokes	明	明	

MÍNG, be bright, be clear [A]

"Sun" (日) + "moon" (月) = "light, be bright."

明天 **míngtiān** tomorrow [A]
聪明 **cōngmíng** be intelligent [B]
明白 **míngbái** to understand [C]
黑白分明 **hēi bái fēn míng** in sharp contrast (literally, with black and white clear(ly marked))

听 495 7 strokes	丨	𠃌	𠮛
	𠯈	𠯈	𠯈
	听		

TĪNG, to listen [A]
Said to be a new meaning-meaning compound, but "mouth"(口) + "ax"(斤) = "to listen"…? The old form had "ear" as one of its meaning parts.
听见 **tīngjiàn** to hear [A]
听说 **tīngshuō** to hear it said that… [A]
听写 **tīngxiě** dictation, do dictation (in class) [A] 聽

| 今 496 4 strokes | 丿 | 人 | 仌 |
| | 今 | | |

JĪN, be of/at the present time, be contemporary [A]

今天 **jīntiān** today [A]
今日 **jīnrì** today, the present time, "these days" [C]
古今 **gǔjīn** past and present
今生 **jīnshēng** this life

念 497 8 strokes	丿	人	仌
	今	今	念
	念	念	

NIÀN, to study [A]
This character is supposed to be a meaning-meaning compound: "be present" (今) + the "heart" (心) radical (for "mind") = "to have present in the mind, to study."
想念 **xiǎngniàn** to miss, to remember longingly [B]
念书 **niànshū** to study, do some serious reading [C]

孝 498 7 strokes	一	十	土
	耂	孝	孝
	孝		

XIÀO, filial piety; family name [D]
The character combines meanings: the "old" (耂) radical + the "child" (子) radical = "filial piety."
孝心 **xiàoxīn** filial piety, love and respect for parents
孝子 **xiàozǐ** filial son

教 499 11 strokes	一	十	土
	耂	孝	孝
	孝攵	教攵	教

JIĀO, to teach; JIÀO, to tell; religion; family name [A]
教 looks like a meaning-meaning compound: old (耂) + child (子) + a hand holding a stick (for discipline)(攵). In fact, "old" used to be "crisscross" and was the character the child was being taught to write.
教书 **jiàoshū** to teach

曷	丨	冂	日	**HÉ, what? why?** The form at the top is the "say" (曰) radical, not the "sun" (日) radical. This character is now bookish.
	曰	尸	昻	
500 9 strokes	昜	曷	曷	

喝	丨	冂	口	**HĒ, to drink; HÈ, to shout [A]** Hé (500, above) gives the sound; the "mouth" radical gives the meaning. 喝茶 **hē chá** to drink tea 大吃大喝 **dà chī dà hē** to pig out, to eat and drink extravagantly
	口曰	吗	喝	
501 12 strokes	喝	喝	喝	

豕	一	厂	了	**SHĬ, pig. PIG radical (194)** The character is a picture of a pig.
	豕	豕	豕	
502 7 strokes	豕			

家	丶	八	宀	**JIĀ, home, house, family; specialist; family name (rare) [A]** Jiā combines meanings: "pig" under "roof" = "home." Some commentators say the pig is really outside the house. 家乡 **jiāxiāng** hometown, ancestral home [B] 家长 **jiāzhǎng** head of a family [D] 家母 **jiāmǔ**　my mother
	宀	宀	宀	
503 10 strokes	家	家	家	

户	丶	乛	㝵	**HÙ, door; a measure for households; family name. DOOR radical (86) [B]** This character is a picture. The student should distinguish it from "corpse" 尸 (440, p. 89). 户口 **hùkǒu**　population; household [D] 三户人家 **sānhù rénjiā** three households
	户			
504 4 strokes				

101

方	`	亠	宁	**FĀNG, square; direction; locality; family name. SQUARE radical (85) [A]**
	方			**Fāng** may originally have been a picture of a man leaning hard to one side—the original character for 旁 **páng** "side"—(875). By tradition, "square" radical. It gives the sound in several characters (below).
505 **4 strokes**				方便 **fāngbiàn** be convenient [A] 东方 **dōngfāng** the East, the Orient [B]

房	`	宀	긐	**FÁNG, house, building; family name [B]**
	户	户	户	"Door" gives the meaning; **fāng** (505, above) gives the sound.
506 **8 strokes**	房	房		房子 **fángzi** house, building; room [B] 房东 **fángdōng** landlord [D] 房事 **fángshì** sexual intercourse (between husband and wife)

访	`	讠	讠	**FĂNG, to look for; to dig up (the news); to visit [B]**
	讠	讠	访	The "side-word" radical here may help with the meaning. 方 is phonetic.
507 **6 strokes**				訪

纺	乚	纟	纟	**FĂNG, to reel, to spin; silk [A]**
	纟	纩	纩	The "silk" radical ("side-silk (纟)") suggests the meaning.
508 **7 strokes**	纺			纺车 **fángchē** spinning wheel 紡

仿	丿	亻	亻	**FĂNG, to copy, imitate; to resemble [B]**
	仃	仿	仿	仿古 **fǎnggǔ** to build or design, be built or designed, on an ancient model or models
509 **6 strokes**				

防

510
6 strokes

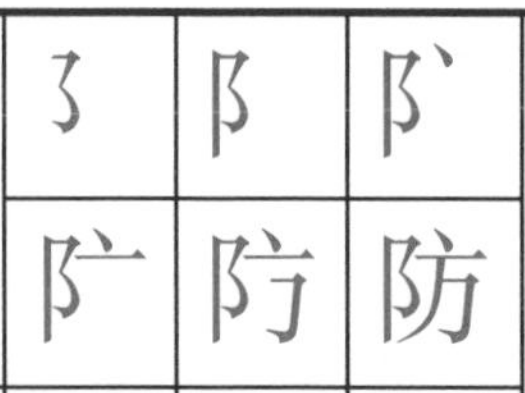

FÁNG, to guard against [B]

The "left ear" ("mound") suggests the meaning (perhaps as a metonymy for ramparts). 方 **fāng**, as with several characters on these pages, gives the sound.

妨

511
7 strokes

FÁNG, to hinder [C]

The "woman" radical, in a use which appears to be sexist, suggests the meaning "to hinder." Scholarly articles have been written on such a bias in the writing system. The scribes and script-masters, of course, were all male. 方 **fāng** (505, p. 102) is the phonetic.

放

512
8 strokes

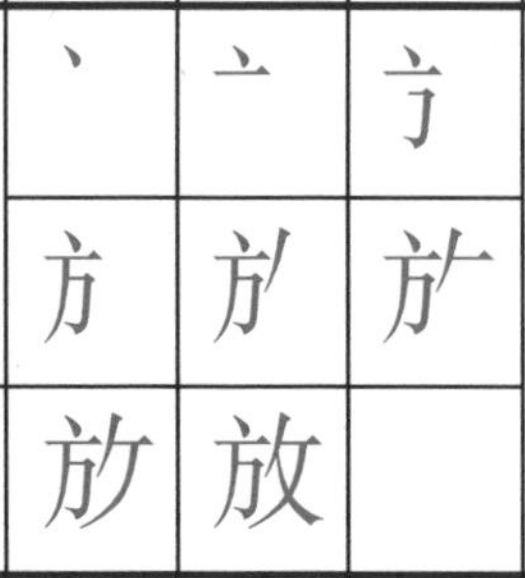

FÀNG, to lay down; to put; to tend; to lend; to fire (a weapon) [A]

放心 **fàngxīn** to be at ease about [B]
放大 **fàngdà** to enlarge, to magnify [B]
放手 **fàngshǒu** to let go of [C]
放学 **fàngxué** to get out of class, get out of school [C]

楼

513
13 strokes

LÓU, a building of two or more stories; family name [A]

楼房 **lóufáng** building of two or more stories [C]
下楼 **xiàlóu** to go downstairs
楼下 **lóuxià** downstairs

樓

至

514
6 strokes

ZHÌ, to reach, to arrive at; REACH radical (171) [B]

The character is a picture of a bird alighting, from which came the idea of "to reach, to arrive at."

至今 **zhìjīn** up to the present time [B]
至少 **zhìshǎo** at least [B]

屋 515 9 strokes	﹁	﹁	尸	**WŪ, a room [A]**
	尸	尸	戽	The "corpse" radical here is supposed to mean "to lie or sit," and the character is explained as "where you come (reach) to lie or sit down—your room."
	屋	屖	屋	屋子 **wūzi** room [A] 房屋 **fángwū** houses, buildings [C]

地 516 6 strokes	一	十	土	**DÌ, the earth; soil; place [A]**
	圫	坩	地	地方 **dìfāng** place [A] 土地 **tǔdì** land [B] 地点 **dìdiǎn** place, site [B] 地位 **dìwèi** job, status [B] 地下 **dìxià** be underground; be secret [B] 地支 **dìzhī** earthly branch(es): see 44, p. 9. 谢天谢地 **xiètiān xièdì** Thank God!

戊 517 5 strokes	一	厂	尺	**WÙ, halberd; the fifth "heavenly stem." HALBERD radical (138)**
	戌	戊		戊 is a picture of a halberd—a lance with an ax-like blade in the middle. Distinguish from 戈 the "lance" radical (30, p. 7). On the "heavenly stems," see *Lin Yutang's Dictionary* 1451f.

成 518 6 strokes	一	厂	厉	**CHÉNG, to perfect; to become; family name [A]**
	成	成	成	成就 **chéngjiù** accomplishment [B] 成立 **chénglì** to set up [B] 成长 **chéngzhǎng** grow up, mature [B] 成分 **chéngfèn** component(s); class status (Marxist/Maoist concept) (also written 成份) [B] 成人 **chéngrén** an adult [D]

城 519 9 strokes	一	十	土	**CHÉNG, city wall; city [A]**
	圹	圹	坊	The "earth" radical gives the meaning, and **chéng** (preceding character) gives the sound. 城乡 **chéngxiāng** town and country 长城 **Chángchéng** the Great Wall
	城	城	城	

交

520
6 strokes

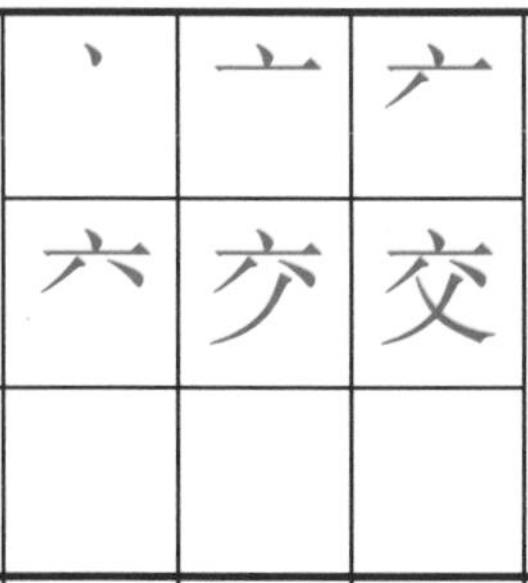

JIĀO, to hand over, to exchange

The original meaning of this character was "to cross;" it was a picture of a man with crossed legs. Distinguish it from "pattern" 文 (215, p. 44). 交 gives the sound in several common characters (see following).

交易	**jiāoyì**	to trade [B]
交手	**jiāoshǒu**	fight hand-to-hand [D]

校

521
10 strokes

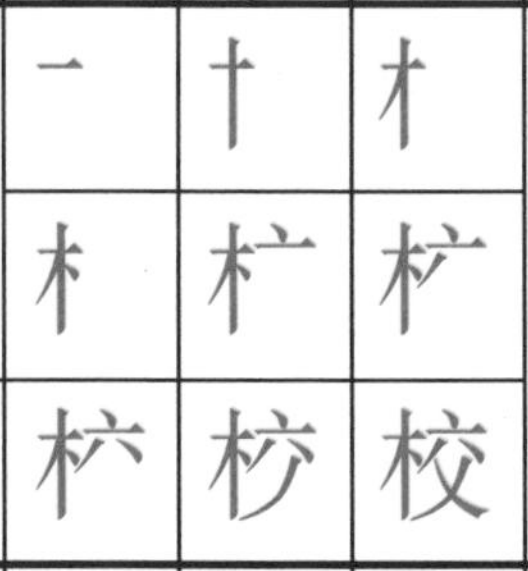

XIÀO, school [A]; JIÀO, to check, collate

学校	**xuéxiào**	school [A]
校长	**xiàozhǎng**	principal (of a school); college president [B]
校对	**jiàoduì**	to proofread

较

522
10 strokes

JIÀO, to compare [A]

交 **jiāo** (520, above) gives the sound. The significance of the "car" radical in this character is not clear. Karlgren (*AD* 357) sees a connection with chariot competitions.

較

饺

523
9 strokes

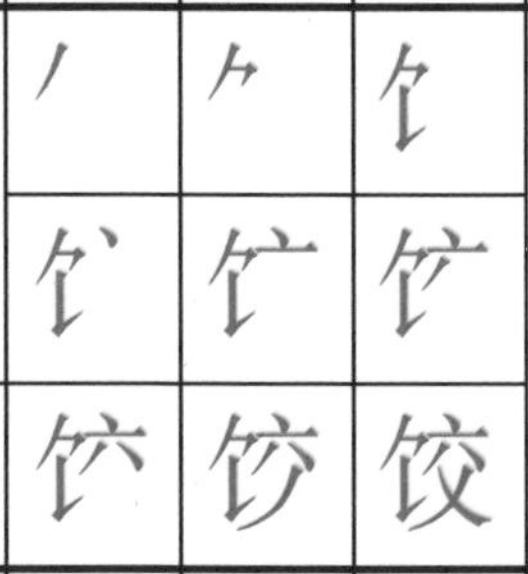

JIǍO, dumpling [A]

This is a sound-meaning compound: the "side-food" radical for meaning, 交 **jiāo** (520, above) for sound.

饺子	**jiǎozi**	dumpling (stuffed with meat and vegetables)

餃

郊

524
8 strokes

JIĀO, suburb; outskirts of a city [B]

The "city" (now called "right ear"—see 191, p. 39) gives the meaning. 交 **jiāo** (520, above) gives the sound.

郊外	**jiāowài**	outskirts, suburban

效 525 10 stroks	丶	亠	广
	六	夳	交
	刻	効	效

XIÀO, effect; to imitate; to devote [B]
效力 **xiàolì** to render a service to; an effect [D]
效能 **xiàonéng** efficacy
仿效 **fǎngxiào** to imitate; to follow the example of
生效 **shēngxiào** be in effect; become effective

狡 526 9 strokes	ノ	犭	犭
	犭丶	犷	犷
	犷	狡	狡

JIǍO, be crafty, be cunning [C]
The "dog" (on the left) may allude to small animals (see 183, p. 37) and some idea that such are cunning. In English, we say "foxy" and "to outfox someone."

胶 527 10 strokes	丿	刀	月
	月	月丶	胪
	胪	胪	胶

JIĀO, be sticky; glue; sticky stuff; plastic; rubber [C]
The "moon/meat" radical on the left, with the significance here of "meat," perhaps suggests the meaning. 交 **jiāo** (520, p. 105) gives the sound.

膠

咬 528 9 strokes	丨	冂	口
	口丶	咁	咛
	咛	咛	咬

YǍO, to bite; to incriminate an innocent person with false testimony [B]

用 529 5 strokes	丿	冂	月
	月	用	

YÒNG, to use [A]
Scholars say, "This shows an arrow shot into a bull's-eye, so 'fit to the purpose, usable, to use'."
作用 **zuòyòng** function; to affect [B]
用力 **yònglì** put effort into [B]
运用 **yùnyòng** use, put into practice [B]
用心 **yòngxīn** motive; diligently [C]
用人 **yòngrén** servant [D]

甫	一	厂	丆
	万	肎	甫
530 7 strokes	甫		

FŬ, to begin; just, only (bookish)

铺	丿	𠂆	⻒
	𠂉	𨨏	𨥉
531 12 strokes	钌	铕	铺

PÙ, to store; PŪ, to spread [B]
The character is a sound-meaning compound. The "gold" radical gives the meaning, and **fŭ** (530, above) gives the sound.
铺子 **pùzi**   a store, a shop
铺张 **pūzhāng** be extravagant

铺

官	丶	丷	宀
	宀	宁	宇
532 8 strokes	官	官	

GUĀN, mandarin; (bodily) organ [B]
This may be "a picture of many people under a roof: the people's roof," city hall; by metonymy, the mandarins. The bottom is *not* 臣 (Pt. 2, p. 216b) or 巨 (Pt. 2, p. 238b).
官方 **guānfāng** governmental [D]
官话 **guānhuà** "Mandarin" language
五官 **wǔ guān** the five organs (ears, eyes, lips, nose, tongue)

馆	丿	𠂊	饣
	饣丶	饣宀	饣宁
533 11 strokes	馆	馆	馆

GUĀN, public building (embassy, museum); public accommodation (hotel, eatery, teahouse); family name [A]
Guān (532) gives the sound—and maybe the meaning; for "eatery," the "food" radical, of course, helps with the meaning.
饭馆 **fànguǎn**   restaurant [C]
天文馆 **tiānwénguǎn** planetarium
        (天文 = astronomy)

館

尼	ㄱ	ㄱ	尸
	尸	尼	
534 5 strokes			

NÍ, nun [D]
Looking now like "corpse" 尸 (440, p. 89) + "ladle" 匕 (41, p. 9), this character was once "person" beside "person" and meant "be beside, be near." The meaning "nun" appears to have come by sound-loan.

107

呢 **535** 8 strokes	丨 口┐ 吚	冂 口コ 呢	口 呢	**NE, a grammatical particle [A]; NÍ, wool-stuff** NÍ (534) gives the sound; the mouth here warns that the character may be a particle. Chao's *Grammar* says that ne may signal a question, a deliberate pause, or a mild warning (pp. 801f.) The meaning "wool-stuff" comes by sound-loan. 我呢 **Wǒ ne** What about me?
所 **536** 8 strokes	ˊ 戶 戶	厂 戶 所	斤 斦	**SUŎ, place; which? what? family name [A]** "Door" and "ax" here combine to mean "to build a living place," whence "place." Other meanings by sound-loan. 所以 **suǒyǐ** therefore [A] 所有 **suǒyǒu** all; to own; possessions [A] 所在 **suǒzài** place [C]
汽 **537** 7 strokes	` 氵 汽	ˋ 汇	氵 汽	**QÌ, gas, steam [A]** The character combines meanings: "water" + "breath" (vapor) = "steam." 汽车 **qìchē** automobile [A] 汽水 **qìshuǐ** carbonated drink, soda water [A]
舟 **538** 6 strokes	ˊ 舟	丿 舟	力 舟	**ZHŌU, boat. BOAT radical (182) [D]** The "boat" radical is a picture of a boat. 舟车 **zhōuchē** (bookish) boat and car; (by metonymy) journey 舟子 **zhōuzi** (bookish) boatman
船 **539** 11 strokes	ˊ 舟 舢	丿 舟 船	力 舟 船	**CHUÁN, boat [A]** 汽船 **qìchuán** steamship [C] 下船 **xiàchuán** disembark 船长 **chuánzhǎng** master, captain, of a ship 船首 **chuánshǒu** the bows of a boat, prow

飞	㇆	飞	飞	**FĒI, to fly [A]** Fēi is a picture, somewhat abbreviated, of a flying bird. 飞船 **fēichuán** blimp, airship [D] 飞舟 **fēizhōu** a very fast boat (speed-boat)
540 **3 strokes**				飛
几	丿	几		**JǏ, several, a few; how many? [A]; JĪ, (small) table. TABLE radical (30)** A picture of a table. Other meanings by sound-loan. Distinguish from 儿 (67, p. 14). As a radical, 几 may appear a bit different, as in 风 **fēng** wind (819, p. 164), 朵 **duǒ** flower, etc. 几点了 **jǐ diǎn le** What time is it?
541 **2 strokes**				幾
机	一	十	才	**JĪ, machine, mechanism; crucial point; opportunity; be quick-witted [A]** 飞机 **fēijī** airplane [A] 机子 **jīzi** (colloquial) loom, small machine, trigger 机会 **jīhuì** opportunity [A] 唱机 **chàngjī** a record-player, phonograph
	木	杉	机	
542 **6 strokes**				機
行	㇒	㇒	彳	**XÍNG, to go, do, perform; be okay [A]; behavior, conduct [B]; HÁNG, row (e.g., of trees), line (of verse) [B]; business firm, "hong" [C]** "Step" (50, p. 10) + "step" (now slightly corrupted) = "to go." 行李 **xínglǐ** baggage [B] 行人 **xíngrén** pedestrian(s) [C] 行业 **háng yè** trade, profession
	彳	行	行	
543 **6 strokes**				
圭	一	十	土	**GUĪ, jade tablets or jade batons used in the old days as symbols of authority** Note that in **guī** "earth" appears twice. These jade symbols were the tokens used in conferring fiefs (land). 圭表 **guībiǎo** old Chinese sundial (it measured the length of the year and of the 24 solar terms)
	圭	丰	圭	
544 **6 strokes**				

街 545 12 strokes	ノ	彳	彳
	徃	徃	徍
	徍	街	街

JIĒ, a street (A)

Jiē is a sound-meaning compound. "Go" gives the meaning; **guī** (544, p. 109) at one time gave the sound.

街道 **jiēdào** street; neighborhood [B]
大街 **dàjiē** boulevard [B]
唐人街 **Tángrén jiē** Chinatown [A]

封 546 9 strokes	一	十	土
	圭	丰	圭
	圭	封	封

FĒNG, to seal up [C]; a measure for letters; a family name [A]

信封 **xìnfēng** envelope [A]
封口 **fēngkǒu** to seal up (a letter, a wound); to end a debate

定 547 8 strokes	丶	八	宀
	空	宁	宇
	定	定	

DÌNG, be calm, stable; to settle (a matter); subscribe; family name [A]

The character combines meanings: first "set right" (正 600, p. 121) things under your "roof" 宀 (40) to have a settled life. 正 now looks more like 疋 (326, p. 66).

一定 **yídìng** certainly; fixed, set [A]
不一定 **bùyídìng** not necessarily, not for sure [A]

怎 548 9 strokes	ノ	亠	仁
	乍	乍	乍
	怎	怎	怎

ZĚN, how? why? [A]

The character is supposed to be a meaning-meaning compound: "suddenly" 乍 (451, p. 91) + "heart/mind" = bewilderment = the questions "how? why?"

怎么 **zěnme** how? why? [A]
不怎么 **bùzěnme** not very

| 从 549 4 strokes | ノ | 人 | 从 |
| | 从 | | |

CÓNG, to follow; from [A]; a family name

Two persons, one following the other.

从不 **cóngbù** never [B]
从没 **cóngméi** has/have never [B]
从此 **cóngcǐ** from now (then) on [B]
从事 **cóngshì** go in for, deal with [B]

從

110

回	丨	冂	冂	**HUÍ, to return; a time, occurrence; Muslim; a family name [A]**
	冋	回	回	The character is supposed to symbolize going around something until you return to the starting point.
550 6 strokes				回想 **huíxiǎng** bring back to mind, recollect [C] 回家 **huíjiā** to return home 下回 **xiàhuí** next time

到	一	乙	厶	**DÀO, to arrive at; verb-ending, indicating successful completion of the action of the verb; family name [A]**
	丢	至	至	The "reach" radical gives the meaning; **dāo** (232, p. 47) gives the sound.
551 8 strokes	到	到		从…到… **cóng…dào…** from…to… [A] 到了 **dào le** [some subject] has arrived 看到 **kàndào** to see 想不到 **xiǎngbudào** be unexpected [A]

倒	丿	亻	亻	**DÀO, on the contrary; be flipped, be upside down; DǍO, to fall, topple**
	仁	伝	侄	
552 10 strokes	倖	倒	倒	

坐	丿	人	人丿	**ZUÒ, to sit down; to travel by [A]**
	人人	从	坐	**Zuò** is a picture of two people sitting on the earth.
553 7 strokes	坐			坐下 **zuòxià** to sit down 坐船 **zuò chuán** to travel by boat 坐飞机 **zuò fēijī** to travel by plane

座	丶	亠	广	**ZUÒ, a measure-word for buildings, mountains, cities, clocks, tombs [A]**
	庆	庆	庐	座位 **zuò wèi** a seat [B] 一座山 **yízuò shān** one mountain
554 10 strokes	座	座		

111

来 555 7 strokes	一	〒	〒
	立	平	来
	来		

LÁI, to come; a family name [A]
Lái once meant "wheat" and was a picture of growing wheat. It means "to come" by sound-loan.
回来 **huílai** to return [A]
未来 **wèilái** the future [B]
来回 **láihuí** to make a round-trip; back and forth [C]
来客 **láikè** guest, visitor [C]

| 去 556 5 strokes | 一 | 十 | 土 |
| | 去 | 去 | |

QÙ, to go; to cause to go; get rid of. GO radical (133) [A]
Qù was a cup (now "cocoon" 厶 (46, p. 10) with a lid (now "earth" 土 (34)). Why it should mean "to go" is unclear.
回去 **huíqù** to return, go back [A]
下去 **xiàqù** to go down
说来说去 **shuō lái shuō qù** to say over and over

起 557 10 strokes	一	十	土
	丰	丰	走
	起	起	起

QǏ, to rise, to raise [A]
Jǐ (297, p. 60) suggests the sound in this character; the "walk" radical is supposed to help with the meaning.
起来 **qǐlai** to stand up, to get up (as, out of bed); **qǐlai**, a verb-ending, indicating "up:" 站起来, stand up; or "begin:" 唱起来, begin singing
起飞 **qǐfēi** to take off (airplane)

昨 558 9 strokes	丨	冂	日
	日	旷	旷
	昨	昨	昨

ZUÓ, yesterday [A]
The "sun" radical suggests the meaning; **zhà** (451, p. 91) once gave the sound.
昨天 **zuótiān** yesterday [A]
昨儿 **zuór** (colloquial) yesterday

| 旦 559 5 strokes | 丨 | 冂 | 日 |
| | 日 | 旦 | |

DÀN, dawn [C]
The character is a picture of the sun just above the horizon, and it suggests "dawn." It gives the sound in a few characters.
元旦 **Yuándàn** New Year's Day [C]
一旦 **yídàn** in one day, pronto, right away [D]
旦夕 **dànxī** (bookish) in the morning or the evening—pretty soon

但	ノ	亻	仈	**DÀN, but, only; family name [A]**
	伃	伃	但	但是 **dànshì** but [A] 不但 **búdàn** not only [A] 但愿 **dànyuàn** if only; I wish that
560 7 strokes	但			

担	一	扌	扌	**DĀN, to carry on a pole on your shoulder (between two persons) [B]** The side-hand radical gives the meaning; **dàn** (559, p. 112) gives the sound.
	扡	扣	扣	
561 8 strokes	扣	担		擔

胆	丿	刀	月	**DĂN, gall bladder; courage; inside of a thermos bottle [B]** The "moon/meat" radical (as "meat") gives the meaning. 旦 **dàn** is the phonetic.
	月	肌	肌	
562 9 strokes	肌	胆	胆	膽

早	丨	冂	日	**ZĂO, be early; long ago; Good morning! [A]** 早饭 **zǎofàn** breakfast [A] 早上 **zǎoshàng** in the (early) morning [A] 早已 **zǎoyǐ** long ago; for a long time [C] 早日 **zǎorì** soon; at an early date [D] 早点 **zǎodiǎn** breakfast [D]
	日	旦	早	
563 6 strokes				

免	丿	勹	勹	**MIĂN, to escape [B]** **Miǎn** is supposed to be a picture of a running hare, whence "to escape." Do not confuse it with **tù** 兔 "hare" (Pt. 2, p. 244b). The "dot" in "hare" 兔 is the key. 免得 **miǎnde** to save (as, from inconvenience); to avoid [C] 免税 **miǎnshuì** to be exempt from taxes
	夕	乌	乌	
564 7 strokes	免			

113

晚	丨	刀	日
	旷	旷	晔
565 11 strokes	晔	晚	晚

WǍN, be late; evening; family name [A]

"Sun" for meaning, **miǎn** (564) for sound (once upon a time).

晚上 **wǎnshang** in the evening; at night [A]
晚饭 **wǎnfàn** supper [A]
晚会 **wǎnhuì** soiree, evening party [A]
晚报 **wǎnbào** evening newspaper [C]

工	一	丁	工
566 3 strokes			

GŌNG, work. WORK radical (48) [A]

工 is a carpenter's square; so, "work."

工厂 **gōngchǎng** factory, mill [A]
工作 **gōngzuò** work, job [A]
工人 **gōngrén** workman [A]
工夫 **gōngfu** time, effort [B]
工会 **gōnghuì** labor union [B]
分工 **fēn gōng** to divide the labor [C]

经	ㄥ	幺	纟
	纟	经	经
567 8 strokes	经	经	

JĪNG, warp (of fabric); pass through; literary classic; family name [A]

Right half: a picture of threads run across a loom; the "silk" radical reclarifies. Other meanings derived from "warp."

经常 **jīngcháng** every day, often [A]
已经 **yǐjīng** already [A]
曾经 **céngjīng** have done it [B]

經

还	一	丆	不
	不	不	还
568 7 strokes	还		

HÁI, still, yet; HUÁN, to return [A]

The upper right-hand part of 还 has nothing to do with the negator of verbs 不 —it is a shorthand way to suggest the upper right-hand part of the traditional character (see below, this frame).

还是 **háishi** still, yet [A]

還

前	丶	丷	丷
	广	前	前
569 9 strokes	前	前	前

QIÁN, front, in front of [A]

从前 **cóngqián** in the past [A]
前天 **qiántiān** the day before yesterday [B]
前方 **qiánfāng** ahead; the front [C]
前后 **qiánhòu** in front and back; from beginning to end [C]
前门 **qiánmén** (at) the front door
前两天 **qiánliǎngtiān** the past two days

114

剪 570 11 strokes	`	``	丷
	广	疒	首
	前	前	剪

JIǍN, scissors; to cut with scissors [B]
前 (569, p. 114) suggests the sound. The "knife" radical helps with the meaning.

箭 571 15 strokes	ノ	⺦	⺮
	⺮	𥫗	𥫗
	筲	箭	箭

JIÀN, arrow [B]
前 (569, p. 114) suggests the sound.
箭头 **jiàntóu** arrowhead; arrow (sign)

煎 572 13 strokes	`	``	丷
	首	前	前
	前	煎	煎

JIĀN, to fry; to simmer in water [C]
前 (569, p. 114) suggests the sound. The "fire-dots" give the meaning.

时 573 7 strokes	｜	冂	日
	日	旷	时
	时		

SHÍ, time [A]
The "sun" radical helps with the meaning. If 寸 "thumb; inch" can be thought of as suggesting *measurement,* then 时 should be fairly easy to remember.
时间 **shíjiān** time [A]
时时 **shíshí** often, all the time [C]
时常 **shícháng** often [C]

時

候 574 10 strokes	亻	亻	伫
	伫	伫	伫
	伫	候	候

HÒU, to wait; to pay the bill; climate; a period of time [A]
时候 **shíhòu** time [A]
问候 **wènhòu** to ask after someone [B]
火候 **huǒhòu** time required to cook something

115

| 百 575 6 strokes | 一 | 丆 | 厂 | **BǍI, one hundred [A]** **Bái** (282, p. 57) gives the sound; "one" suggests that the meaning is numerical. 老百姓 **lǎobǎixìng** common folks [B] 百花齐放, 百家争鸣 **bǎihuā qífàng, bǎijiā zhēngmíng** "Let 100 flowers bloom, let 100 schools of thought contend." (Mao Tsetung) [D] (花= 787, 齐= Pt. 2, p. 217b, 放 = 512, 争 = 709, 鸣 = Pt. 2, p. 268a) |
| | 百 | 百 | 百 | |

| 为 576 4 strokes | 丶 | 丿 | 力 | **WÈI, for; WÉI, to be, do, act [A]** 为什么 **wèishénme** why? [A] 为了 **wèile** for; in order to [A] 为止 ... **wéizhǐ** up to ..., until ... [C] 为首 ... **wéishǒu** with ... as leader [C] 为难 **wéinán** be embarrassed; give somebody a hard time [C] 為 |
| | 为 | | | |

第 577 11 strokes	丿	𠂉	𠂊	**DÌ, a prefix to numbers (forms ordinals) [A]** 第一 **dìyī** first, the first 第四天 **dìsì tiān** the fourth day 第三者 **dìsānzhě** the third one
	⺮	竺	竺	
	笃	第	第	

| 年 578 6 strokes | 丿 | 𠂉 | 仁 | **NIÁN, year [A]** 去年 **qùnián** last year [A] 今年 **jīnnián** this year [A] 明年 **míngnián** next year [A] 年纪 **niánjì** age (a person's) [A] 一百年 **yìbǎinián** a hundred years; a lifetime |
| | 仁 | 㐃 | 年 | |

| 凵 579 2 strokes | ∟ | 凵 | | **KǍN, bowl. BOWL radical (38)** **Kǎn** is a picture of a bowl. |

116

| 中 | └ | └┘ | 屮 | **CHÈ, sprout. SPROUT radical (61)** The "sprout" radical is a picture of a sprout. |
| 580 3 strokes | | | | |

CHÚ, to come/go out; to produce [A]
Picture of a sprout coming out of a bowl.
出版 **chūbǎn** to publish; put out [B]
出来 **chūlái** to come out [A]
出去 **chūqù** to go out [A]
出口 **chūkǒu** exit, way out [A]
出现 **chūxiàn** to appear, emerge [A]
出生 **chūshēng** be born [B]
出门 **chūmén** be away from home

581 5 strokes

DĚNG, to wait; to equal; rank; "etc." [A]
Although the authorities all equate 等 with English "etc.," 等 often seems rather just to signal the list's end.
等候 **děnghòu** to wait for [C]
等到 **děngdào** by the time that … [C]
马、牛、羊、等 **mǎ, niú, yáng, děng** horses, cows, sheep, etc. OR (better): horses, cows, and sheep.

582 12 strokes

KUÀI, be fast; soon; be happy; be sharp [A]
快车 **kuàichē** express train
快刀 **kuài dāo** sharp knife
飞快 **fēikuài** be very fast; be very sharp
快点 **kuàidiǎn** "Faster, please."

583 7 strokes

MÀN, be slow [A]
慢车 **mànchē** local train
快慢 **kuàimàn** "the fast and the slow of it," i.e. speed
慢走 **mànzǒu** Watch your step! "Take care of yourself!" (said to a departing guest)

584 14 strokes

117

再	一	厂	冂	**ZÀI, again; another, more [A]** 再见 **zàijiàn** Goodbye! So long! [A] 再三 **zàisān** over and over, repeatedly [C] 再说 **zài shuō** and furthermore [C] 再给五个 **zài gěi wǔge** give five more
585 6 strokes	丙	再	再	

着	丶	丶丶	丷	**ZHE, (after verbs) continues doing; (after imperative verbs) intensifies the command [A]** See next two items. (For more on 着, see Chao's *Grammar* 248-51, 446-47.) Note: 着 is not 看 (161, p. 33). 她吃饭着呢 **tā chīfànzhe ne** She's eating at the moment. 等着 **děngzhe** Just you wait!
	兰	兰	羊	
586 11 strokes	着	着	着	

着	丶	丶丶	丷	**ZHÁO, to touch; to feel [A]; ZHÁOLE (着了) (after verbs) did it right! Oh dear!** See preceding and following items. 着忙 **zháo máng** get busy, feel pressed 着火了 **zháohuǒle** catches fire 这回你可说着了 **zhèihuì nǐ kě shuō zháole** Right on! You said it! 我买着了 **wǒ mǎi zháole** Yeah! I bought it!
	兰	兰	羊	
587 11 strokes	着	着	着	

着	丶	丶丶	丷	**ZHUÓ, to wear; to apply, to use [C]** See preceding two items. 着手 **zhuó shǒu** put a hand in, start [C] 着重 **zhuó zhòng** to emphasize [C] 着想 **zhuó xiǎng** consider, focus on [D] 着笔 **zhuó bǐ** to start to write (or paint) 着力 **zhuó lì** apply some elbow grease 着意 **zhuó yì** do with the brain turned on
	兰	兰	羊	
588 11 strokes	着	着	着	

件	丿	亻	仁	**JIÀN; a measure for events, official documents, articles of clothing, pieces of furniture [A]** 文件 **wénjiàn** documents, papers [B] 零件 **língjiàn** component; spare part; accessory [C] 一件事 **yíjiàn shì** an event, a matter, an affair
589 6 strokes	仁	仨	件	

井	一	二	丰	**JĬNG, well, mineshaft [B]** 井, say the scholars, depicts the traditional eight-family village, with a central area cultivated by all families for tax purposes: in the central area was the village well (sometimes in ancient characters marked with a big dot) (Karlgren *AD* 1084)
590 4 strokes	井			

礼	丶	冫	礻	**LĬ, ritual; manners [A]** As often, the "sign" radical appears in a character related to religion.* 礼帽 **lǐmào** top hat 礼金 **lǐjīn** cash given in congratulation or for respect <div align="right">禮</div>
591 5 strokes	礻	礼		

拜	一	二	三	**BÀI, to worship [B]** The radical is "hand" (27, p. 6) slightly distorted (compare with 161, p. 33). **Bài** originally had two "hands" + "to lower." "Lower the hands" = "to worship." 礼拜 **lǐbài** to worship; to pay homage to the gods; week [C] 礼拜天 **lǐbài tiān** Sunday [B]
592 9 strokes	手	手	手	
	手	手	拜	

拿	丿	人	合	**NÁ, to pick up [A]** The character combines meanings: "to join" + "hand" = "to pick up." 拿…来说 **ná … lái shuō** as to… [C] 拿起来 **náqǐlái** to pick up 拿走 **názǒu** to take away 拿住 **názhù** to hold onto firmly 拿着 **názhe** Hold on to it! Hang on!
593 10 strokes	合	合	拿	

进	一	二	丰	**JÌN, to enter [A].** 井 (590, above) gives the sound imperfectly. 进去 **jìnqù** to go in [A] 进来 **jìnlái** to come in [A] 进行 **jìnxíng** to make progress with; to pull strings [A] 进口 **jìnkǒu** entrance, way in; to enter port; to import [B] 进入 **jìnrù** to enter [B] <div align="right">進</div>
594 7 strokes	井	进	进	
	进			

* See 450, p. 90, on 礼's significance in Confucian China. In the traditional character (see below, this frame), the right half is a ritual dish holding flowers.

送 595 9 strokes	丶	丷	丷
	丷	关	关
	关	诶	送

SÒNG, to send off, to see off; to give as a present; to deliver [A]

送行　sòngxíng　to see off [B]
送礼　sònglǐ　　to send a present [C]
不送　búsòng　　(guest) Don't bother to see me off; (host) Excuse me for not…
买一送二　mǎiyī sòngèr　buy one, get one free

因 596 6 strokes	丨	冂	冃
	团	闵	因

YĪN, cause, because [A]

Karlgren says the basic meaning is "cause" in a legal sense and explains the character as "a man (the 'big' radical) in prison."

因为　yīnwèi　because [A]
因此　yīncǐ　because of this [B]

信 597 9 strokes	丿	亻	亻
	亻	亻	信
	信	信	信

XÌN, sincerity; to believe; letter (as in "business letter, personal letter") [A]

The character shows "a man standing by his word," whence "sincere; to believe."

相信　xiāngxìn　to believe [A]
信心　xìnxīn　　confidence, trust [B]
回信　huí xìn　　to write back; a reply (written or oral) [B]
信念　xìnniàn　faith, belief [C]

万 598 3 strokes	一	丁	万

WÀN, ten thousand; family name [A]

The "one" radical (top) suggests a number.

千万　qiānwàn　10 million; by all means [B]
万万　wànwàn　(intensifies negation) absolutely (not…), never; 100 million [C]
万一　wànyī　just in case; what if; eventuality; one ten-thousandth, tiny bit [C]

萬

紧 599 10 strokes	丨	丨丨	丨丨丷
	丨丨又	竖	竖
	竖	紧	紧

JǏN, be tense, be urgent, be tight [A]

紧张　jǐnzhāng　be excited; be tense; be exciting [A]
要紧　yàojǐn　be important [B]
太紧　tàijǐn　be too tight (as in shoes)

緊

120

正	一	丁	下	**ZHÈNG, be true; truly; be straight, upright; be in the midst of (doing) [A]**
	正	正		正 gives the sound in several characters (see below) in which rectification seems to be part of the meaning.*
600 **5 strokes**				正在 **zhèng zài** be in the midst of [A] 正好 **zhèng hǎo** be just right; it just happens that… [B] 正常 **zhèngcháng** be normal [B]
政	一	丁	下	**ZHÈNG, government; political administration [A]**
	正	正	正	正 gives the sound. The significance of "knock" is unclear.
601 **9 strokes**	政	政	政	政客 **zhèngkè** politician (pejorative)
整	一	冂	束	**ZHĚNG, to tinker with; to give trouble; whole, exactly [A]**
	敕	敕	敕	正 is phonetic. The top part— 束 "bundle, to bind" + "to knock" means "to correct; imperial orders."
602 **16 strokes**	整	整	整	整个 **zhěnggè** whole, entire [B] 整整 **zhěngzhěng** whole, entire [D] (两) 点整 **(liǎng) diǎn zhěng** (2) o'clock sharp [C]
证	、	讠	讠	**ZHÈNG, proof, to prove; permit [B]**
	订	证	证	证明 **zhèngmíng** to prove; to testify; certificate, I.D. [B]
603 **7 strokes**	证			证书 **zhèngshū** certificate, credentials [C] 证件 **zhèngjiàn** papers, credentials [C] 證
征	⼂	⼃	彳	**ZHĒNG, 1) To go on a trip; to go on an expedition; 2) evidence; to examine evidence; to summon to court; to recruit or levy [B]**
	行	彳	征	The "step" radical may help with the meaning. 正 (600, above) gives the sound.
604 **8 strokes**	征	征		徵 (2nd meanings only)

*Karlgren, in "Word-classes in Chinese" (*Bulletin of the Museum of Far Eastern Antiquities* V (1933)) and "Cognate Words in the Chinese Phonetic Series" (*BMFEA* XXVIII (1956)) advances the idea that

疒	`	亠	广	**"SICK" radical (127)**
	疒	疒		The "sick" radical represents a person stretched out on a bed, whence "sick." Compare the "bed" radical (1033, p. 207). Not in modern use as an independent character.
605 **5 strokes**				

症	亠	广	广	**ZHÈNG, sickness, disease; pronounced ZHĒNG in a couple of not-common terms [C]**
	疒	疒	疒	症结 **zhēngjié** the crux of the matter
606 **10 strokes**	疞	症	症	癥

必	ノ	心	心	**BÌ, must [A]**
	必	必		必要 **bìyào** be necessary, essential [B] 必定 **bìdìng** certainly 未必 **wèibì** not necessarily 必得 **bìděi** must
607 **5 strokes**				

夜	`	亠	广	**YÈ, night [A]**
	疒	疒	夜	半夜 **bànyè** midnight
608 **8 strokes**	夜	夜		

岁	ノ	山	山	**SUÌ, harvest; year; be … years old [A]**
	屮	岁	岁	他几岁了 **tā jǐsuì le** How old is he? (assuming less than ten) 岁月 **suìyuè** years [D]
609 **6 strokes**				歲

(*cont'd from p. 121*)
a common *phonetic* in a series of characters may indicate the scribes' belief that the words of the serie:
are cognate.

忘 610 7 strokes	﹅　亡　亡 广　忘　忘 忘	**WÀNG, to forget; to overlook [A]** The "heart" radical ("heart-mind") for meaning, **wáng** (85, p. 18) for sound. Compare with 86, and note that "side-heart" + **wáng** means "be busy" [忄 + 亡 = 忙] while "heart" + **wáng** means "to forget." 忘八　**wángbā**　tortoise; cuckold (abusive); note the change to **wáng**). (Also written 王八.)
差 611 9 strokes	﹅　丷　丷 丷　丷　羊 差　羊　差	**CHÀ, to differ; to fall short, to owe [A]; CHĀ, to differ; difference (arithmetical); mistake; CHĀI, to send; to commission; official** Distinguish 差 from 着 (586–88, p. 118). 差别　**chàbié**　difference [C] 差不多　**chàbuduō**　be almost the same 差事　**chāishì**　job, official assignment
开 612 4 strokes	一　二　于 开	**KĀI, to open; to start; to drive (a car); to boil [A]** 开学　**kāi xué**　school/term opens [A] 开会　**kāi huì**　hold or attend a meeting [B] 开明　**kāimíng**　be enlightened [B] 开口　**kāi kǒu**　start to talk [C] 开饭了　**kāi fànle**　Dinner's ready! [C] 开玩笑　**kāi wánxiào**　to joke, ridicule [A]　開
关 613 6 strokes	﹅　丷　丷 丷　羊　关	**GUĀN, to shut [A]; a barrier; family name [C]** 关心　**guānxīn**　be concerned about [A] 关头　**guāntóu**　moment, point in time [C] 关门　**guānmén**　to shut the door 关税　**guānshuì**　customs duty　關
刻 614 8 strokes	﹅　亠　亥 歹　亥　亥 刻　刻	**KÈ, quarter of a hour [A]; to carve, engrave [B]; be stingy, be sarcastic** The original meaning was "carve." "Knife" gave the meaning, **hài** (331, p. 67) suggested the sound. 立刻　**lìkè**　immediately, right away 木刻　**mùkè**　a woodcut, wood engraving 三点一刻　**sāndiǎn yíkè** 3:15 (a quarter past three)

内	丨	冂	内	**NÈI, inside [A]**
	内			Nèi is a picture of a person entering a space marked off by the "borders" radical.
615				内容 **nèiróng** content, substance [A] 内地 **nèidì** interior (of a country) [D] 内在 **nèizài** be inherent, intrinsic [D] 内心 **nèixīn** heart; innermost being [D] 三天内 **sāntiānnèi** within three days
4 strokes				

呐	丨	卩	口	**NE, particle indicating two closely related questions, a pause ("as for …"), a mild warning, a continuing state ("still"), an antagonistic retort ("Whadda ya mean, …?"), "as much as …," "really, even" [A]**
	叫	呐	呐	(See Chao's *Grammar*, pp. 801-03.)
616	呐			… 着呐 ….zhene "Oh, yes, … is true." (See Chao's *Grammar*, pp. 809-10.)
7 strokes				

丙	一	厂	厂	**BǏNG, fish tail; the third "heavenly stem" (used to enumerate headings in an outline, like "C"—third letter of the Western alphabet). [C]**
	丙	丙		See *Lin Yutang's Dictionary* 1451f for an account of the "heavenly stems."
617				
5 strokes				

过	一	寸	寸	**GUÒ, to go over [A]**
	寸	讨	过	过来 **guòlái** to come over[A] 过去 **guòqù** to go over; to die; in the past [A] 过年 **guònián** to celebrate the New Year [B] 过分 **guòfèn** be excessive, go over the (due) measure [C]
618				過
6 strokes				

自	丿	厂	白	**ZÌ, nose; self; from. SMALL NOSE radical (180) [B]** (Distinguish from 目 "eye," 129.)
	白	自	自	A picture. Compare with the radical 鼻 (Pt. 2, p. 231b). 自己 **zìjǐ** self, oneself [A] 自我 **zìwǒ** self- (before 2-syllable verbs) [B]
619				自从 **zìcóng** from, since [B] 自学 **zìxué** to study independently [B]
6 strokes				自行车 **zìxíngchē** bicycle [B]

124

采	一	㇒	ㅠ	CǍI, to cull, to pick, to pick out, to gather; to extract, to mine; bright colors; CULL radical (197) [B]
	ㅠ	亚	平	采取 **cǎiqǔ** to take; to adopt [B] 采用 **cǎiyòng** to adopt, to use [B]
620 8 strokes	采	采		(first six meanings only) 採

彩	㇒	ㅠ	亚	CǍI, be ornamented; good luck; colorful [A] 五彩 **wǔcǎi** be multi-colored
	平	采	采	
621 11 strokes	彩	彩	彩	

菜	卝	艹	艹	CÀI, vegetables; course or dish in a Chinese meal [A]
	艹	艹	苙	点菜 **diǎncài** to choose dishes (from a menu) 菜地 **càidì** vegetable plot 一道菜 **yídào cài** one course (of a meal)
622 11 strokes	莘	莘	菜	

踩	丨	冂	口	CǍI, to trample underfoot; to step on [B]
	무	무	뮤	
	뮤	跘	踩	
623 15 strokes				

丁	一	丁		DĪNG, person; nail; be strong; single; the fourth "heavenly stem" (used to enumerate items in an outline, like "D"—fourth letter of the Western alphabet); a family name [C]
				For more on the "heavenly stems," see *Lin Yutang's Dictionary* 1451f.
624 2 strokes				尼古丁 **nígǔdīng** nicotine 丁字街 **dīngzìjiē** T-shaped junction

125

打	一	丁	扌	**DĂ**, to beat [A]; from [C]; **DÁ**, a dozen [C]
	扩	打		打听 **dǎtīng** to inquire [B] 打开 **dǎkāi** to open 打扮 **dǎban** to put on make up; dress up 打入 **dǎrù** to branch out (in business); to force your way in
625 5 strokes				打字机 **dǎzìjī** typewriter 打交道 **dǎjiāodào** make contact with; have dealings with [C]

算	丿	𠂉	𥫗	**SUÀN**, to add up; to add in; to consider as … [A]
	𥫗𥫗	竺	笡	打算 **dǎsuàn** to plan to [A] 算了 **suànle** That's enough! Forget it! 心算 **xīnsuàn** do arithmetic in your head 笔算 **bǐsuàn** do arithmetic with pencil and
626 14 strokes	筲	算	算	paper

认	丶	讠	认	**RÈN**, to recognize; to admit [A]
	认			The "side-word" radical for meaning, **rén** "person" (replacing a complex phonetic) to suggest the sound.
627 4 strokes				认为 **rènwéi** to think, feel, deem [A] 认真 **rènzhēn** be conscientious [A] 认得 **rènde** to recognize [B] 认字 **rènzì** to be literate 認

识	丶	讠	讠	**SHÍ**, to know; knowledge [A]; **ZHÌ** (bookish) to remember; a mark, sign
	讠	识	识	认识 **rènshi** to recognize, to know [A] 常识 **chángshí** general knowledge [C] 识别 **shíbié** to distinguish, discern [D] 识字 **shízì** be literate
628 7 strokes	识			識

底	丶	亠	广	**DĬ**, foundation; bottom [B]
	广	庀	庍	底下 **dǐxia** underneath, below [B] 底子 **dǐzi** background, origin, foundation; original copy 年底 **niándǐ** year's end
629 8 strokes	底	底		

路 — 630 — 13 strokes

Stroke order: 丨 口 卩 卩 卩 足 趴 跻 路

LÙ, road; kind, sort; family name [A]

The "foot" radical for meaning ("road"); the other part once gave the sound.

路上 **lùshang** on the road; en route [B]
路口 **lùkǒu** (road) intersection [C]
路过 **lùguò** to go past [C]
路子 **lùzi** approach, means; "pull" [D]
走路 **zǒulù** to walk

病 — 631 — 10 strokes

Stroke order: 亠 广 广 疒 疒 疒 疒 疔 病 病

BÌNG, sickness, be sick [A]

The "sick" radical + **bǐng** (617) for sound.

看病 **kànbìng** to see a doctor; to examine a patient [A]
病人 **bìngrén** an invalid, a patient [B]
病房 **bìngfáng** sickroom, ward [B]
生病 **shēngbìng** to get sick [C]
病情 **bìngqíng** patient's condition [C]

邦 — 632 — 6 strokes

Stroke order: 一 二 三 丰 邦 邦

BĀNG, nation [D]

邦交 **bāngjiāo** diplomatic relations

帮 — 633 — 9 strokes

Stroke order: 一 二 三 丰 邦 邦 邦 帮 帮

BĀNG, to help; clique, group [A]

Bāng (632) gives the sound. "Cloth" is abbreviated from an earlier "riches," perhaps with the idea "help (collaboration) is important in creating wealth."

帮忙 **bāngmáng** to help [B]
帮手 **bāngshǒu** helper
一帮人 **yìbāng rén** gang, clique

幫

绑 — 634 — 9 strokes

Stroke order: 乚 幺 纟 纟 纟 纟 绐 绑 绑

BǍNG, to bind, to tie; to kidnap [C]

The "silk" radical is there for the meaning, 邦 **bāng** (632) for the sound.

綁

垂 635 8 strokes	一	二	千
	手	乭	乖
	垂	垂	

CHUÍ, to droop [C]

Chuí was originally a picture of a tree with drooping leaves.

垂直 **chuízhí** be perpendicular, vertical [C]
垂老 **chuílǎo** (bookish) to be getting old
垂青 **chuíqīng** (bookish) to appreciate (a person), favor a person

睡 636 13 strokes	刂	𝄃⺊	𝄃⺊
	盰	盰	盰
	盰	睡	睡

SHUÌ, to sleep; to lie down [A]

Chuí (635) is probably in 睡 to give the sound, but 睡 can also be explained as a meaning-meaning compound: "eye" + "to droop"= "to nod off, to sleep."

睡衣 **shuìyī** pyjamas
睡意 **shuìyì** sleepiness, desire to sleep

带 637 9 strokes	一	十	卄
	卅	丗	芇
	芇	带	带

DÀI, belt; to wear around the waist; to bring along [A]

带头 **dàitóu** to take the lead; to take the initiative; to set an example [C]
带路 **dàilù** to show or lead the way [C]
带孩子 **dài háizi** to bring up a child

| 犬 638 4 strokes | 一 | 𠂇 | 大 |
| | 犬 | | |

QUǍN, dog. DOG radical (96) [D]

The "dog" radical was a picture of a dog, corrupted over time to "big" + "dot." Care should be taken to distinguish the "dog" radical from "big" 大 (61, p. 13) and from 太 (98, p. 20). Note that there is also a "side-dog" radical (183, p. 37).

哭 639 10 strokes	丨	口	叩
	叩	叩	叩
	哭	哭	哭

KŪ, to cry, to howl [A]

Kū combines meanings: "dog" + "mouth" = "to howl, to cry." This was originally the top part of 丧 "to mourn"– traditional form 喪 — (Pt. 2, p. 269a); the bottom was a person, hidden in the grave.

哭笑不得 **kū-xiào bùdé** not know whether to laugh or cry; find a thing both painful and amusing

| 平 640 5 strokes | 一 | 丁 | 二 |
| | 立 | 平 | |

PÍNG, to weigh; be calm, level, flat [A]

Píng is a picture of a scale in balance.

平常	**píngcháng**	be ordinary [B]
平等	**píngděng**	be equal [B]
平原	**píngyuán**	a plain (flatland) [B]
平方	**píngfāng**	(in math) square [B]
平时	**píngshí**	in ordinary times [B]
平行	**píngxíng**	of equal rank; parallel [C]

评 641 7 strokes	丶	讠	讠
	讠	讠	讠
	评		

PÍNG, to comment on, criticize; to judge [A]

"Words" + "to weigh" can easily be seen as a meaning-meaning compound for "to criticize, to judge." Karlgren sees 640 and 641 as standing for the same word, etymologically (*AD* 743).

評

苹 642 8 strokes	一	十	艹
	艹	芒	苎
	芏	苹	

PÍNG, first syllable of 苹果 *píngguǒ,* **"apple" [A]**. (For 果, see 690, p. 139)

平 *píng* (640, above) gives the sound. The "grass" radical (as indicative of plants, flora) helps with the meaning.

应 643 7 strokes	丶	亠	广
	广	应	应
	应		

YĪNG, to promise; ought; a family name; YÌNG, to respond; to turn out to be true [A]

| 应用 | **yīngyòng** to put into practice [B] |
| 应得的 | **yīng déde** ought to be gotten; be deserved |

應

| 当 644 6 strokes | 丨 | 丷 | 丷 |
| | 丷 | 当 | 当 |

DĀNG, to serve as; in the presence of; the very same; DǍNG, to think (mistakenly) that; DÀNG, to think (mistakenly) that; to pawn [A]

应当	**yīngdāng** ought to (do) [B]
当时	**dāngshí** (at) that time [B]
当店	**dàngdiàn** pawnshop
当 … 的时候	**dāng... de shíhòu** just when... [B]

當

法	`	` ̣	氵
	氵	汁	泮
645 **8 strokes**	法	法	

FǍ, method, way, law; doctrine [A]

法文 **fǎwén** French language [A]
法子 **fǎzi** way, method [C]
法令 **fǎlìng** laws and decrees [C]
说法 **shuōfǎ** wording; version [C]
法院 **fǎyuàn** law court [C]
法官 **fǎguān** a judge [D]
法人 **fǎrén** (law) person; corporation [D]

怕	⺀	⺀⺀	忄
	忄	忄	怕
646 **8 strokes**	怕	怕	

PÀ, to fear [A]

"White"+"heart"= "to fear." **Bái** "white" is probably there to give the sound (but English has "lily-livered"—from an earlier "white-livered").

可怕 **kěpà** be frightening, scary [B]*
怕人 **pàrén** be shy (afraid of people); be frightening (making people fear)*
怕太太 **pàtàitai** be afraid of your wife

完	`	⺀	宀
	宀	宀	宀
647 **7 strokes**	完		

WÁN, to finish; family name [A]

完成 **wánchéng** to complete [A]
用完 **yòngwán** to use up, be used up
完儿完 **wánr wán** (colloquial) be kaput, finished, "done for"

办	フ	力	力
	办		
648 **4 strokes**			

BÀN, to manage; to punish [A]

The "strength" radical (suggesting exertion) may help with the meaning.

办法 **bànfǎ** method, way [A]
办事 **bànshì** do a job; manage [B]
办公 **bàngōng** to work (in an office); to take care of official business [B]
置办 **zhìbàn** to purchase

辦

觉	`	⺀	⺀⺀
	⺌	⺍	⺍
649 **9 strokes**	觉	觉	觉

JUÉ, to feel; JIÀO, to sleep [A]

觉得 **juéde** to feel [A],
睡觉 **shuìjiào** to sleep [A]
听觉 **tīngjué** sense of hearing

覺

---

*Note the typical versatility of the Chinese verb here: 1) 可怕, can/should be feared (passive); 2a) 怕人, fears people (is shy)(transitive); 2b) 怕人 causes people to fear (transitive-causative). (The terms "passive," "transitive," etc. here are not intended to be part of an analysis of Chinese grammar, but

错 650 13 strokes	ノ	⼂	钅
	钅	钅	钅艹
	钳	错	错

CUÒ, to make a mistake [A]

不错 **búcuò** be pretty good [A]
错字 **cuòzì** incorrectly written character; misprint [C]
错过 **cuòguò** to miss a chance
错觉 **cuòjué** illusion, wrong impression

錯

坏 651 7 strokes	一	⼗	土
	圤	圢	坏
	坏		

HUÀI, be bad, rotten, sly [A]

The right-hand part of 坏 has nothing to do with the negator of verbs 不. It is just a short-hand way to suggest the right-hand part of the traditional character (see below, this frame).

车坏了 **chē huàile** The car broke down.

壞

河 652 8 strokes	、	⼆	氵
	汀	汀	河
	河	河	

HÉ, river [A]

Kě (106, p. 22) gives the sound; the "three-dots water" radical, of course, gives the meaning.

河道 **hédào** river course, riverbed [D]
河口 **hékǒu** mouth of a river
河马 **hémǎ** hippopotamus

鱼 653 8 strokes	ノ	⼂	伫
	鱼	鱼	鱼
	鱼	鱼	

YÚ, fish; family name. FISH radical (210) [A]

飞鱼 **fēiyú** flying fish
鱼网 **yúwǎng** fishnet
金鱼 **jīnyú** goldfish
煎鱼 **jiān yú** fry fish

魚

| 永 654 5 strokes | 、 | ⼁ | ⼆ |
| | 永 | 永 | |

YǑNG, be eternal [A]

The character is supposed to be a picture of water currents and thus suggests "go on and on" like flowing water: "be eternal."

永远 **yǒngyuǎn** forever, always [A]
永不 **... yǒngbu...** never...
永生 **yǒngshēng** (religious term) eternal life; be immortal

rather a "quick and dirty" way to help native speakers of English and other Indo-European languages deal with Chinese verbs and get from Chinese sentences the same picture as the Chinese speaker had in his/her mind.)

样	木	木`	木``
	杧	栏	栏
655 10 strokes	样		

YÀNG, kind, sort [A]

样子 **yàngzi**　style [A]
这样 **zhèyàng**　in this way; so [A]
怎样 **zěnyàng**　how?; in a certain way [A]
一样 **yíyàng**　be alike
怎么样 **zěnmeyàng**　how?; …, how about it?; How's everything?; in a certain way, in any way [A]

樣

条	ノ	ク	冬
	冬	夅	夅
656 7 strokes	条		

TIÁO, a twig; a long, narrow thing, a strip; section; a measure for roads, rivers, fishes, some animals; a note (short message) [A]

条件 **tiáojiàn**　terms, conditions [A]
便条 **biàntiáo**　brief note [B]
条子 **tiáozi**　a strip; short note [D]
一条鱼 **yìtiáo yú**　a fish

條

冫	丶	冫	
657 2 strokes			

BĪNG, ice. ICE radical (8)

Note the similarity between the "ice" radical and the "three-dots-water" radical (77, p. 16). The "ice" radical has two dots instead of three.

次	丶	冫	冫`
	沪	汋	次
658 6 strokes			

CÌ, a time; a measure for times or occasions [A]; be next (in order); be inferior to [C]

三次 **sāncì**　three times
次要 **cìyào**　second most important [C]
下次 **xiàcì**　next time
首次 **shǒucì**　the first time
真次 **zhēncì**　be really inferior, be awful

短	ノ	⻌	⻌
	午	矢	矢`
659 12 strokes	矩	短	短

DUĂN, be short (opposite of long); to lack [A]

The first example below illustrates a favorite Chinese technique of word-formation, putting two contraries together to form an abstract noun: "the long and the short of it" = "length."

长短 **chángduǎn**　length [D]
短少 **duǎnshǎo**　be deficient, to lack

比 660 4 strokes	一 比	上	比ˊ	**BǏ, set side by side, to compare. COMPARE radical (123)** The modern character looks like "ladle" + "ladle" (41, p. 9). The old forms have two people standing side by side. In any case, there are two similar objects side by side, as if for comparison. 比较 **bǐjiào** to compare [A]
及 661 3 strokes	丿	乃	及	**JÍ, to reach, together with; and; see** 来得及 **and** 来不及, **below. [B]** 及时 **jíshí** be timely; be seasonable; promptly, without delay [B] 及早 **jízǎo** as soon as possible; at an early date [D] 来得及 **láidejí** there's still time, it can be done [B] 来不及 **láibují** it's too late to do it now [B]
极 662 7 strokes	一 木 极	十 朾	才 极	**JÍ, to reach an extreme; extremely; pole (extreme point) [A]** 及 **jí** (661, above) gives the sound. (verb) + 极了 ...**jíle** be extremely...: e.g., 好极了 **hǎojíle** Superb! Great! [A] 极力 **jílì** with all your strength [D] 极点 **jídiǎn** extreme point
级 663 6 strokes	乚 纟	纟 级	纟 级	**JÍ, level, class, grade; a measure for levels, classes, and grades [A]** 及 **jí** (661, above) gives the sound.
吸 664 6 strokes	丨 叽	叮 吸	口 吸	**XĪ, to inhale; to soak up [B]** The "mouth" radical helps with the meaning; 及 **jí** (661, above) at one time helped with the sound.

南 665 9 strokes	一	十	十
	市	市	南
	南	南	南

NÁN, south; family name [A]

English-speakers say "southwest"; Chinese speakers "westsouth." See also 666.

南方 **nánfāng** south; S. China [B]
西南 **xīnán** southwest; SW China [B]
东南 **dōngnán** southeast; SE China [B]
南极 **nánjí** South Pole
南京 **Nánjīng** Nanjing (the city)

北 666 5 strokes	⎸	⼅	⼅
	⼅	北	

BĚI, north [A]

北方 **běifāng** the North [B]
东北 **dōngběi** northeast; NE China [B]
西北 **xīběi** northwest; NW China [B]
北京 **Běijīng** Beijing
城北 **chéngběi** north of the city

背 667 9 strokes	⼅	⼅	⼅
	⼅	⼅	⼅
	背	背	背

BÈI, back; to turn one's back on; be bad; to memorize; to recite; BĒI, to carry on the back [B]

背后 **bèihòu** in back of; behind someone's back
背包 **bēibāo** knapsack

揹 (BĒI only)

左 668 5 strokes	一	𠂇	𠂇
	左	左	

ZUǑ, left (opposite of right) [A]

左手 **zuǒshǒu** left hand
想左了 **xiǎngzuǒle** to think incorrectly

右 669 5 strokes	一	𠂇	𠂇
	右	右	

YÒU, right (opposite of left) [A]

左右 **zuǒyòu** left and right; alternately
左右开弓 **zuǒyòu kāi gōng** fire away left and right; be ambidextrous
十个左右 **shíge zuǒyòu** approximately ten [B]

左 … 右 … do something repeatedly, e.g.
左思右想 **zuǒ sī yòu xiǎng** keep thinking about it

134

边 670 5 strokes	ヲ 讠カ	カ 边	`カ	**BIĀN, side, region; family name [A]** 北边 **běibiān** north side, N region [A] 里边 **lǐbiān** inside [A] 左边 **zuǒbiān** left side [B] 边 + verb-1 + 边 + verb-2 **biān…biān…** do 1 and 2 simultaneously, e.g. 边干边学 **biān gàn biān xué** work (do) and study, learn on the job [B] 邊
牙 671 4 strokes	一 牙	二	牙	**YÁ, tooth; family name. TOOTH radical (99) [B]** The "tooth" radical is a picture. It gives the sound in several common characters (see the following). 门牙 **ményá** incisor 犬牙 **quǎnyá** canine tooth; dog's fang
呀 672 7 strokes	丨 吖 呀	冂 吘	口 呀	**YĀ, an exclamation of surprise; an onomatopoetic sound, e.g., for the creaking of a door ; YA, used for euphonic reasons in place of** 啊 **(108, p. 22) when the word before the particle ends with an open vowel [A]** 牙 **yá** (671, above) gives the sound.
讶 673 6 strokes	ヽ 讠	讠 讶	讠 讶	**YÀ, (bookish) be surprised; amazement, wonder [C]** This is another character in which 牙 **yá** (671, above) gives the sound. 訝
芽 674 7 strokes	一 芒 芽	十 芒	++ 芽	**YÁ, bud, sprout, shoot [C]** The "grass" radical gives the meaning; 牙 **yá** (671, above) gives the sound. Karlgren sees 671 and 674 as standing for the same word, etymologically (*AD* 208).

135

面	一	厂	厂	**MIÀN, face; flour, noodles [A]**
	币	币	而	The character is a picture of a face. Now it stands, by sound-loan, for an homonymous word meaning "flour, noodles" (in the traditional character, 面 had been the phonetic, with the meaning element "wheat:" see below).
675 9 strokes	面	面	面	版面 **bǎnmiàn** layout; space on a whole page 麵 ("flour, noodles" only)

穿	﹅	丷	宀	**CHUĀN, to pierce; to thread; to don, to wear [A]**
	宀	穴	空	Analyzed, 穿 is "cave" (454, p. 91) over "tooth," but the logic…perhaps "tooth" → "make a hole in" → "pierce."
676 9 strokes	空	穿	穿	看穿 **kànchuān** to see right through 穿戴 **chuāndài** clothing, apparel 穿着 **chuānzhuó** clothing, apparel

近	一	厂	斤	**JÌN, be near [A]**
	斤	沂	沂	斤 (342, p. 69) gives the sound, "halt" (90, p. 19) the meaning. 近来 **jìnlái** recently [B] 远近 **yuǎnjìn** distance (compare 长短 in 659, p. 132); far and near
677 7 strokes	近			远近闻名 **yuǎnjìn wénmíng** have your name heard far and near: be famous 邻近 **línjìn** be near; be close to

凶	丿	乂	区	**XIŌNG, be cruel; be unlucky (bring bad luck); be calamitous [C]**
	凶			The "bowl" radical in this character used to be a pit, and the X shape was a person falling, legs up, into the pit: "calamity."
678 4 strokes				凶手 **xiōngshǒu** murderer, (figurative senses) butcher 行凶 **xíngxiōng** to commit physical assault or murder

离	亠	宀	文	**LÍ, to part from; from [A]**
	卤	卤	卤	离 once meant "hobgoblin" and was a picture of that creature (with the bottom part being hind legs and a tail). Now in sound-loan for "to part from; from."
679 10 strokes	离	离	离	离开 **líkāi** to leave [A] 离别 **líbié** to part from (for long) [D] 离间 **líjiān** to cause a rift between 離

脸 680 11 strokes	刀	月	肝	**LIǍN, face [A]** The "moon/meat" radical here (as "meat") helped with the meaning; the righthand part once helped with the sound. 门脸 **ménliǎn** facade 笑脸 **xiào liǎn** a smiling face 不要脸 **búyào liǎn** be shameless, have no conscience 脸盆 **liǎnpén** washbasin 臉
	肸	肸	脸	
	脸	脸	脸	

数 681 13 strokes	`	``	䒑	**SHÙ, number; SHǓ, to enumerate [A]** 数学 **shùxué** mathematics [A] 数字 **shùzì** numeral, digit; quantity [B] 数目 **shùmu** number, amount [C] 岁数 **suìshù** (person's) age [C] 数数儿 **shǔshùr** to count ("to enumerate the numbers") 數
	半	米	米	
	娄	数	数	

洗 682 9 strokes	`	``	氵	**XǏ, to wash [A]** 洗脸 **xǐliǎn** to wash your face 洗手 **xǐshǒu** (figuratively, as in English) to wash your hands of something; (of a criminal) to go straight 洗礼 **xǐlǐ** baptism (literally, "the washing ritual"); (figuratively) a severe test 洗衣机 **xǐyījī** washing machine [B]
	氵	氵	汖	
	泩	泩	洗	

往 683 8 strokes	´	⁄	彳	**WǍNG, to go; bygone; toward [A]** 往往 **wǎngwǎng** often, frequently [B] 往常 **wǎngcháng** as was habitual [C] 往来 **wǎnglái** 来往 **láiwǎng** deal, to deal, do business with; come and go [C] 往事 **wǎngshì** past events; the past [D] 往日 **wǎngrì** (in) bygone days [D] 往东 **wǎngdōng** eastward
	彳	彳	行	
	徃	往		

每 684 7 strokes	´	⁄	仁	**MĚI, each [A]** 每天 **měitiān** every day 每次 **měicì** each time 每一个 **měi yíge** each, each one
	勹	匂	每	
	每			

怪	⟍	⺍	忄
	忄	忆	怪
685 8 strokes	怪	怪	

GUÀI, to blame; to consider weird; to be weird [B]

奇怪 **qíguài** be peculiar, be weird [B]
怪话 **guàihuà** cynical remark; complaint
别怪她 **bié guài tā** Don't blame her
怪不得 **guàibude** no wonder; so *that*'s the reason; don't blame...

然	ノ	ク	夕
	夕	夕⼀	夗
686 12 strokes	㹺	㹸	然

RÁN, be right; so, like this [A]

然 once meant "to roast;" it combined meanings: "meat" (deformed) + "dog" + "fire." Other meanings by sound-loan.

然后 **ránhòu** afterward [A],
当然 **dāngrán** certainly; naturally [A]
自然 **zìrán** be natural (大自然: Nature) [B]
必然 **bìrán** certainly [B]

午	ノ	⺅	⺊
	午		
687 4 strokes			

WǓ, noon; the 7ᵗʰ "earthly branch" [A]

午 once meant "to knock against" and was a picture of a battering ram. Distinguish from 干 (223, p. 45). "Noon" by sound-loan. On the "branches," see 44, p. 9.

下午 **xiàwǔ** afternoon [A]
午饭 **wǔfàn** noon meal, lunch [A]
正午 **zhèngwǔ** high noon

许	⟍	讠	讠'
	讠	许	许
688 6 strokes			

XǓ, to permit; to promise; perhaps; family name [A]

许多 **xǔduō** a lot; many things [A]
许可 **xǔkě** to permit; permission [D]
许愿 **xǔyuàn** to make a vow (to a god); to promise a reward

許

才	一	十	才
689 3 strokes			

CÁI, substance; natural capacity; talent, genius; then (not till then); only [A]

Distinguish from 寸 "thumb" (237, p. 48) and from 扌 ("side-hand") (28).

人才 **réncái** talented person; (colloquial) handsome man [B]
天才 **tiāncái** genius, talent [C]
才能 **cáinéng** talent, ability [C]

138

果 690 8 strokes	丨	冂	日
	曰	旦	甲
	甲	果	

GUǑ, fruit; result; really [A]

Guǒ is a picture of fruit on a tree.

水果　**shuǐguǒ**　fruit [A]
结果　**jiēguǒ**　result [A]
果然　**guǒrán**　indeed, certainly [B]
果仁　**guǒrén**　nut

课 691 10 strokes	丶	讠	订
	订	评	评
	评	课	课

KÈ, lesson, course; class section [A]

下课　**xiàkè**　class dismissed [A]
课本　**kèběn**　textbook [A]
课文　**kèwén**　text [A]
课时　**kèshí**　class hour [D]

課

棵 692 12 strokes	木	朾	机
	柯	柯	栖
	椑	椑	棵

KĒ, a measure for trees and heads of cabbage [A]

三棵大白菜　**sānkē dàbáicài**　three heads of Chinese cabbage ("bok choy" in most American Chinatowns)

世 693 5 strokes	一	十	卅
	卅	世	

SHÌ, world, generation; family name [A]

世 is three "ten" 十 radicals (the vertical stroke on the left is bent for the sake of design) written together to suggest "thirty years: a generation."

世纪　**shìjì**　century [B]
今世　**jīnshì**　this age; be contemporary
世上　**shìshang**　in this world, on earth

介 694 4 strokes	丿	八	介
	介		

JIÈ, between; to regard as important [A]

介入　**jièrù**　to intervene, get involved
介子　**jièzi**　meson (term from physics: particle of intermediate mass, between baryons 重子[**zhòngzi** "heavy ones"] and leptons 轻子[**qīngzi** "light ones"—see Pt. 2, p. 218a for 轻 "be light"].)

139

界	丨	冂	日	**JIÈ, boundary; world; scope [A]** 世界 **shìjiè** world [A] 边界 **biānjiè** border [C] 国界 **guójiè** national boundaries, borders 新闻界 **xīnwénjiè** journalistic circles
	用	田	甲	
695 **9 strokes**	畀	界	界	

价	丿	亻	仁	**JIÀ, price, value [B]** 价钱 **jiàqián** price [C] 原价 **yuánjià** original price 讲价 **jiǎngjià** to haggle, discuss price 租价 **zūjià** rental
	价	价	价	
696 **6 strokes**				價

海	氵	冫	氵	**HǍI, sea; a family name [A]** 海关 **hǎiguān** customs house; Customs [B] 海外 **hǎiwài** overseas, abroad [D] 上海 **Shànghǎi** Shanghai 地中海 **Dìzhōnghǎi** Mediterranean Sea
	汇	海	海	
697 **10 strokes**	海	海		

部	丶	亠	亠	**BÙ, set, portion, part; department; a measure for vehicles; family name (rare) [A]** 部分 **bùfen** portion, part [A] 部门 **bùmén** department [B] 部长 **bùzhǎng** department head [B] 部首 **bùshǒu** a "radical"—an element of the Chinese writing system
	立	立	音	
698 **10 strokes**	咅	部		

黄	一	艹	艹	**HUÁNG, yellow; family name [A]** 黄金 **huángjīn** "the yellow metal," i.e. gold [D] 黄豆 **huángdòu** soyabean 黄河 **Huáng hé** the Yellow River 黄了 **huángle** (collquial) to have fallen through, have come to nothing (literally, "to have turned yellow")
	艹	艹	苗	
699 **11 strokes**	苗	黄	黄	(田 10)

总	`	˅	⼾	**ZŎNG, to add together; always; probably; surely [A]**
	⼧	兯	户	总是 **zŏngshì** always [A] 总共 **zŏnggòng** altogether [C] 总得 **zŏngděi** must, have to [C]
700 **9 strokes**	总	总	总	总算 **zŏngsuàn** at last; on the whole [C] 总数 **zŏngshù** total, total amount [D] <div align="right">總</div>

连	一	七	左	**LIÁN, to connect; continuously; including; company (military); even; family name [A]**
	车	车	诈	连忙 **liánmáng** at once, promptly [B] 连连 **liánlián** (colloquial) repeatedly 连年 **liánnián** in consecutive years; year after year
701 **7 strokes**	连			连... 都(也)... **lián ... dou (yě)** even (see Chao's *Grammar*, p. 766) [B] 連

只	⎸	⼞	口	**ZHĬ, just, only; ZHĬ, a measure for animals, birds, boats; single [A]**
	只	只		只好 **zhǐhǎo** can do nothing but... [A] 只有 **zhǐyǒu** can do nothing but... [B] 只是 **zhǐshì** but; only [B] 只要 **zhǐyào** so long as [B]
702 **5 strokes**				只得 **zhǐdé** can do nothing but... [C] <div align="right">(zhī only) 隻</div>

特	⼂	⼇	牛	**TÈ, be special [A]**
	牛	牜	牜	特别 **tèbié** special, especially [A] 特点 **tèdiǎn** special feature [D] 特定 **tèdìng** be specifically designated [D]
703 **10 strokes**	牜	牜	特	特地 **tèdì** for a specific purpose [D] 特意 **tèyì** same as 特地 [D]

洋	`	ˇ	氵	**YÁNG, ocean; be foreign [B]**
	氵	氵	洋	The "water" radical gives the meaning, and "sheep" (**yáng**) gives the sound. 洋鬼子 **yángguǐzi** "foreign devil," foreigner (derogatory)
704 **9 strokes**	洋	洋	洋	大西洋 **Dàxīyáng** the Atlantic 太平洋 **Tàipíngyáng** the Pacific

余	ノ	人	亼	**YÚ, surplus; remainder [B]; (bookish) I, me; family name**
	仐	仐	仐	其余 **qíyú** the rest of it [B] 余数 **yúshù** balance, remainder; complement of a number 余闲 **yúxián** spare time, leisure
705 7 strokes	余			(surplus, remainder only) 餘

除	⻖	⻖	⻖	**CHÚ, except; to divide (arithmetic); to remove [A]**
	阶	阶	阶	除了... 以外 **chúle...yǐwài** other than... [A] 除外 **chúwài** except, excluding [D] 除夕 **chúxī** (on) New Year's Eve [D] 除去 **chúqù** in addition to; to remove
706 9 strokes	阶	除	除	

江	、	冫	氵	**JIĀNG, river; family name [A]**
	氵	汀	江	长江 **Chángjiāng** the "long river," i.e., the Yangtse 江西 **Jiāngxī** Kiangsi (province) 江山 **jiāngshān** rivers and mountains; landscape; (by metonymy) nation
707 6 strokes				

全	ノ	人	亼	**QUÁN, complete, completely; all, the whole; family name [A]** Distinguish from 金 "gold" (218, p. 44).
	仐	仐	全	完全 **wánquán** complete(ly); perfectly [A] 全部 **quánbù** the whole thing; completely 全面 **quánmiàn** overall; be comprehensive [B] 全力 **quánlì** with all your strength [D] 全心全意 **quánxīnquányì** wholeheartedly [D]
708 6 strokes				

争	ノ	⺈	刍	**ZHĒNG, to argue, to fight [B]** The character shows two hands struggling over an object (the hand on top is abbreviated).
	刍	刍	争	争取 **zhēngqǔ** to work hard for [B] 争气 **zhēngqì** be determined; do your best to make a good showing [D]
709 6 strokes				爭

净 710 8 stroks	`	⺡	⺡

JÌNG, to clean, be clean; net (as opposed to gross); everywhere [A]
干净 **gānjìng** be clean [A]
净得 **jìngdé** net profit
净重 **jìngzhòng** net weight

淨

HÚ, Tartars; Mongols; be foolish; beard, mustache; family name [B]
胡子 **húzi** beard, mustache [B]
胡说 **húshuō** to talk nonsense, to blather; Nonsense! Bunkum! [C]
胡来 **húlái** not know what you're doing; to act like a fool, make trouble; to blunder [D]

HÚ, lake [A]
湖北 **Húběi** Hubei (province)
湖南 **Húnán** Hunan (province)
江湖 **jiānghú** rivers and lakes; all over the country
江湖 **jiānghu** traveling con artists (entertainers, fake doctors, and the like) or itinerant performers and the like

SHĀNG, quotient; commerce; merchant; family name [A]
商人 **shāngrén** businessman [A]
商船 **shāngchuán** merchant ship
商会 **shānghuì** chamber of commerce
进口商 **jìnkǒushāng** importer

YÈ, business, profession, course of study; property; family name. BUSINESS radical (140) [A]
业 is thick foliage at the top of a tree, to suggest productive activity and prosperity.
商业 **shāngyè** business, commerce [B]
业余 **yèyú** spare time; amateur [B]
重工业 **zhònggōngyè** heavy industry [D]

業

| 民 715 5 strokes | ⁊ | ⊐ | ⊨ |
| | ⼾ | 民 | |

MÍN, folk, people [A]*

人民 **rénmín** the common people [A]
民主 **mínzhǔ** democracy, be democratic [B]
民间 **mínjiān** among the people; folk
(adjective); non-governmental [C]
民用 **mínyòng** for civil use, civil [C]
民事 **mínshì** relating to civil law [D]
民意 **mínyì** the will of the people [D]

党 716 10 strokes	⼌	⼩	⼩⼂
	⼩⼀	⼩⼀	学
	岩	学	党

DǍNG, association; political party; family name [B]

国民党 **Guómíndǎng** Kuomingtang,
Nationalist Party
民主党 **Mínzhǔdǎng** Democratic Party
入党 **rùdǎng** to join or be admitted to a
political party (or to the Party)
党报 **dǎngbào** party newspaper

黨

| 产 717 6 strokes | ⼂ | ⼀ | ⼇ |
| | 亠 | 立 | 产 |

CHǍN, to produce, product; property [A]
Distinguish 厂 (229, p. 46), 广 (363), and 產
(Pt. 2, p. 236b).
出产 **chūchǎn** to produce; production output
[D]
产业 **chǎnyè** property (real estate) [D]
特产 **tèchǎn** special local product [D]
共产党 **Gōngchǎndǎng** Communist
Party [B]

產

斩 718 8 strokes	一	七	车
	车	车ˊ	轩
	轩	斩	

ZHǍN, to behead; to cut to pieces ; (dialect) to cheat somebody; to blackmail [D]

The character is explained as "a chariot with axes in it."

斩除 **zhǎnchū** to eradicate, extirpate
斩首 **zhǎnshǒu** to behead

斬

暂 719 12 strokes	车	车ˊ	轩
	轩	斩	斩
	暂	暂	暂

ZÀN, temporarily [B]

暂时 **zànshí** temporarily [B]
暂且 **zànqiě** for a short time [D]
短暂 **duǎnzàn** be brief, transient [D]
暂定 **zàndìng** be provisional, temporary

暫

*In *Han-Ying Cidian*, 民 is one of 11 "left-over" characters, not classified under a radical.

144

准 720 10 strokes	冫	氵	沪
	沪	汇	汇
	汇	准	准

ZHǓN, water-level; standard; to deem to meet a standard, to permit, allow; to cause to meet a standard, to regulate; to be up to a standard, be accurate; quasi-

准时 **zhǔnshí** to be on time [B]
准许 **zhǔnxǔ** to permit [D]
水准 **shuǐzhǔn** standard, level
准保 **zhǔnbǎo** for sure

準

| 久 721 3 strokes | 丿 | 勹 | 久 |

JIǓ, to last for a long time [A]

长久 **chángjiǔ** be long (in time), long-lasting [C]
永久 **yǒngjiǔ** eternally, permanently [D]
很久没见 **hěnjiǔ méijiàn** "Long time no see," (as in the English borrowing) "It's been quite a while since I last saw you."

| 发 722 5 strokes | 一 | 乄 | 乡 |
| | 发 | 发 | |

FĀ, to send out, to bring out, to shoot; a measure for rounds (ammunition); **FÀ**, hair [A]
The traditional form: the bow 弓 may help with the meaning "to shoot." 殳 "club" was once an arrow 矢. "Hair" is by sound-loan.

发生 **fāshēng** to happen [A]
发现 **fāxiàn** to discover [A]
头发 **tóufa** hair
(hair only) 髮 (other meanings) 發

堂 723 11 strokes	丷	丷丷	丷丷
	丷丷	丷丷	丷丷
	堂	堂	

TÁNG, hall; a measure for classes and sets of furniture [A]

堂堂 **táng táng** be impressive; have high aspirations and bold vision

| 讲 724 6 strokes | 丶 | 讠 | 讠 |
| | 讠 | 讲 | 讲 |

JIǍNG, to speak; to be conscientious about [A]

讲话 **jiǎnghuà** to talk, make a speech [B]
听讲 **tīng jiǎng** to attend a lecture [B]
讲课 **jiǎngkè** to teach, to lecture [C]
讲学 **jiǎngxué** an academic subject
讲明 **jiǎngmíng** to clarify, to explain

講

种 725 9 strokes	一 禾 和	二 禾 和	千 和 种	**ZHǑNG**, kind, sort, species [A]; **ZHÒNG**, to plant, to sow, to grow [B]; **CHÓNG**, family name (rare) 种子 **zhǒngzi** seed [B] 种地 **zhòngdì** to farm, till the soil [D] 种种 **zhǒngzhǒng** all kinds of [D] 种马 **zhǒngmǎ** stud 種
傅 726 12 strokes	亻 伃 僡	仁 侼 傅	仨 傅 傅	**FÙ**, to teach; a teacher; to put on, to apply; family name [A] 傅粉 **fùfěn** to make up, put on face powder
专 727 4 strokes	一 专	二	专	**ZHUĀN**, be sole, be unique; solely; family name (rare) [B] 专 gives the sound in a number of characters (see the next few items). 专门 **zhuānmén** be special, specialized [B] 专家 **zhuānjiā** an expert, specialist [B] 专心 **zhuānxīn** concentrate on [B] 专业 **zhuānyè** specialty (profession or field of study) [B] 專
传 728 6 strokes	丿 仁	亻 传	仁 传	**CHUÁN**, to transmit; **ZHUÀN**, record, biography [B] 传说 **chuánshuō** to spread a rumor; rumor, legend [C] 传真 **chuánzhēn** facsimile [D] 传教 **chuánjiào** to proselytize 自传 **zìzhuàn** autobiography 傳
转 729 8 strokes	一 车 转	土 车 转	车 车	**ZHUǍN**, to turn [B] 转变 **zhuǎnbiàn** to transform [B] 转告 **zhuǎngào** pass the word [B] 转入 **zhuǎnrù** to shift to, move over to [C] 转交 **zhuǎnjiāo** to transmit [D] 轉

146

砖	一	厂	石	**ZHUĀN, brick [C]** 砖厂 **zhuāngchǎng** brickyard
730 9 strokes	石	石	矿 砖 砖	磚

虫	丨	冂	口	**CHÓNG, bug. BUG radical (174) [B]** 虫 is said to be a picture of a bug. The traditional form, presumably twice reclarified, has two more bugs (see below). 虫子 **chóngzi** bug; worm [B]
731 6 strokes	中	虫	虫	蟲

虽	丨	冂	口	**SUĪ, although [A]** 虽然 **suīrán** although [A] 虽说 **suīshuō** (colloquial) although
732 9 strokes	尸	吕	吕 虽	雖

象	⺈	仱	臽	**XIÀNG, 1) elephant; image [B]; 2) to present an image of, to look like; picture, portrait, statue; such as… [A]** 象 gets meanings marked "2" by being the short form of 像 (see next item). Originally a picture of an elephant. Other meanings by sound-loan.* 现象 **xiànxiàng** phenomenon (B) (meanings marked "2" only)
733 11 strokes	牟	象	象 象	像

像	亻	亻	伫	**XIÀNG, to present an image of, to look like; picture, portrait, statue; such as … [A]** Karlgren (AD 797) says 像 stands for the same word as 象 (733, above)—reclarified, then, with the "person" radical. 像样 **xiàngyàng** be up to standard/ acceptable/ appropriate/decorous/ decent [D]
734 13 strokes	伊	傍	像 像	

*Karlgren, however, sees a semantic (or metonymic) progression: elephant → ivory → carved ivory → carved things generally → portrait, statue (AD 797).

亮 735 9 strokes	丶	亠	广
	亠	古	亭
	亭	亭	亮

LIÀNG, be bright; to show

明亮 **míngliàng** be well-lit; be bright and clear; to become clear [B]
亮相 **liàngxiàng** (Beijing opera) to strike a pose; to state your views
天亮了 **tiān liàng le** It's already daylight.

越 736 12 strokes	土	丰	未
	走	走	起
	越	越	越

YUÈ, to pass over, to exceed; (if repeated) the more.... the more...; family name [B]

越... 越... **yuè... yuè...** the more..., the more... [B]
越来越... **yuè lái yuè...** more and more... [B]
越过 **yuèguò** to get across; to negotiate [D]
越界 **yuèjiè** overstep a boundary; cross a border
越南 **Yuènán** Vietnam

敢 737 11 strokes	⼇	又	孑
	丣	爭	耳
	玣	敢	敢

GǍN, to dare, to be so bold as to ... [A]

敢情 **gǎnqing** (dialect) Oh, so …; really (intensifier)
不敢当 **bùgǎndāng** I don't deserve such a compliment.

并 738 6 strokes	丶	丷	丷
	兰	羊	并

BÌNG, be side by side; and; actually; moreover [B]

并且 **bìngqiě** furthermore [B]
合并 **hébìng** to merge [D]
并不 **bìngbù** certainly not (intensifies the negation)
并行 **bìngxíng** to implement (two things) at the same time

| 瓦 739 4 strokes | 一 | 厂 | 瓦 |
| | 瓦 | | |

WǍ, tile; watt (electrical term). WÀ, to cover with tile, to tile over (a roof). TILE radical (98)

瓦工 **wǎgōng** bricklaying, tiling, plastering; bricklayer, tiler, plasterer
瓦时 **wǎshí** watt-hour (electrical term)

瓶

740
10 strokes

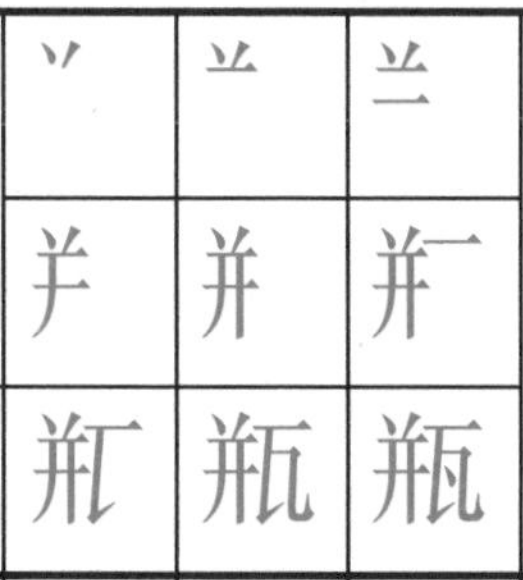

PÍNG, bottle, vase [A]
瓶子 **píngzi** vase, bottle [B]

拼

741
9 strokes

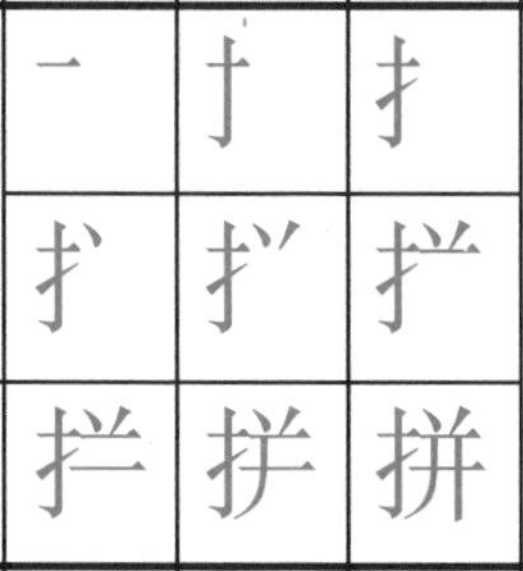

PĪN, to put together; to fight or work furiously [B]
拼音 **pīnyīn** to spell

非

742
8 strokes

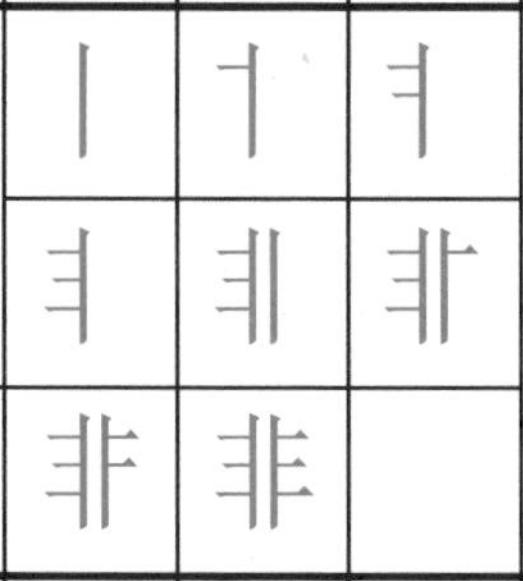

FĒI, be wrong; be false; not. WRONG radical (205) [A]
非常 **fēicháng** exceptionally [A]
是非 **shìfēi** right and wrong [C]
并非 **bìngfēi** It's not that... [D]
胡作非为 **hú zuò fēi wéi** to act barbarously and behave wrongly; to commit many outrages
非...不可 **fēi...bù kě** must … [B]

造

743
10 strokes

ZÀO, to manufacture, to build; party to a lawsuit [B]
造句 **zàojù** sentence-making [B]
造反 **zàofǎn** to rebel [D]
造爱 **zào'āi** to make love
造汽车 **zào qìchē** to manufacture cars

于

744
3 strokes

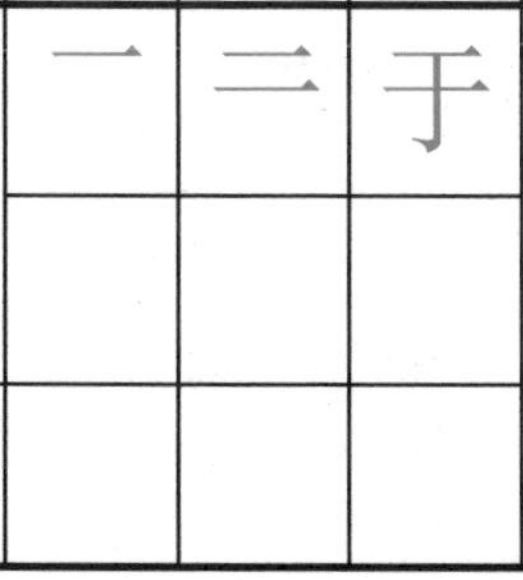

YÚ, on, to, at, than; family name [B]
In old texts, often written 於.
于是 **yúshì** hence, as a result [B]
等于 **děngyú** be equal to, be equivalent to [B]
敢于 **gǎnyú** to dare to [C]
多于 **duōyú** be more than
于今 **yújīn** up till now, up till the present
于我 **yúwǒ** the way I see it,...; with reference to me

束	一	厂	〒	**SHÙ, bundle; to bind; family name [A]** Distinguish from 束 the "thorn" radical (Pt. 2, p. 229b) 束手　**shùshǒu**　be helpless, be powerless to act; "my hands are tied..."
	〒	申	束	
745 7 strokes	束			

树	一	十	十	**SHÙ, a tree; to plant, cultivate; to set up [A]** 树林　**shùlín**　a grove, woods [B] 树木　**shùmù**　trees [C] 果树　**guǒshù**　fruit tree [C] 树干　**shùgàn**　tree trunk, trunk [D] 树枝　**shùzhī**　branch, twig 树立　**shùlì**　to set up, establish 爬树　**páshù**　to climb trees
	木	权	权	
746 9 strokes	权	树	树	樹

皮	一	厂	广	**PÍ, bark, leather, skin, fur; a family name. SKIN radical (153) [B]** 皮带　**pídài**　leather belt [D] 皮革　**pígé**　leather; hide [D] 皮包　**píbāo**　briefcase, leather handbag 皮鞋　**píxié**　leather shoes
	庐	皮		
747 5 strokes				

活	丶	丶	氵	**HUÓ, to live, be alive [A]; be lively; be movable [C]; work; product** 生活　**shēnghuó**　life; to live [A] 活儿　**huór**　work; product [A] 活力　**huólì**　vitality [D] 活字　**huózì**　(printing) type, movable type
	氵	汇	汗	
748 9 strokes	汗	活	活	

石	一	厂	石	**SHÍ, rock; a family name [B]; DÀN, a picul (133-1/3 pounds). ROCK radical (136)** The "mouth" is supposed to be a rock that has rolled to the foot of a cliff. 石头　**shítou**　stone, rock [B] 石头子儿　**shítouzǐr**　(colloquial) pebble 石像　**shíxiàng**　stone statue 石英　**shíyīng**　quartz
	石	石		
749 5 strokes				

150

				SĪ, silk; trace, a bit; a unit of weight (0.0005 gram) [B]
丝	∠	∠	纟	真丝 **zhēnsī** real silk 粉丝 **fěnsī** vermicelli 一丝不差 **yìsī búchà** there's no difference at all
	纟	丝		
750 5 strokes				絲

				YÌ, also. ALSO radical (162)
亦	ヽ	亠	广	This was originally a drawing of a man with a stroke on either side to indicate the armpits; it meant "armpit." It came to mean "also" by sound-loan.
	亣	亦	亦	
751 6 strokes				

				BIÀN, change [A]
变	ヽ	亠	广	变成 **biànchéng** to change into, become [A] 变革 **biàngé** to transform [C] 事变 **shìbiàn** incident; emergency [D] 变更 **biàngēng** to change, alter, modify [D] 变脸 **biànliǎn** suddenly become hostile 转变 **zhuǎnbiàn** to change
	亣	亦	亦	
752 8 strokes	变	变		變

				BÙ, step, pace; on foot; a family name [A]
步	丨	卜	止	步行 **bùxíng** to walk, go on foot [D] 步子 **bùzi** step; pace [D]
	止	牛	步	
753 7 strokes	步			

				JŪ, to reside; family name [B]
居	⌐	⊐	尸	尸 here is a person lying down or sleeping (rather than a corpse) and helps with the meaning: where you sleep is where you reside. 古 in former times helped with the sound.
	尸	尸	尺	邻居 **línjū** neighbor [B] 居民 **jūmín** resident [C]
754 8 strokes	居	居		居然 **jūrán** unexpectedly [C] 居住 **jūzhù** to reside [C]

剧	⊐	尸	尸	**JÙ**, stage play; be severe; be intense [B]
	尸	尸	居	京剧 **jīngjù** Beijing Opera
755 10 strokes	居	剧	剧	劇

据	扌	扩	扩	**JÙ**, according to; to take in your hand; evidence, proof [B]
	护	护	捽	据说 **jùshuō** it is said… [B] 占据 **zhànjù** to occupy (by force)
756 11 strokes	捽	据	据	據

炎	ノ	⺌	⺍	**YÁN**, to blaze; to be very hot; inflammation [D]
	火	尖	炏	"Fire" over "fire" = "to blaze, to be very hot." 发炎 **fāyán** to become inflamed; inflamma-tion [D]
757 8 strokes	步	炎		

谈	讠	讠	讠	**TÁN**, to chat, to talk about; a family name [A]
	讠	讠	讠	The "word" radical gives the meaning; **yán** (757, above) here has the sound value **tán**. See also 759, below.
758 10 strokes	谈	谈	谈	谈话 **tánhuà** to talk [B]; statement [C] 谈天 **tántiān** chit-chat [D] 谈心 **tánxīn** have a heart-to-heart talk; heart-to-heart talk 談

淡	氵	氵	氵	**DÀN**, to be weak, thin, insipid, pale [B]
	沙	淡	淡	淡水 **dànshuǐ** fresh water 看得很淡 **kànde hěn dàn** be indifferent to 生意很淡 **shēngyì hěn dàn** business is bad
759 11 strokes	淡	淡	淡	

152

| 击 | 一 | 二 | 十 | **JĪ**, to beat, to hit; bump into; an assault [D] |
| 760 5 strokes | 击 | 击 | | 擊 |

陆	阝	阝	阝	**LÙ**, land; family name [B] 大陆 **dàlù** continent, mainland [B] 陆地 **lùdì** land, dry land [C]
	阝	阣	陆	
761 7 strokes	陆			陸

| 丸 | 丿 | 九 | 丸 | **WÁN**, bullet, BB, pill, ball. BULLET radical (66) [C] The student should distinguish **wán** from 凡 (768, p. 154) and from 刃 (Pt. 2, p. 227b). 鱼丸 **yúwán** fishball (food) |
| 762 3 strokes | | | | |

执	一	十	扌	**ZHÍ**, to take hold of, to manage, to direct [B] 执行 **zhíxíng** to carry out, put into effect [B] 执法 **zhífǎ** to enforce the law [D] 固执 **gùzhi** be stubborn, obstinate [D]
	扌	执	执	
763 6 strokes				執

热	一	十	扌	**RÈ**, to be hot; to make hot, to heat [A] 热情 **rèqíng** enthusiasm, zeal; be enthusiastic, zealous [A] 热爱 **rè'ài** to love ardently [B] 热心 **rèxīn** be enthusiastic; be warm-hearted [B] 热带 **rèdài** the tropics [C] 炎热 **yánrè** be blazing hot [D] 热力学 **rèlìxué** thermodynamics
	扌	执	执	
764 10 strokes	执	热	热	熱

153

斗 765 4 strokes	`	＇	⸺	**DÒU**, to fight [B]; **DǑU**, unit of volume equal to 316 cubic inches, usually translated as "peck." PECK radical (82) A picture: the old scoop used to measure out pecks. Now mainly used, by sound-loan, for **dòu** "to fight." Traditionally, "to fight" (see below) was written with a good meaning-meaning compound: two kings in a confined space. ("to fight" only) 鬥
	斗			

市 766 5 strokes	`	亠	广	**SHÌ**, market, marketplace; municipality; standard system of weights and measures [A] 市长 **shìzhǎng** mayor [C] 市民 **shìmín** townsfolk, residents of a city 黑市 **hēishì** black market 市容 **shìróng** the appearance of a city 市寸 **shìcùn** Chinese standard inch (≈3.333 cm/1.312 inch)
	亣	市		

闹 767 8 strokes	`	冫	门	**NÀO**, to make a disturbance; be disturbed by; to get (perhaps with difficulty) [B] The traditional form combined meanings: "to fight in the marketplace" (see 765, 766). The modern form, a market at the city gate, can also be understood as combining meanings. 热闹 **rènào** be lively; have a hot time [B] 闹笑话 **nào xiàohuà** make a fool of yourself [C] 鬧
	门	闩	闬	
	闹	闹		

凡 768 3 strokes	丿	几	凡	**FÁN**, be common, be ordinary; all [B] 凡 is said to combine meanings: an object (the dot) thrown under a table may be any old thing you would leave under the table. 凡是 **fánshì** all those who are [C] 平凡 **píngfán** be ordinary [C] 凡人 **fánrén** an ordinary fellow, a bloke

恐 769 10 strokes	一	丁	工	**KǑNG**, to fear [B]; perhaps, maybe 恐怕 **kǒngpà** be afraid that; "probably" [B] 恐水病 **kǒng shuǐbìng** hydrophobia (literally, "fear water sickness")
	卫	巩	巩	
	巩	恐	恐	

| 阴 770 6 strokes | 乛 | 阝 | 阴 | YĪN, be dark, be shaded; "yin" in "yin and yang;" be cloudy; be crafty; secret; lunar; negative; incised; to deceive; family name [A] |
| | 阴 | 阴 | 阴 | 阴天 **yīntiān** be overcast
树阴 **shùyīn** shade of a tree
阴部 **yīnbù** private parts
阴门 **yīnmén** vaginal opening
阴户 **yīnhù** vaginal opening　　陰 |

| 阳 771 6 strokes | 乛 | 阝 | 阳 | YÁNG, sun, solar; "yang" in "yin and yang;" be open; positive; male organ; to cut in relief; family name [A] |
| | 阳 | 阳 | 阳 | 太阳 **tàiyáng** sun [A]
太阳能 **tàiyángnéng** solar energy [D]
阳极 **yángjí** (term from electricity) positive pole, anode　　陽 |

| 虍 772 6 strokes | 丨 | 上 | 上 | HǓ, tiger. TIGER radical (173)
This is a picture of a tiger. The independent character for tiger is 虎 **hǔ**, which looks like the radical reclarified with "legs" (see Pt. 2, p. 216b). |
| | 广 | 庐 | 虍 | |

| 号 773 5 strokes | 丨 | 冂 | 口 | HÀO, to call out, cry out; appellations, means of identification; name, size, number, sign, mark; command; bugle [A] |
| | 旦 | 号 | | 问号 **wènhào** question mark
记号 **jìhào** mark, sign [D]
十一号 (楼) **shíyīhào (lóu)** number 11 (building)
今天几号 **jīntiān jǐhào** What's today's date? 十号 **shíhào** The tenth.　　號 |

| 乛 774 2 strokes | 乛 | 乛 | | No pronunciation. Radical (31), "top of 予" (see next item). |
| | | | | |

				YǓ, to give, grant; YÚ, I [C]
予	ㄱ	マ	マ	The student should learn to tell 予 from the "child" radical 子 (44, p. 9), from 于 (744), and from the "spear" radical 矛 (Pt. 2, p. 226a).
	予			予以 **yǔyǐ** to grant, to give [D]
775 4 strokes				

				YÙ, beforehand; to anticipate [A]
预	マ	ㄱ	予	预先 **yùxiān** beforehand [C]
	予	予	予	预报 **yùbào** a forecast [C]
				预告 **yùgào** (give) advance notice [C]
				预见 **yùjiàn** foresee, foresight [D]
776 10 strokes	预	预	预	预算 **yùsuàn** make plans [D]
				预言 **yùyán** prophesy, prophecy [D]
				预定 **yùdìng** subscribe [D] 預

				BÈI, to prepare, to get ready for [A]
备	丿	ク	夂	准备 **zhǔnbèi** to get ready, to intend to [A]
	冬	各	各	预备 **yùbèi** to get ready, to plan; preparation [B]
				备用 **bèiyòng** be reserve, extra, spare [D]
777 8 strokes	备	备		备马 **bèimǎ** to saddle a horse 備

				XĪ, be loose; be rare; to hope [A]
希	丿	メ	乄	The four strokes at the top are supposed to show the loose mesh of a cloth; the "cloth" radical is there to help develop this meaning. The meaning "hope" (the most common modern meaning of this character) is by sound-loan.
	乑	矛	希	
778 7 strokes	希			

				WÀNG, to look for; to expect; towards; family name [A]
望	丶	亠	亡	希望 **xīwàng** hope, to hope for [A]
	訠	切	朗	看望 **kànwàng** to pay a visit to, to call on [D]
779 11 strokes	朗	望	望	名望 **míngwàng** prestige

156

红

780
6 strokes

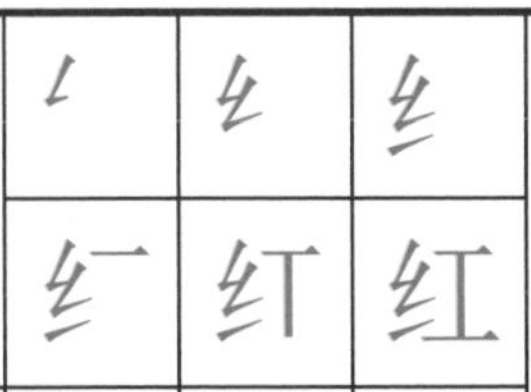

HÓNG, be red; red [A]; popular; dividend, bonus

红茶 **hóngchá** "black" tea [B]
脸红 **liǎnhóng** to blush; to get red-faced with anger or other excitement
红人 **hóngrén** favorite of an important person
红十字会 **Hóng Shízì Huì** Red Cross

紅

切

781
4 strokes

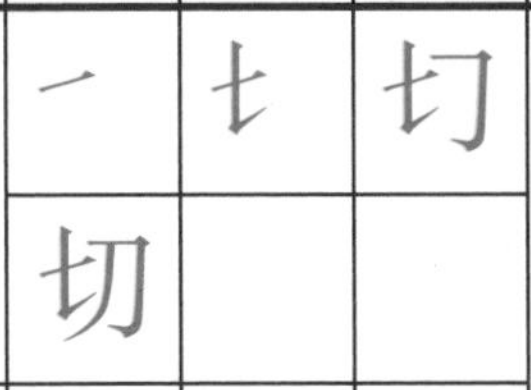

QIĒ, to slice, to carve; tangent in geometry; QIÈ, sure to; be close to [A]

A "knife" in the character for "to slice, carve" obviously helps with the meaning. Meanings for **qiè** seem to be by sound-loan.

亲切 **qīnqiè** be closely related to [B]
切身 **qièshēn** be personal; be of importance to a person
切合 **qièhé** to suit, to go well with

代

782
5 strokes

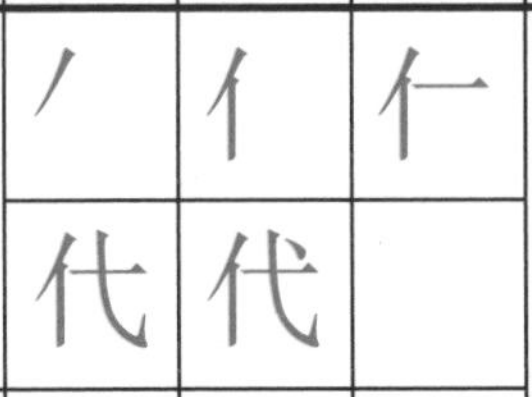

DÀI, to take the place of; an age [A]

代表 **dàibiǎo** to represent; on behalf of... (representing...); a representative [A]
现代 **xiàndài** be contemporary; modern times [A]
古代 **gǔdài** ancient times [B]
代号 **dàihào** code name [D]
代数 **dàishù** algebra

袋

783
11 strokes

DÀI, bag, pocket [B]

The "gown" radical gives the meaning in this character; **dài** (782) gives the sound.

口袋 **kǒudài** bag, pocket [B]
睡袋 **shuìdài** sleeping bag

接

784
11 strokes

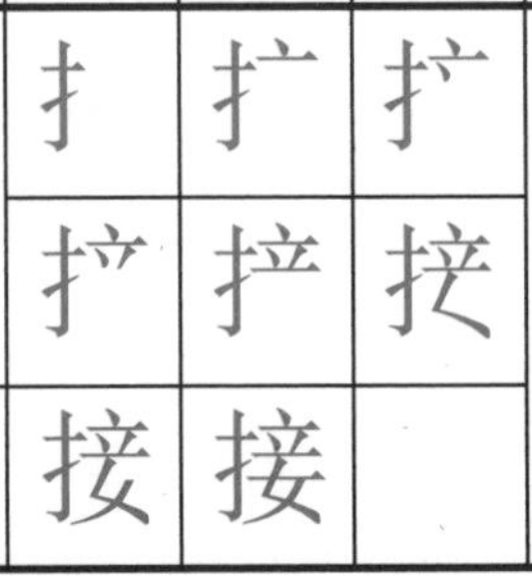

JIĒ, get; connect; meet; catch; take over [A]

接着 **jiēzhe** to catch; to follow closely [A]
接见 **jiējiàn** to receive a visitor; to grant an interview [B]
接到 **jiēdào** to receive, answer (telephone) [B]
接近 **jiējìn** be close to [B]
接受 **jiēshòu** to accept [C]
接连 **jiēlián** in succession [C]
接二连三 **jiē'èr liánsān** one after another [D]

和	一	二	千	**HÉ**, and, with; to make peace; **HUÒ**, to mix; **HUO**, a verb-suffix: "comfortably" [A]; **HÚ**, complete a set in mahjong
	禾	禾	利	和平 **hépíng** peace; be mild (as, medicine) [B]
785 8 strokes	和	和		和气 **héqì** be gentle, be amiable, be kind [D] 和尚 **héshang** Buddhist monk [D]
化	丿	亻	仁	**HUÀ**, to change; to melt; to evaporate; works like English suffixes –ize, -ify [A]
	化			If "man" + "ladle" suggests "alchemy" to you, you can use that as a mnemonic for 化. "Alchemy" = "to transmute, to change."
786 4 strokes				化学 **huàxué** chemistry [A] 化工 **huàgōng** chemical industry [C] (工业)化 **(gōngyè) huà** to (industrial)ize [B]
花	一	十	++	**HUĀ**, flower, blossom; be flowery; design; cotton; to spend; fireworks [A]
	艹	艹	花	花生 **huāshēng** peanut [C] 花样 **huāyàng** design, pattern [D] 放花 **fànghuā** to set off fireworks
787 7 strokes	花			一束花 **yíshù huā** a bunch of flowers
华	丿	亻	仁	**HUÁ**, flowers; glory; be magnificent; be prosperous; the best part, "cream" of...; Chinese; **HUÀ**, a family name
	化	华	华	Distinguish from 毕 (1039, p. 208). 中华民国 **Zhōnghuá Mínguó** The Republic of China
788 6 strokes				中华人民共和国 **Zhōnghuá Rénmín Gònghéguó** The People's Republic of China 華
哗	丨	刂	口	**HUÁ**, noise, clamor; **HUĀ**, onomatopoetic: clang! or gurgle gurgle! (sic) [C]
	吖	吖	吖	
789 9 strokes	吵	吵	哗	嘩, 譁 (譁 = **huá** only)

声	一	十	士	**SHĒNG, sound, tone; to declare; reputation [A]** 声音 **shēngyīn** sound [A] 声明 **shēngmíng** to declare; declaration [C]
	吉	吉	吉	
790 **7 strokes**	声			聲

让	丶	讠	让	**RÀNG, to yield, to allow; to lower (in price); to offer; to step aside; to cause, to make; by [A]** 让步 **ràngbù** to concede, to compromise [D] 让位 **ràngwèi** to abdicate; to give way to 让茶 **ràngchá** to offer somebody tea.
	让	让		
791 **5 strokes**				讓

类	丶	丷	丷	**LÈI, kind, type; resemble [B]** 人类 **rénlèi** mankind [B] 同类 **tónglèi** be of the same kind [D] 分类 **fēnlèi** to classify [D] 类别 **lèibié** class (resulting from a classification); category
	平	米	米	
792 **9 strokes**	类	娄	类	類

休	丿	亻	亻	**XIŪ, to rest; to cease; to divorce [A]** 休 combines meanings and is supposed to show a man resting under a tree, whence "to rest." 休学 **xiūxué** to drop out (of school) 休业 **xiūyè** to close a business (for a holiday or vacation); to cease operations
	什	休	休	
793 **6 strokes**				

息	丿	亻	亻	**XĪ, to breathe; to rest ; to stop; to cease; a family name [A]** 息 is supposed to combine "nose" + "heart" to suggest "to breathe." (The significance of "heart" is, perhaps, obscure.) 休息 **xiūxī** to rest [A] 信息 **xìnxī** information, news [C]
	自	自	自	
794 **10 strokes**	息	息	息	

式	一	二	丁	**SHÌ, form, fashion, model, style [B]** 新式 **xīnshì** new style [C] 式样 **shìyàng** style, type [D]
	工	式	式	
795 6 strokes				

癶	フ	ヌ	ヌ´	**BÒ, back-to-back; be opposed. BACK radical (154)** The character shows two feet—the "toe" radical 止 (246, p. 50)—faced away from each other, that is, back to back. Hence the idea "back." Not seen as an independent character now.
	ヌ冫	癶		
796 5 strokes				

豆	一	厂	厂	**DÒU, flask; bean, pea. FLASK radical (191) [B]** The character is a picture of a flask. The meaning "bean, pea" is by sound-loan. 豆子 **dòuzi** bean, pea [C] 土豆 **tǔdòu** potato [B]
	豆	豆	豆	
797 7 strokes	豆			

登	フ	ヌ	ヌ冫	**DĒNG, to go up; to press down on with the foot; to publish [B]** Distinguish from 凳 (Pt. 2, p. 266a). 登报 **dēngbào** to publish (in a newspaper or magazine) 登山 **dēngshān** mountain-climbing
	癶	癶	𣥠	
798 12 strokes	𥧌	登	登	

灯	丶	丷	丬	**DĒNG, lantern, lamp [A]** The "fire" radical here gives the meaning; **dīng** (624, p. 125) gives the sound. 灯火 **dēnghuǒ** lights [C] 点灯 **diǎndēng** to light a lamp 花灯 **huādēng** colored lantern
	火	灯	灯	
799 6 strokes				燈

160

普	丷	丱	丱	**PǓ**, be general, be universal; a fam... [B]
	丱	並	普	普 combines meanings: "side by side" (738, p. 128) + "sun" to suggest "all the places the sun shines:" "universal, general."
800 **12 strokes**	普	普	普	普天下 **pǔtiānxià** all over the world; everywhere 普希金 **Pǔxījīn** Pushkin (the Russian poet)
甬	ㄱ	マ	𠄌	**YǑNG**, bulk measure: ten "pecks;" name of a river in Zhejiang (Chekiang) province; short for Ningbo (the city—which is on the Yong River)
	甬	甬	甬	甬 originally meant "a big bell" and was a picture, with the hook at the top by which the bell could be hung. "Ten pecks" is by sound-loan.
801 **7 strokes**	甬			甬道 **yǒngdào** covered passage, corridor
通	ㄱ	マ	𠄌	**TŌNG**, to go through; to be thoroughgoing, to be universal [A] 通过 **tōngguò** to go through; to pass in a parliamentary meeting [A]
	甬	甬	甬	通知 **tōngzhī** to inform; a notice [A] 通常 **tōngcháng** be general, be usual [C] 普通 **pǔtōng** be universal; be widespread
802 **10 strokes**	甬	诵	通	or common [B] 普通话 **pǔtōnghuà** "Mandarin" Chinese [B]
雷	宀	雨	雨	**LÉI**, thunder; mine (military weapon); family name [B]
	雨	雨	雨	雷雨 **léiyǔ** thunderstorm
803 **13 strokes**	雪	雷	雷	
申	｜	冂	日	**SHĒN**, to stretch; to state, to inform; Shanghai; the ninth "earthly branch;" family name. STRETCH radical (144). On the "earthly branches," see *Lin Yutang's Dictionary* 1451f.
	日	申		申 is a picture of two hands stretching an object (the "down" radical).
804 **5 strokes**				申请 **shēnqǐng** to apply for 申报 **shēnbào** to report (to a superior); to declare (to Customs)

电	丨	冂	日
	日	电	
805 5 strokes			

DIÀN, electricity; lightning [A]
The "twist" radical ㇄ is a streak of lightning falling (the traditional form—see below, this frame—has rain above). The other part, 申 (804) either suggests the stretching clouds or gives the sound. (See Karlgren *AD*, 869).
电灯 **diàndēng** electric light [A]
电话 **diànhuà** telephone [A]
电气 **diànqì** electricity [D]

電

神	丶	㇇	礻
	礻	礻	祁
806 9 strokes	衵	神	神

SHÉN, spirit; god; family name [A]
神经 **shénjīng** nerve [B]
神话 **shénhuà** mythology, myth [C]
神气 **shénqì** air, manner; be spirited; be cocky, show 'attitude' [C]
神情 **shénqíng** expression, look [C]
神奇 **shénqí** be magical, miraculous
精神病 **jīngshénbìng** mental illness; nervous disease

伸	丿	亻	们
	们	伯	伸
807 7 strokes	伸		

SHĒN, to stretch, to extend [B]
申 (804, above) gives the sound; it also appears to help with the meaning.
伸手 **shēnshǒu** to stretch out your hand; to ask for help [D]

婶	乚	女	女
	妒	妒	妒
808 11 strokes	婶	婶	婶

SHĚN, wife of your father's younger brother; aunt; polite address to a woman about your mother's age
"Aunt" is not really a good translation, given the precision with which familial relationships are identified in Chinese culture and language.
婶母 **shěnmǔ** wife of your father's younger brother; aunt
婶子 **shěnzi** (colloquial) same as 婶 [C]

审	丶	八	宀
	宀	宁	审
809 8 strokes	审	审	

SHĚN, be careful; to examine closely; to interrogate; (bookish) to know; (bookish) indeed, truly [C]
审定 **shěndìng** to examine and approve [D]
审理 **shěnlǐ** to try a case [D]
审美 **shěnměi** to appreciate beauty [D]

收

810
6 strokes

SHŌU, to put away; to receive; to collect [A]

收入	**shōurù**	income; to earn [B]
收成	**shōuchéng**	harvest [D]
收回	**shōuhuí**	to recall; to countermand [D]
收买	**shōumǎi**	to buy; to bribe [D]
收支	**shōuzhī**	income and expenditures [D]
收音机	**shōuyīnjī**	a radio [B]
收起来	**shōuqǐlái**	to put away

耒

811
5 strokes

Radical (130), "top of 春" (see next).

春

812
9 strokes

CHŪN, spring (the season); a family name [A]

春 is supposed to show vegetation burgeoning in the sun.

春天	**chūntiān**	springtime [A]
青春	**qīngchūn**	youth [C]
春意	**chūnyì**	the feeling of early spring; thoughts of love

兆

813
6 strokes

ZHÀO, omen; a family name [D]

兆 shows the cracks on the heated tortoise shell which were anciently used in China for divination. (Read the note in 159, p. 32.)

兆头	**zhàotou**	omen
预兆	**yùzhào**	signs of the times
吉兆	**jízhào**	a good omen

跳

814
13 strokes

TIÀO, to leap [A]

The "foot" radical gives the meaning; **zhào** (813, above) is supposed to give the sound.

跳远	**tiàoyuǎn**	broad jump [D]
跳高	**tiàogāo**	high jump [D]
心跳	**xīntiào**	heart palpitations

挑 815 9 strokes	一 丁 扌 扌 扌 扌 扎 挑 挑	**TIĀO**, carrying pole (with bucket or basket on each end); to carry in such a way; measure for a pair of buckets or baskets so carried (一挑 = *two* buckets or baskets); to select; **TIĀO**, to probe [B] 一挑水 **yìtiāo shuǐ** two buckets of water carried on a pole
逃 816 9 strokes	丿 丿 丬 兆 兆 兆 兆 逃 逃	**TÁO**, to run away [B] The "halt" radical gives the meaning here (suggesting, as it often does, motion rather than stasis). 兆 **zhào** (813, above) is the phonetic element, giving a (near-) rhyme rather than an homonymous sound. 逃跑 **táopǎo** to run away [D]
杀 817 6 strokes	丿 乂 乄 矛 矛 杀	**SHĀ**, to kill; to tighten (a belt); to add up; to sting (as antiseptic on a cut); to hurt; to reduce; to brake, to stop [B] In script reform, the meaning part—the "club" radical (see below, this frame) disappeared, leaving only the traditional sound element. 自杀 **zìshā** to commit suicide [D] 杀人 **shārén** to commit murder 杀气 **shāqì** to look or act like you wanted to kill somebody 殺
处 818 5 strokes	丿 勹 夂 处 处	**CHÙ**, place; **CHǓ**, to dwell [A] 处 has "follow/slow" + "man," but "follow/slow" was originally a picture of a stool, suggesting a man sitting outside his home to get some air. 处分 **chǔfèn** to discipline, to punish [B] 处于 **chǔyú** to be (in a certain condition/ position) 处处 **chùchù** everywhere; in every way [C] 處
风 819 4 strokes	丿 几 风 风	**FĒNG**, wind; news; custom; rumor; desire. WIND radical (121) [A] 风力 **fēnglì** wind-power; wind force [B] 风气 **fēngqì** general mood; common practice [C] 风尚 **fēngshàng** prevailing custom [D] (Distinguish from 风向 **fēngxiàng** 885, p. 178) 风闻 **fēngwén** get wind of 風

俗	ノ	イ	仆	**SÚ, be vulgar, be common [B]**
	仏	伀	伀	The "valley" radical 谷 is supposed to suggest "ravines, mountain country;" with the addition of "man," we get "hillbilly," hence "uncultivated, vulgar."
820 9 strokes	伀	俗	俗	风俗 **fēngsú** custom [B] 俗气 **súqì** be in poor taste

死	一	厂	歹	**SǏ, to die; be dead; stubbornly [A]** 死 combines meanings. The "ladle" radical is corrupted from an earlier "man" radical, and "man" + "bone chips" i s supposed to suggest death.
	歹	歹'	死	
821 6 strokes				死亡 **sǐwáng** to die; death [C] 死尸 **sǐshī** corpse 死党 **sǐdǎng** diehards, sworn followers

题	日	旦	早	**TÍ, theme, subject [A]** 问题 **wèntí** question, problem [A] 题目 **tímù** topic, title, heading; problem, exercise [B] 出题 **chūtí** to set questions (for an exam)
	是	是	是	
822 15 strokes	是	题	题	题

秋	一	二	千	**QIŪ, autumn [A]** In China, after the grain is threshed, it is common to stack and burn the unusable stalks. These "grain fires" are a part of the autumn scene; whence, perhaps, this character.
	千	禾	禾	
823 9 strokes	禾'	秒	秋	秋天 **qiūtiān** autumn [A]

凉	冫	冫	广	**LIÁNG, be cool, be cold; LIÀNG, to make or become cool [A]** The "ice" radical appears in this character for the meaning. Traditionally, often written as 凉 (where the meaning element is "water").
	冫	泸	泸	
824 10 strokes	泸	凉	凉	凉快 **liángkuài** be cool; to cool off [A] 着凉 **zháoliáng** to catch cold [C] 凉水 **liángshuǐ** cold water, unboiled water [C]

165

员	丨	冂	口	**YUÁN, be round (but see 826); person with certain duties, member [A]** "Mouth" + "cowrie" is supposed to suggest roundness. The meaning "member," etc. is by sound-loan.
	严	吊	员	
825 **7 strokes**	员			教员 **jiàoyuán**　teacher [B] 会员 **huìyuán**　member [D] 海员 **hǎiyuán**　sailor 员工 **yuángōng**　staff, personnel　　員

圆	丨	冂	冂	**YUÁN, be round; to make plausible; make excuses; currency (*yuan*: the monetary unit of China); a coin [A]**
	冈	同	圆	This character is now often used rather than 员 (825) to mean "be round." The character is reclarified with the "surround" radical. See also 元 (89, p. 18).
826 **10 strokes**	圆	圆		圓

改	㇕	㇆	己	**GǍI, to change [A]** 改变 **gǎibiàn**　to change, change [A] 改革 **gǎigé**　to reform, improve [B] 改进 **gǎijìn**　to make better [B] 改造 **gǎizào**　to remake, to reform [B] 改正 **gǎizhèng**　to correct (an error) [B] 改良 **gǎiliáng**　to improve, improvement [C]
	㔾	孑	改	
827 **7 strokes**	改			

楚	木	林	梵	**CHǓ, be distinct; a family name [A]** 清楚 **qīngchu**　be clear; see clearly, understand [A] 楚楚 **chǔchǔ**　be clear; be neat; be dainty; delicate 一清二楚 **yìqīngèrchǔ**　be *very* clear
	梵	梵	梵	
828 **13 strokes**	楚			

留	㇒	㇈	乊	**LIÚ, to keep; to stay; ask someone to stay; leave behind; family name [A]** 留念 **liúniàn**　accept or keep (souvenir) [A] 留意 **liúyì**　to be careful, attentive [D] 留心 **liúxīn**　to be careful [D] 留声机 **liúshēngjī**　record player 留学生 **liúxuéshēng**　student studying abroad [A]
	乊	乊	乊	
829 **10 strokes**	留	留	留	

召 830 5 strokes	フ	刀	刀	**ZHÀO, to summon; SHÀO, a place name; a family name [B]**
	召	召		The meaning "to summon" comes by combining "mouth" for meaning with **dāo** 刀 (knife," 131, p. 27) for sound.
				召开 **zhāokāi** to convene [B]

绍 831 8 strokes	⺃	纟	纟	**SHÀO, to join together [A]**
	纟	纟	纟	The "silk" radical suggests the meaning; **zhào, shào** (830, above) gives the sound.
	绍	绍		介绍 **jièshào** to introduce [A]
				紹

管 832 14 strokes	⺮	⺮	⺮	**GUǍN, reed, pipe; to manage; to guarantee; family name [B]**
	⺮	竺	竺	管理 **guǎnlǐ** to manage [B]
	管	管	管	管子 **guǎnzi** tube, pipe [C]
				管道 **guǎndào** a pipeline [C]

劝 833 4 strokes	丁	又	劝	**QUÀN, to exhort [B]**
	劝			The "strength" radical gives the meaning in this character. The "right hand" is simply a scribble to replace the traditional complicated phonetic (see below, this frame).
				劝告 **quàngào** to urge; exhortation [C]
				劝说 **quànshuō** to advise [D]
				勸

安 834 6 strokes	丶	八	宀	**ĀN, be peaceful, be at ease; peace; to install; family name [A]**
	安	安	安	安 is a famous meaning-meaning character: "one woman under your roof means peace."
				安心 **ānxīn** be calm; to focus your mind on [B]
				安定 **āndìng** be secure, be steady [C]
				安全 **ānquán** be safe; safety [B]
				安全第一 **ānquándìyī** Safety first!

167

按	一	扌	扌
	扌	扩	扩
835 **9 strokes**	扩	按	按

ÀN, to press with the finger or thumb; according to [B]

按时　**ànshí**　be on time [A]
按着　**ànzhe**　according to
按月　**ànyuè**　by the month
按理　**ànlǐ**　logically, . . .

案	丶	丷	宀
	安	安	宰
836 **10 strokes**	宰	案	

ÀN, table; case at law; bill (legislative); legal record [B]

Ān (834) gives the sound; the "tree" radical suggests "table."

方案　**fāng'àn**　plan, program [B]
案件　**ànjiàn**　law case [D]
案情　**ànqíng**　details of a case; a case [D]
办案子　**bàn ànzi**　to handle a legal case

求	一	丁	寸
	寸	求	求
837 **7 strokes**	求		

QIÚ, to reach for; to beg [A]

求得　**qiúdé**　to try to achieve … [D]
乞求　**qǐqiú**　to beg for, to implore [D]
求乞　**qiúqǐ**　to beg
求亲　**qiúqīn**　to seek a marriage alliance;
　　　　　　　to propose

救	十	寸	求
	求	求	求
838 **11 strokes**	救	救	

JIÙ, to rescue, to save [B]

求救　**qiújiù**　　to ask for help
救生　**jiùshēng**　to save a life
救火车 **jiùhuǒchē**　fire engine

光	丨	丷	丷
	业	光	光
839 **6 strokes**			

GUĀNG, light, brightness, be bright; only [B]; to make bright [C]; be bare; all used up; only (adverb)

阳光　**yángguāng**　sunlight [B]
光明　**guāngmíng**　light; be bright, be prom-
　　　　　　　　ising [B]
光亮　**guāngliàng**　be bright, luminous [D]
光阴　**guāngyīn**　　time
用光了　**yòngguāng le**　to be used up

| 论 840 6 strokes | 丶 | 讠 | 讠 |
| | 讠 | 讠 | 论 |

LÙN, to discuss; theory; works like English suffix –ism to form words meaning "theory of" or "doctrine of," e..g. "materialism," "evolutionism," etc. **LÚN**, first syllable in *Analects* (Confucian book) [A]

论文 **lùnwén** dissertation, essay [B]
无论 **wúlùn** no matter; regardless of … [B]
论点 **lùndiǎn** argument, thesis [D] 論

亭 841 9 strokes	丶	亠	广
	亠	亠	亠
	亭	亭	亭

TÍNG, kiosk [C]

亭子 **tíngzi** kiosk, pavilion [D]
书亭 **shūtíng** bookstall

停 842 11 strokes	亻	亻	亻
	停	停	停
	停	停	

TÍNG, to stop [A]

停止 **tíngzhǐ** to stop (doing something) [B]
停留 **tíngliú** to tarry, stay for a while [C]
停车 **tíngchē** to park
停火 **tínghuǒ** cease-fire
暂停 **zhǎntíng** to suspend; (sports) a timeout

随 843 11 strokes	阝	阝	阝
	阝	阝	阝
	隋	隋	随

SUÍ, to follow; any, all; family name [B]

随便 **suíbiàn** at your convenience; as you like; be casual, be informal [B]
随时 **suíshí** at any time [B]
随手 **suíshǒu** conveniently; without trouble [C]
随后 **suíhòu** soon afterwards [C]
随意 **suíyì** at will [D]
随着 **suízhe** along with … [D] 隨

量 844 12 strokes	冂	一	旦
	昌	昌	昌
	量	量	

LIÁNG, to consider carefully; to weigh, to measure [B]; **LIÀNG**, quantity, volume, capacity [C]

The bottom part used to be 重 "be heavy" (323, p. 65), for the meaning; it has been corrupted into "village." The "sun" 日 at the top was originally just an object being weighed

169

倍 845 10 strokes	亻	亻′	亻′	**BÈI, times, fold [A]** 倍数　**bèishù**　a multiple [D] 三倍　**sānbèi**　three times as much, three- 　　　　　fold 成倍　**chéngbèi** to double, be doubled 加倍　**jiābèi**　to double
	亻宀	亻宀′	位	
	倍	倍	倍	

贱 846 9 strokes	丨	冂	刂	**JIÀN, be cheap; be humble; be unresponsive [C]** The cowrie 贝 is here, as often, to suggest money, monetary value, value. 戋 **jiān** gives the sound. 贱卖　**jiànmài** to sell at a low price 贱骨头 **jiàngǔtou** (insulting) "rat," 　　　　　　low-life　　　　　　　**賤**
	贝	贝`	贝`	
	贬	贱	贱	

危 847 6 strokes	丿	丿⁻	匃	**WĒI, danger; be lofty; family name [A]** The character is explained as "a man on top of a cliff, looking down at something that has fallen off." 危机　**wēijī**　crisis [B] 危楼　**wēilóu**　tall building 病危　**bìngwēi** be critically ill
	产	夗	危	

险 848 9 strokes	阝	阝	阝	**XIĂN, be dangerous; be difficult to get through or to [A]** 危险　**wēixiǎn** be dangerous; danger [A] 冒险　**màoxiǎn** to forge ahead despite the 　　　　　danger [D] 险些　**xiǎnxiē** nearly, almost 天险　**tiānxiǎn** natural barrier (e.g., a 　　　　　mountain)　　　　　　**險**
	阝个	阝今	阝今	
	险	险	险	

厚 849 9 strokes	一	厂	厂	**HÒU, be thick; be generous; family name [B]** 厚实　**hòushi**　(colloquial) be thick 厚道　**hòudào** be kind and honest 厚意　**hòuyì**　kindness, thoughtfulness 厚脸皮 **hòuliǎnpí** "have thick skin on your 　　　　　　face," i.e., be brazen
	厈	戸	戸	
	厚	厚	厚	

既	ㄱ	ㅋ	ㅋ	**JÌ, be finished; since, now that; already; a family name [B]**
	刂	刂	旷	既然　　**jìrán**　　this being the case, … [B] 既…也…　**jì…yě…**　both … and … [B] 既…又…　**jì…yòu…**　both … and … [B] 既是　　**jìshì**　　this being the case, …
850 9 strokes	旷	旷	既	

辰	一	厂	厂	**CHÉN, be early; the fifth "earthly branch." EARLY radical (187) [D]**
	厂	辰	辰	辰 can mean "early" in the sense "early in the day" or "early in the year." One modern scholar (Guo Moruo) thinks it is a picture of a stone tool used in ancient times to break the soil for cultivation. On the "branches," see *Lin Yutang's Dictionary* 1451f.
851 7 strokes	辰			

晨	㇑	冂	日	**CHÉN, morning [A]**
	尸	尸	启	This appears to be a meaning-meaning compound: "early" + "sun" (suggesting "day") = "morning."
852 11 strokes	晨	晨	晨	

振	十	扌	扩	**ZHÈN, to shake, to flap; to rise up with spirit [C]**
	扩	护	护	振动　**zhèndòng**　(physics) vibration 振作　**zhènzuò**　to bestir yourself, get a move on
853 10 strokes	折	振	振	

震	一	一	二	**ZHÈN, to shake, to shock, to vibrate; to be very excited/shocked/astonished [C]**
	二	雪	雪	震动　**zhèndòng**　to quake, shake, vibrate 震中　**zhènzhōng**　(geological term) epicenter (i.e, of an earthquake)
854 15 strokes	震	震	震	

唇	厂	厂	尸	**CHÚN, lip, lips [C]** 上唇 **shàngchún** upper lip 下唇 **xiàchún** lower lip 唇舌 **chúnshé** squabble, argument
	厔	厔	辰	
855 10 strokes	辰	唇	唇	屑

研	一	丆	丆	**YÁN, to grind finely; to do research, to investigate thoroughly [A]** The "rock" radical 石 (749, p. 150) suggests the meaning; the rest of the character in former times helped with the sound.
	石	石	石	
856 9 strokes	矿	矿	研	

究	丶	丷	宀	**JIŪ, to look into [A]** 研究 **yánjiū** research, to do research; knowledge [A] 究办 **jiūbàn** to prosecute and settle a case 研究所 **yánjiūsuǒ** research institute, "think-tank" [B] 研究生 **yánjiūshēng** graduate student [C]
	宀	宂	宂	
857 7 strokes	究			

实	丶	丷	宀	**SHÍ, fruit; be solid; be true, real [A]** 实现 **shíxiàn** to come true [A] 实在 **shízài** truly [B] 实用 **shíyòng** be practical [B] 实行 **shíxíng** put into practice [B] 实话 **shíhuà** truth [C] 切实 **qièshí** be feasible; conscientiously [C] 事实求是 **shìshíqiúshì** Seek truth from facts! [B]
	宀	宀	空	
858 8 strokes	实	实		實

简	𠂉	𥫗	𥫗	**JIǍN, to be simple; to make simple, to abridge; letter correspondence [A]** 简直 **jiǎnzhí** simply, frankly [B] 简便 **jiǎnbiàn** be simple and convenient [C] 简化 **jiǎnhuà** to simplify [D] 简易 **jiǎnyì** be simple and easy [D] 简要 **jiǎnyào** be brief and to the point [D]
	筲	筲	简	
859 13 strokes	简	简	简	簡

同	丨	冂	冂	**TÓNG, be the same; with, together [A]**
	冋	同	同	同意 **tóngyì** to agree [A] 同学 **tóngxué** classmate [A] 同时 **tóngshí** at the same time; moreover [A] 同样 **tóngyàng** be the same, be equal [B] 同屋 **tóngwū** share a room; room-mate [B] 同情 **tóngqíng** to sympathize with [B] 同胞 **tóngbāo** be siblings/countrymen [C] 胡同 **hútòng** lane, alley (note: **tòng**) [C]
860 6 strokes				

铜	丿	乍	乍	**TÓNG, brass, copper, bronze [B]**
	乍	钅	钌	The "side-gold" radical helps with the meaning. **Tóng** (860) gives the sound. 黄铜 **huángtóng** bronze 红铜 **hóngtóng** copper 铜像 **tóngxiàng** bronze statue
861 11 strokes	钌	钌	铜	銅

洞	丶	冫	氵	**DÒNG, cave, hole; incisively [B]**
	汀	汩	洞	洞穿 **dòngchuān** to pierce; to understand thoroughly 洞穴 **dòngxué** cave
862 9 strokes	洞	洞	洞	

筒	⺮	⺮⺮	竹	**TǑNG, tube, large cylinder [C]**
	筥	筒	筒	
863 12 strokes	筒	筒		

选	丿	乍	丬	**XUǍN, to choose; a choice; selections, an anthology [B]**
	生	牛	先	选民 **xuǎnmín** voter [D] 选手 **xuǎnshǒu** contestant [D] 选取 **xuǎnqǔ** to choose [D] 选定 **xuǎndìng** decide after careful selection [D] 文选 **wénxuǎn** anthology 普选 **pǔxuǎn** general election
864 9 strokes	迗	选	选	選

昏 865 8 strokes	一	厂	戶	**HŪN, dusk, darkness [B]** The top of this character used to be **dǐ** "foundation, bottom, go down" (bottom part of 底, 629, above), and the character was a meaning-meaning compound: "go down" + "sun" = "darkness, dusk." 黄昏 **huánghūn** evening
	氐	氐	昏	
	昏	昏		

婚 866 11 strokes	〈	女	女厂	**HŪN, marriage [B]** Hūn (865) gives the sound. The "woman" radical 女 helps with the meaning. 结婚 **jiéhūn** to get married [B] 离婚 **líhūn** to get divorced [B] 婚礼 **hūnlǐ** marriage ceremony
	女厂	娇	娇	
	婚	婚	婚	

| 丁

867
1 stroke | 丁 | | | **No pronunciation. Radical (6). "Top of 刁 diáo"** |
| | | | | |

| 习

868
3 strokes | 丁 | 刁 | 习 | **XÍ, to practice; practice, habit [A]**
习惯 **xíguàn** be accustomed to; custom, habit [A]
习俗 **xísú** custom, convention [D]
习题 **xítí** exercises (schoolwork) [D]
习气 **xíqì** bad practice, evil habit
研习 **yánxí** to study

習 |
| | | | | |

| 羽

869
6 strokes | 丁 | 刁 | 习 | **YǓ, wings. WINGS radical (183) [B]**
羽毛 **yǔmáo** feather [D]
党羽 **dǎngyǔ** member of a clique (pejorative) |
| | 习习 | 羽 | 羽 | |

加	コ	力	加	**JIĀ, to add, to increase, plus... [A]**
	加	加		加工 **jiāgōng** process (manufacturing) [B] 加以 **jiāyǐ** moreover [B]* 加入 **jiārù** to add; to join [C] 加热 **jiārè** heating [D] 加重 **jiāzhòng** to make/become heavier [D] 加快 **jiākuài** to speed up
870 5 strokes				

驾	コ	力	加	**JIÀ, to harness; to pull (a cart); to drive, pilot, or sail (car, airplane, boat) [A]**
	加	加	驾	The "horse" helps with the meaning; **jiā** (870) gives the sound.
871 8 strokes	驾	驾		駕

架	コ	力	加	**JIÀ, frame; a measure for airplanes [B]**
	加	加	架	**Jiā** (870) gives the sound; "tree" 木 helps with the meaning. 书架 **shūjià** bookshelf [B] 绑架 **bǎngjià** to kidnap 架子 **jiàzi** frame; outline; stance; hauteur [C] 打架 **dǎjià** come to blows, engage in fisti- cuffs [C]
872 9 strokes	架	架	架	一架飞机 **yíjià fēijī** an airplane

咖	丨	冂	叮	**KĀ, GĀ, used to write foreign words [A]**
	叮	叻	咖	咖 is used, for sound-value alone, to write such borrowed foreign words as "coffee." 咖喱 **gālí** curry 咖啡 **kāfei** coffee
873 8 strokes	咖	咖		咖啡馆 **kāfeiguǎn** coffeehouse; café

称	ノ	二	千	**CHĒNG, to weigh; name; CHÈN, to own; to suit [B]**
	禾	禾	秒	称号 **chēnghào** title, designation [D] 名称 **míngchēng** name [D] 称道 **chēngdào** to commend [D] 简称 **jiǎnchēng** abbreviated name [D] 称心 **chènxīn** to suit one's
874 10 strokes	秒	称	称	wishes [D] 稱

*加以may also appear before two-syllable verbs with a resumptive function: Example: "选择他们的长处加以跟从 *xuǎnzé tāmende chángchu* **jiāyǐ** *gēncóng* (I'll) pick out their good

旁	亠	亠	立	**PÁNG, other; side; beside [A]** 旁 gives the sound in several common characters (see below). 旁边　**pángbiān**　beside; the area near [A] 旁人　**pángrén**　other people 旁听　**pángtīng**　to audit (a course) 旁白　**pángbái**　aside (in a play)
875 **10 strokes**	产	产	立	
	产	旁	旁	

傍	亻	亻	广	**BÀNG, to approach, be close to [B]** 傍晚　**bàngwǎn**　near evening; at dusk [B]
	伫	倅	倅	
876 **12 strokes**	倅	傍	傍	

榜	木	栌	栌	**BĂNG, announcement; a posted list of names [B]** 榜样　**bǎngyàng**　model (for emulation), example [B]
	栌	梓	椁	
877 **14 strokes**	榜	榜		

膀	丿	刀	月	**BĂNG, upper arm; shoulder; PĀNG, to swell up [B]**
	扩	护	胪	
878 **14 strokes**	膆	膀	膀	

磅	丆	石	矿	**BÀNG, pound (unit of weight); scales (for weighing); to weigh; point (in typography) [C]**
	矿	碎	碎	
879 **15 strokes**	磅	磅		

(*cont'd from p. 175*)
points and **thereto** follow" (Confucius, the English version is intended to be illustrative, not idiomatic); or "A 加以 VERB," "as to A, …" 择: Pt. 2, p. 220b.

如 880 6 strokes	㇈	㇈	女	**RÚ, be like; be as good as; according to; if [A]** 如今 **rújīn** nowadays [B] 如果 **rúguǒ** if [B] 如同 **rútóng** be like, as [C] 如此 **rúcǐ** as follows [C] 如下 **rúxià** as follows, as below [C] 如意 **rúyì** be satisfied [D]
	女	如	如	

决 881 6 strokes	丶	冫	冖	**JUÉ, to decide; decidedly; to execute (a person); to burst [A]** 决定 **juédìng** to decide; decision [A] 决心 **juéxīn** determination [B] 决口 **juékǒu** be breached; to burst (as, a dyke, a dam) [C] 决不 **juébù** be determined to do/not to do (something) [D]
	冖	决	决	

性 882 8 strokes	㇒	㇀	忄	**XÌNG, nature, temperament; sex [B]** "Heart" is for meaning, **shēng** "birth" for sound; or 性 and 生 are cognate words; or 性 combines meanings: what's in you at birth, "temperament, disposition." 性别 **xìngbié** sexual difference, sex [B] 性能 **xìngnéng** performance, function (of a machine) [C] 性情 **xìngqíng** temperament [D] 性交 **xìngjiāo** sexual intercourse
	忄	忄	忙	
	性	性		

呆 883 7 strokes	丨	冂	口	**DĀI, be stupid; be idiotic; to stay, to remain [B]** 呆板 **dāibǎn** be inflexible, rigid 呆子 **dāizi** stupid person; fool; enthusiast (see next item) 发呆 **fādāi** to stare like a fool, be in a daze 书呆子 **shū dāizi** "bookworm" 呆在家里 **dāi zài jiālǐ** to stay at home 獃
	旦	早	呆	
	呆			

保 884 9 strokes	㇒	亻	亻	**BǍO, to protect; guarantee, surety [B]** 保留 **bǎoliú** to retain; to hold in reserve [B] 保险 **bǎoxiǎn** insurance; be safe; be certain (to happen) [C] 保管 **bǎoguǎn** to take care of; surely [C] 保重 **bǎozhòng** Take care of yourself! [D] 保全 **bǎoquán** to keep intact; to preserve
	伄	伄	但	
	伄	保	保	

| 向 885 6 strokes | ′ | ⼁ | 冂 | **XIÀNG, toward, to face; habitually in the past; family name [A]** Distinguish from 尚 (448, p. 90) 想来 **xiànglái** always, all along [C] 向往 **xiàngwǎng** to look forward to [D] 向着 **xiàngzhe** to turn towards, to face; (colloquial) to take somebody's side 一向 **yíxiàng** up till now; consistently 风向 **fēngxiàng** wind direction |
| | 冋 | 向 | 向 | |

响 886 9 strokes	⼁	Ⅱ	Ⅱ	**XIǍNG, a sound; to sound [A]** 响应 **xiǎngyìng** to respond [B] 响亮 **xiǎngliàng** be loud and clear; to resonate [C] 响声 **xiǎngshēng** sound, noise [D]
	Ⅱ′	叮′	叫	
	响	响	响	響

借 887 10 strokes	ノ	⼈	仁	**JIÈ , to lend; to borrow [A]** 借口 **jièkǒu** to use as an excuse; excuse [C] 借入 **jièrù** to borrow 借出 **jièchū** to lend 借给 **jiègěi** to lend 借据 **jièjù** notes (receipts for loans) 借光 **jièguāng** Excuse me (polite)
	仁	什	供	
	借	借	借	

视 888 8 strokes	丶	⼆	ネ	**SHÌ, to look, to look at [A]** Distinguish from the next two characters. 电视 **diànshì** television [A] 视觉 **shìjué** vision, visual sense [D] 视力 **shìlì** sight, vision [D]
	⽰	衤	初	
	初	视		视

规 889 8 strokes	一	二	丰	**GUĪ, (drawing) compasses; rule, regulation; to correct (a fault); fee [B]** Distinguish from the preceding (888) and following (890) characters. 规定 **guīdìng** to stipulate; to set, formulate [B] 规劝 **guīquàn** to admonish 校规 **xiàoguī** school regulations
	夫	刲	却	
	规	规		規

| 观 890 6 strokes | フ | ス | 刈 |
| | 刈 | 观 | 观 |

GUĀN, to look at, view [A]
The "see" radical 见 gives the meaning. The "right hand" 又 is just a scribble to replace the traditional complicated phonetic element (see below). Distinguish from the preceding two characters.
观点 **guāndiǎn** viewpoint [B]
观念 **guānniàn** con... [C]
观看 **guānkàn** to watch [C]   觀

社 891 7 strokes	丶	礻	礻
	礻	礻	社
	社		

SHÈ, society [A]
This character combines meanings: "sign" + "earth" = "altar to the spirits of the land" (original meaning), "tutelary deity, village, society."
社会 **shèhuì** society [A]
社论 **shèlùn** editorial; leading article [C]
社员 **shèyuán** a member of a club

度 892 9 strokes	丶	亠	广
	广	庐	庐
	庐	庹	度

DÙ, to pass through; degree, rule, extent; family name [A]
度过 **dùguò** to pass through (a period of time) [B]
高度 **gāodù** altitude [B]
度数 **dùshù** degree
度日如年 **dù rì rú nián** to pass days like years (i.e., time creeps by)

| 由 893 5 strokes | 丨 | 冂 | 日 |
| | 由 | 由 | |

YÓU, to test with, be up to (someone); from, by; cause; family name [B]
自由 **zìyóu** freedom [B]
由于 **yóuyú** be due to [B]
理由 **lǐyóu** reason [B]
由此可见 **yóucǐ kějiàn** "From this, it can be seen" (i.e., "therefore") [D]

命 894 8 strokes	丿	人	合
	介	合	合
	合	命	

MÌNG, destiny, fate; life, order [B]
生命 **shēngmìng** life [B]
革命 **gémìng** to carry out a revolution; revolution [B]
命令 **mìnglìng** order, command [B]
命运 **mìngyùn** destiny, fate [B]
拼命 **pīnmìng** to risk your life; to give your all [B]
命名 **mìngmíng** to give a name to [D]
算命 **suànmìng** tell somebody's fortune

展	ㄱ	ㄹ	尸	**ZHĂN, to unroll; to postpone; family name [A]**
	尸	尸	屌	发展 **fāzhǎn** to develop, development [A] 展开 **zhǎnkāi** to open out [B] 展出 **zhǎnchū** to unfold, open out [B] 展望 **zhǎnwàng** look into the distance; look
895 10 strokes	屌	展	展	into the future; to predict [D] 展现 **zhǎnxiàn** unfold in front of your eyes [D]

替	二	夫	耒	**TÌ, for, in place of, to substitute [B]**
	耚	替	替	代替 **dàitì** to represent; representing... (i.e., in place of...) [B] 替代 **tìdài** to replace, substitute for [D] 替工 **tìgōng** substitute workman 替身 **tìshēn** substitute, scapegoat
896 12 strokes	替			替死鬼 **tìsǐguǐ** scapegoat

丢	一	二	千	**DIŪ, to lose [A]**
	壬	丢	丢	Note that this character is simply 去 **qù** "to go" with a "left" radical over it. 丢人 **diūrén** "to lose face" [D] 丢脸 **diūliǎn** "to lose face"
897 6 strokes				

体	丿	亻	仁	**TĬ, body [A]**

	什	仲	休	身体 **shēntǐ** body [A]
				体会 **tǐhuì** to have learned /to know/ from
				     experience [B]
				体面 **tǐmiàn** be pretty; be in good taste;
				     honor; face, appearance [C]

898 7 strokes	体			体现 **tǐxiàn** to incarnate, to embody [C] 体力 **tǐlì** physical strength [C] 体重 **tǐzhòng** weight (of a person) [D] 體

示	一	二	丁	**SHÌ, sign. SIGN radical (132) [A]**
	示	示		Compare this to the "side-sign" radical 礻 already learned (166, p. 34). 展示 **zhǎnshì** to show, to lay bare [D] 示意 **shìyì** to know what you mean or intend
899 5 strokes				

	、	ハ	宀
宗	宀	宁	宇
900 8 strokes	宗	宗	

ZŌNG, ancestor; law case; batch; family name

宗 combines meanings. "Roof" over the "sign" radical (used for spiritual manifestations) suggests the altar to the ancestors which every traditional family has in its home.

祖宗　**zǔzōng**　ancestor
宗教　**zōngjiào**　religion

	'	匚	卬
迎	卬	卬	迎
901 7 strokes	迎		

YÍNG, to face; toward; to meet [A]

欢迎　**huānyíng**　to welcome [A]
迎接　**yíngjiē**　to receive or welcome someone [B]
迎面　**yíngmiàn**　facing each other; the space opposite [D]

	ノ	亻	仁
付	付	付	
902 5 strokes			

FÙ, to hand over; a set [A]

The "thumb" (representing a hand) hands over something to the "(side-) man."

对付　**duìfu**　to deal with; to make do with [B]
付出　**fùchū**　to pay; to expend [D]

	、	亠	广
府	广	广	庐
903 8 strokes	府	府	

FǓ, prefecture; palace [A]

政府　**zhèngfǔ**　government [A]
府上　**fǔshàng**　(your) residence (polite expression)
王府　**wángfǔ**　royal palace

	ノ	亻	亻̀
俯	亻广	亻广	俨
904 10 strokes	俨	俯	俯

FǓ, to bow your head; "please condescend to ..." (old-fashioned honorific form used in official correspondence) [C]

俯视　**fǔshì**　to overlook
俯首　**fǔshǒu**　to bow your head and submit

181

附	阝	阝	阝	**FÙ, to attach; be near, close [A]** 附近 **fùjìn** be near to [A] 附带 **fùdài** in passing; to attach; be supplementary [D] 附和 **fùhè** to echo (viewpoint, opinion); to chime in with [D] 附加 **fùjiā** to add, to attach; be additional, be attached [D] 附属 **fùshǔ** be subsidiary, be affiliated [D]
	阝	阝	附	
905 7 strokes	附			
符	𠂉	竹	竹	**FÚ, symbol; written charm or incantation [B]** 符合 **fúhé** to tally with; (term from physics) coincidence [B] 符号 **fúhào** symbol, insignia [D]
	竹	符	符	
906 11 strokes	符			
腐	广	广	庁	**FǓ, to decay, turn rotten [B]** 腐化 **fǔhuà** to go rotten; to be depraved, degenerate; rot, decay [D]
	庁	庁	腐	
907 14 strokes	腐	腐	腐	
咐	丨	冂	口	**FÙ, second syllable of** 吩咐 **fēnfu, to give somebody an order (instruction), to tell somebody to do something [C]**
	叮	叮	吖	
908 8 strokes	咐	咐		
彡	丿	彡	彡	**SHĀN, streaks. STREAKS radical (63)** The character is a picture. Not in modern use as an independent character.
909 3 strokes				

影 910 15 strokes	日	旦	昌
	昌	景	景
	影′	影	影

YǏNG, shadow, image, photograph [A]
影响 **yǐngxiǎng** to affect, to influence; influence, effect [A]
影子 **yǐngzi** shadow, reflection; trace [B]
阴影 **yīnyǐng** shadow, shade
影射 **yǐngshè** to counterfeit
电影 **diànyǐng** movie [A]
电影院 **diànyǐngyuán** movie-house [C]

| 壬 911 4 strokes | 一 | 二 | 千 |
| | 壬 | | |

RÉN, to carry on the shoulder; be great; the ninth "heavenly stem;" family name

The character seems to show the "knight" carrying some object (the "left" radical) thrown over his shoulder. Originally the character was a picture of the common carrying pole with an object fixed at each end for balance; at the center was the carrier.

| 任 912 6 strokes | ノ | イ | 仁 |
| | 仁 | 任 | 任 |

RÈN, to allow; term of office; responsibility; to employ; to endure; RÉN, family name [A]
任性 **rènxìng** be wilful; be wayward [C]
任意 **rènyì** wilfully; wantonly [C]
任命 **rènmìng** be appointed; be nominated [D]
任用 **rènyòng** to appoint

何 913 7 strokes	ノ	イ	仁
	仁	何	何
	何		

HÉ, what; family name [A]
任何 **rènhé** any [A]; whatever, whichever
如何 **rúhé** how? in what way? how about …? [B]
何必 **hébì** why must…? [C]
几何 **jǐhé** how much? how many? [D]
几何学 **jǐhéxué** geometry

详 914 8 strokes	丶	讠	讠
	讠′	详	详
	详	详	

XIÁNG, in detail; to know [B]
Xiáng is supposed to be a sound-meaning compound, "words" giving the meaning and 羊 **yáng** (156, p. 32) giving—not the full sound, but—the rhyme.

详谈 **xiángtán** discuss in detail
详情 **xiángqíng** detailed information
不详 **bùxiáng** be unknown

183

细

915
8 strokes

XÌ, be fine (not coarse), be thin [A]

Note that the radicals in **xì** are the same as in 累 (49, p. 10), but the position is different. Originally, **xì** had "silk" + "head" = "hair," therefore "fine." Head was corrupted.

详细 **xiángxì** be in detail [B]

細

根

916
10 strokes

GĒN, root; square root; a measure for long, thin things [A]

根本 **gēnběn** be basic, be fundamental; from the beginning [B]
根据 **gēnjù** to base something on; according to; basis [B]
方根 **fānggēn** square root

史

917
5 strokes

SHǏ, history, historian; family name [A]

历史 **lìshǐ** history [A]

使

918
8 strokes

SHǏ, envoy; to use; to cause; with [A]

使用 **shǐyòng** to use, to employ [A]
大使 **dàshǐ** ambassador [C]
使得 **shǐdé** to make; to cause; to be able to use; be all right [C]
使命 **shǐmìng** mission, assignment
大使馆 **dàshǐguǎn** embassy [B]

味

919
8 strokes

WÈI, flavor; odor; a measure for medicines and for courses (of a meal) [B]

味道 **wèidao** flavor [B]
气味 **qìwèi** smell, flavor [C]
味觉 **wèijué** sense of taste
玩味 **wánwèi** to think over, to ponder

乱	一	二	千	**LUÀN, be disorderly, disorder [A]**
	千	舌	舌	内乱 **nèiluàn**　civil war 乱说 **luànshuō**　to speak recklessly; to gossip 乱真 **luànzhēn**　be a good imitation (of a 　painting or sculpture)
920 7 strokes	乱			亂

派	丶	丶	氵	**PÀI, to branch off; to appoint; faction, sect; to levy; to distribute [A]** Subtract the "water-dots," and you have an old character that was a picture of a stream dividing, from which came the meaning "to branch off."
	沪	沪	沪	党派 **dǎngpài**　political party [C] 派别 **pàibié**　faction [D] 气派 **qìpài**　manner, style
921 9 strokes	沪	派	派	派头 **pàitóu**　style, manner 派出所 **pàichūsuǒ** precinct house [C]

助	丨	冂	月	**ZHÙ, to help [A]**
	月	且	助	帮助 **bāngzhù**　to help, help [A] 助手 **zhùshǒu**　helper, assistant [C] 助理 **zhùlǐ**　assistant [D] 助长 **zhùzhǎng** to encourage; to abet [D] 借助 **jièzhù**　using, drawing on, with the 　help of [D]
922 7 strokes	助			助教 **zhùjiào**　teaching assistant

设	丶	讠	讠	**SHÈ, to establish; if [A]**
	讠	设	设	设备 **shèbei**　equipment [B] 设想 **shèxiǎng** to imagine; to take into 　account, have consideration for; 　rough plan, preliminary idea [C]
923 6 strokes				设立 **shèlì**　to set up [D] 设法 **shèfǎ**　to figure out a way; 　to try to 　設

医	一	厂	厂	**YĪ, to heal [A]**
	三	至	医	医生 **yīshēng**　healer, medical doctor [A] 医院 **yīyuàn**　hospital [A] 医学 **yīxué**　medical science [B] 中医 **zhōngyī**　Chinese traditional medicine 　[C]
924 7 strokes	医			醫

185

服	丿	刀	月	**FÚ**, clothes; to take, swallow (medicine); to serve; to obey; be accustomed to; **FÙ**, a measure for doses (term in Chinese medicine) [A]
	月	刖	服	衣服 **yīfu** clothes [A] 服从 **fúcóng** to obey [B] 说服 **shuōfú** to convince [C]
925 8 strokes	服	服		

务	丿	夕	夂	**WÙ**, affairs; must [A]
	冬	务		服务 **fúwù** to serve; service [A] 业务 **yèwù** business, professional work [B] 任务 **rènwù** mission, task [B] 医务 **yīwù** medical [D] 务必 **wùbì** without fail 外务 **wàiwù** foreign affairs
926 5 strokes				服务员 **fúwùyuán** attendant [A]　　務

精	丶	丷	丷	**JĪNG**, essence, spirit; sperm; very; to be essential, pure; be smart [A]
	半	米	米	精力 **jīnglì** personal energy, vigor [B] 精细 **jīngxì** be meticulous [C] 精通 **jīngtōng** to know very well [D] 精心 **jīngxīn** take pains in doing [D] 精美 **jīngměi** be exquisite [D]
927 14 strokes	精	精	精	精简 **jīngjiǎn** to simplify, retrench [D] 精神 **jīngshén** spirit, vitality [A] 精神病 **jīngshénbìng** mental illness, psychosis

奴	乚	女	女	**NÚ**, handmaiden, slave [C]
	奴	奴		The character combines meanings. 奴才 **núcái** slave 奴性 **núxìng** be servile; servile disposition
928 5 strokes				

努	乚	女	女	**NǓ**, to strive, to work hard at [A]
	奴	奴	努	This appears to combine meanings: use the strength or energy of a slave. Or it may represent an extension of meaning of the word behind 奴: "to slave at it."
929 7 strokes	努			努力 **nǔlì** "put your back into it," effort [A]

怒	㇄	㇄	女
	奵	奴	奴
930 9 strokes	怒	怒	怒

NÙ, anger, passion, rage [B]

怒 appears to combine meanings: the heart (emotions) of a slave: anger, passion, rage.

发怒 **fānù** get angry

动	一	二	云
	云	刧	动
931 6 strokes			

DÒNG, to move [A]
活动 **huódòng** be active, activity [A]
运动 **yùndòng** movement (physical), exercise; campaign, movement (political) [A]
动人 **dòngrén** be touching (emotions) [B]
动手 **dòngshǒu** start work; to touch, handle; to hit out [B]
动身 **dòngshēn** to start a journey [B] 動

靠	ノ	㇀	生
	告	告	告
932 15 strokes	靠	靠	靠

KÀO, to lean on, to depend on [B]
可靠 **kěkào** be reliable [B]
靠近 **kàojìn** be near to [B]

彳	彳	夂	
933 2 strokes			

No pronunciation. To march. MARCH radical (36)

This is a picture of a man marching out. The student should distinguish "march" from the "halt" radical, ⻌ (90, p. 19).

建	㇕	㇇	㇕
	彐	聿	聿
934 8 strokes	肂	建	

JIÀN, to set up; Fujian (old style: "Fukien") [A]
建设 **jiànshè** to build, to build up [A]
建立 **jiànlì** to establish [B]
建造 **jiànzào** to build, to make [C]
建交 **jiànjiāo** to establish diplomatic relations [D]

健	ノ	亻	亻冖
	亻彐	亻彐	信
935 **10 strokes**	伊	健	健

JIÀN, to strengthen, be strong; be regular [A]
健全 **jiànquán** to be sound; to make sound, to perfect [C]
健美 **jiànměi** to be strong and good-looking [D]

键	ノ	⺊	乍
	钅	钅彐	钅彐
936 **13 strokes**	钅聿	键	键

JIÀN, key (for a lock; on a piano, type-writer, etc.), bolt [B]

键

墙	土	圢	圹
	坪	坪	墙
937 **14 strokes**	墙	墙	墙

QIÁNG, wall [A]
城墙 **chéngqiáng** city wall

墙, 牆

护	一	丁	扌
	扩	扩	扩
938 **7 strokes**	护		

HÙ, to protect [B]
保护 **bǎohù** to protect [B]
护士 **hùshì** nurse [B]
救护 **jiùhù** to rescue, save

護

莫	一	艹	艹
	艹	芦	昔
939 **10 strokes**	苩	莫	莫

MÒ, don't; none; family name [D]
Anciently, 大 "big" was "grass" 艹, like the top of the character: "the sun going down, disappearing into the grass" (Karlgren AD 638), and the character was pronounced **mù** and meant "dusk, evening." Now sound-loan for "don't," etc. **Mò** is phonetic in several common characters. See the next few items.
莫非 **mòfēi** is it possible that...?

模 940 14 strokes	木	杧	杧
	杧	栉	栉
	栉	栉	模

MÓ, pattern (pronounced MÚ in some compounds) [B]

规模　**guīmó**　dimensions, scope [B]
模式　**móshì**　model; pattern [D]
模子　**múzi**　mold, die
模样　**múyàng** facial appearance, face
模特儿　**mótèr** model

摸 941 13 strokes	扌	扩	扩
	扩	拼	拼
	措	揸	摸

MŌ, to feel with the hand; to grope for; to sneak in or out [B]; to try to find out

The "side-hand" gives the meaning.

摸底　**mōdǐ** to try to find out the real situation or purpose

漠 942 13 strokes	氵	氵	氵
	氵	洪	洪
	洪	淕	漠

MÒ, desert; be indifferent [B]

Although 莫 mò (939, above) gives the sound, this can be read as a meaning-meaning compound: "water" + "none" = desert.

漠漠　**mòmò**　be foggy; be vast and lonely
漠然　**mòrán**　indifferently; apathetically
漠视　**mòshì**　to treat with indifference

寞 943 13 strokes	丶	宀	宀
	宀	帘	宧
	寉	寉	寞

MÒ, be lonely; be deserted [C]

慕 944 14 strokes	艹	艹	艹
	苩	苩	莫
	莫	慕	慕

MÙ, to admire; to hanker for [B]

爱慕　**àimù**　to love, to adore
慕仰　**mùyǎng** to look up to
慕名　**mùmíng** out of admiration for somebody's famous name
慕尼黑　**Mùníhēi** Munich (the Bavarian city)

189

墓 945 13 strokes	⺾	⺾	艹	**MÙ, tomb [C]** 墓地 **mùdì** cemetery
	苩	苴	莫	
	莫	墓	墓	

幕 946 13 strokes	⺾	⺾	艹	**MÙ, stage curtain; measure for acts of a play; (movie) screen [C]** 幕后 **mùhòu** backstage; behind the scenes
	苩	苴	莫	
	莫	幕	幕	

修 947 9 strokes	丿	亻	亻	**XIŪ, to build, to repair; to prune, trim; to study [B]** 修理 **xiūlǐ** to fix [B] 修改 **xiūgǎi** to revise [B] 修建 **xiūjiàn** to build [C] 修正 **xiūzhèng** to amend, revise [C] 自修 **zìxiū** to educate oneself; study period (in school)
	亻	伜	俏	
	修	修	修	

省 948 9 strokes	丨	丿丨	小	**SHĚNG, province [A]; to save [B]** 省得 **shěngdé** lest [C] 省长 **shěngzhǎng** governor of a province [C] 省会 **shěnghuì** provincial capital [D] 省钱 **shěngqián** be economical (be saving of money) 河北省 **Héběi shěng** Hebei (Hopei) Province
	少	少	省	
	省	省	省	

尺 949 4 strokes	ㄱ	ㄱ	尸	**CHǏ, a Chinese "foot" (about 14 English inches); pronounced CHĚ in some compounds; a ruler. FOOT (length) radical (117) [B]** 尺寸 **chǐcun** size (in feet and inches) [C] 尺子 **chǐzi** ruler [C] 市尺 **shìchǐ** Chinese standard foot
	尺			

190

宽 950 10 strokes	`	∧	宀
	宀	宆	宆
	芇	笌	宽

KUĀN, be broad [B]
宽大 **kuāndà** be spacious; to fit loosely; be lenient [D]
宽广 **kuānguǎng** be broad, extensive [D]
宽窄 **kuānzhǎi** "the broad-narrow of it," i.e. width
宽厚 **kuānhòu** be generous
宽容 **kuānróng** be tolerant

寬

系 951 7 strokes	一	乙	乇
	玄	孚	系
	系		

XÌ, 1) department (of a college); system; 2) to connect; be related to; 3) to tie; to haul up or let down on a rope; to remember; be concerned about; to jail [A]
关系 **guānxi** relationship [A]
太阳系 **tàiyángxì** the solar system
社会学系 **shèhuìxué xì** sociology department

係 (2nd meanings) 繫 (3rd meanings)

县 952 7 strokes	l	冂	月
	月	且	县
	县		

XIÀN, a xiàn ("hsien"), administrative district similar to a U.S. county [B]
县城 **xiànchéng** county seat [C]
县长 **xiànzhǎng** magistrate of a **xiàn** [D]

| 公 953 4 strokes | ノ | 八 | 公 |
| | 公 | | |

GŌNG, public; male; be equitable; metric; "Mr.;" grandfather [A]
公里 **gōnglǐ** kilometer [A]
公斤 **gōngjīn** kilogram [A]
公园 **gōngyuán** (public) park [A]
公元 **gōngyuán** Christian era [B]
公开 **gōngkāi** be open; make public [B]
公用电话 **gōngyòng diànhuà** public telephone [B]
公共汽车 **gōnggòngqìchē** public bus [A]

铁 954 10 strokes	ノ	ト	上
	乍	钅	钅
	铲	铗	铁

TIĚ, iron; be strong; family name [B]
铁路 **tiělù** railroad [B]
铁定 **tiědìng** to decide definitely
铁丝 **tiěsī** wire
手无寸铁 **shǒu wú cùn tiě** be completely unarmed, be defenceless

鐵

191

台	乙	厶	台	TÁI, the name of a group of stars; platform, terrace; desk; stand, base; broadcasting station [B]
	台	台		台风 **táifēng** typhoon [D] 电视台 **diànshìtái** television station [B]
955 5 strokes				

抬	一	丁	扌	TÁI, to carry (between two or more people); to raise the price [A]
	扌	扩	扩	抬头 **táitóu** to raise your head; to look up 抬高 **táigāo** to raise, enhance
956 8 strokes	抬	抬		擡

治	丶	丶	氵	ZHÌ, to govern; to heal, to treat [A]
	氵	氵	治	政治 **zhèngzhì** politics [A] 治理 **zhìlǐ** to govern [D] 治安 **zhì'ān** public security, law and order [D]
957 8 strokes	治	治		医治 **yīzhì** to heal, to treat [D] 治病 **zhìbìng** to treat an illness

语	丶	讠	讠	YǓ, language, speech [A] 语言 **yǔyán** language [A] 语法 **yǔfǎ** grammar [A]
	订	讦	讦	语音 **yǔyīn** speech sounds; pronunciation [B] 语气 **yǔqì** tone, manner of speaking; (grammatical) mood [B]
958 9 strokes	语	语	语	语文 **yǔwén** (Chinese) language [C] 四字成语 **sìzìchéngyǔ** a four-character set expression 語

弗	ㄱ	⊐	弓	FÚ, (bookish) not, be unwilling to
	弗	弗		This character originally meant "rope" and was a picture of a piece of rope (the "bow" radical) tying two things—now "left" and "down"— 丿 丨 together. The meanings "not, be unwilling to" come by sound-loan.
959 5 strokes				

费 960 9 strokes	一	一	弓	**FÈI, to waste; expense, fee; family name [B]** 学费 **xuéfèi** tuition fees [B] 费用 **fèiyòng** expense [B] 公费 **gōngfèi** at public expense [B] 费力 **fèilì** require effort, be strenuous [C] 费心 **fèixīn** to take trouble over; (polite) Would you mind to... 费
	弗	弗	弗	
	弗	费	费	

佛 961 7 strokes	ノ	亻	亻	**FÓ, Buddha; FÚ, second syllable of** 仿佛 *fǎngfú*, "to seem, to be more or less the same as; as if" [B] 佛教 **Fójiào** Buddhism
	伊	侣	侣	
	佛			

其 962 8 strokes	一	十	卄	**QÍ, her, his, its, their [A]** 其 gives the sound in several characters. See the next few items 其次 **qícì** next in order; second [B] 其中 **qízhōng** among, in the midst of [B] 其余 **qíyú** the rest [B] 其他 **qítā** other, else [B] 其间 **qíjiān** among, between [D] 其实 **qíshí** actually; in fact 尤其 **yóuqí** especially
	卄	甘	苴	
	其	其		

期 963 12 strokes	十	甘	苴	**QĪ, period; issue (of a magazine); to expect [A]** 期望 **qīwàng** to look forward to [D] 期间 **qījiān** period of time; during [B] 日期 **rìqī** date (calendrical) [B] 期满 **qīmǎn** to expire 星期 **xīngqī** week [A] 星期日 **xīngqīrì** Sunday [A] 星期天 **xīngqītiān** Sunday 星期一 **xīngqīyī** Monday
	其	期	期	
	期	期		

旗 964 14 strokes	亠	方	方	**QÍ, flag [B]** 旗袍 **qípáo** woman's long dress with slit skirt; cheongsam
	方	旃	旃	
	旃	旗	旗	

欺	廿	甘	甚	**QĪ, to cheat [B]; to deceive**
	其	其	欺ʼ	欺负 **qīfu** to bully; to take advantage of 欺骗 **qīpiàn** to deceive, swindle
965 12 strokes	欺ʼ	欺		

棋	木	杧	杜	**QÍ, chess, or any similar board game [C]**
	杣	棋	棋	
966 12 strokes	棋			

韦	一	二	弖	**WÉI, walk off, to walk off in opposite directions; soft leather; family name. WALK OFF radical (91)**
	韦			韦 used to have "foot" at top and bottom to suggest two feet walking in opposite directions.
967 4 strokes				韋

围	丨	冂	冂	**WÉI, to go around; circumference [A]**
	冋	冐	用	包围 **bāowéi** to surround [C] 围巾 **wéijīn** muffler, scarf [C] 围墙 **wéiqiáng** enclosing wall
968 7 strokes	围			圍

伟	丿	亻	仁	**WĚI, be great [A]**
	仨	伃	伟	伟大 **wěidà** be mighty [A]
969 6 strokes				偉

违

970
7 strokes

WÉI, to go against, to disobey [B]

违反 **wéifǎn** to violate, transgress [B]
违法 **wéifǎ** to break the law [D]

違

允

971
4 strokes

YǓN, to consent; be true, sincere [B]

Distinguish from 亢 (1041, p. 209).

允许 **yǔnxǔ** to permit, permission [B]
允从 **yǔncóng** to assent
允当 **yǔndàng** be suitable, satisfactory

充

972
6 strokes

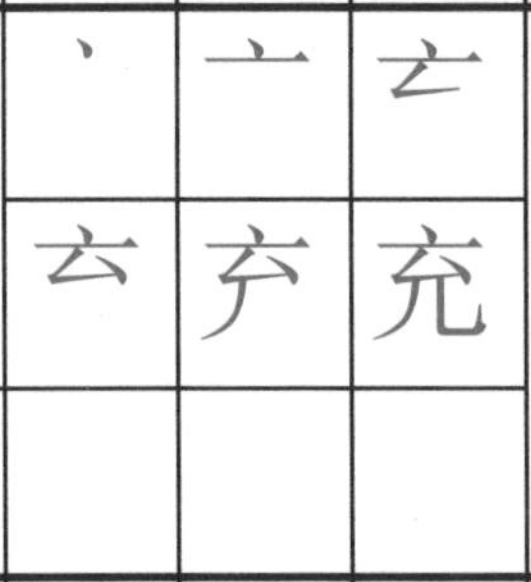

CHŌNG, to fill up; to pretend to be [B]

Distinguish from 亢 (1041, p. 209).

充分 **chōngfèn** be adequate [B]
充足 **chōngzú** be sufficient [B]
充实 **chōngshí** be ample, adequate [C]
充当 **chōngdāng** to serve as, act as [D]
冒充 **màochōng** to impersonate

统

973
9 strokes

TǑNG, to control; all; succession [B]

总统 **zǒngtǒng** president (of a country) [B]
传统 **chuántǒng** tradition; be traditional [B]
统一 **tǒngyī** to unify; unity [B]
系统 **xìtǒng** system; be systematic [B]
统治 **tǒngzhì** to control [B]

統

推

974
11 strokes

TUĪ, to push; to elect; to make excuses; to cut, to clip; to deduce [A]

推动 **tuīdòng** to put into action; to promote; to propel [B]
推进 **tuījìn** give a push to; (military) to advance [B]
推行 **tuīxíng** carry into operation [D]
推理 **tuīlǐ** (logic) inference [D]
推三阻四 **tuīsān-zǔsì** make up all kinds of excuses [D]

答	⺮	⺮⺮	⺮⺮	**DÁ, to answer; DĀ, answer [A]**
	笅	笅	笒	回答 **huídá** to answer, answer [A] 答应 **dāyìng** to answer, to agree to [B] 答案 **dá'àn** answer, solution [B] 答非所问 **dáfēisuǒwèn** to give an irrelevant answer; irrelevant or evasive answer
975 12 strokes	答	答		

货	ノ	イ	亻	**HUÒ, goods; currency [B]**
	化	化	货	国货 **guóhuò** domestic goods (i.e., not imports) 洋货 **yánghuò** imports ("foreign goods") 通货 **tōnghuò** legal tender
976 8 strokes	货	货		貨

咸	一	厂	厂	**XIÁN, salt; (bookish) all; a family name [C]**
	厂	后	咸	
977 9 strokes	咸	咸	咸	(salt only) 鹹

喊	口	旷	旷	**HǍN, to yell [A]**
	听	听	听	喊叫 **hǎnjiào** to cry out [C]
978 12 strokes	喊	喊	喊	

感	厂	厂	后	**GǍN, to feel (emotionally); to move (emotionally); to appreciate [A]**
	咸	咸	咸	感到 **gǎndào** to feel, to sense [A] 感冒 **gǎnmào** the common cold [A] 感谢 **gǎnxiè** to thank, be grateful [A] 感动 **gǎndòng** to move (emotionally) [B] 感觉 **gǎnjué** sense perception; to sense, feel [B]
979 13 strokes	感	感	感	感情 **gǎnqíng** emotion; affection [B] 感想 **gǎnxiǎng** reflections, thoughts [B]

减 980 11 strokes	氵	冫	冫
	厂	店	减
	减	减	

JIǍN, to decrease; "minus" [B]
减少 **jiǎnshǎo** to decrease, to subtract [B]
减产 **jiǎnchǎn** decline in production [D]
减价 **jiǎnjià** to cut prices; hold a sale
五减三 **wǔ jiǎn sān** five minus three

减

形 981 7 strokes	一	二	于
	开	开	形
	形		

XÍNG, form [B]
形势 **xíngshì** appearance, conditions of things; pertain to topography, be topographical [B]
形容 **xíngróng** to describe [B]
形成 **xíngchéng** to take shape [B]
形式 **xíngshì** form, shape [B]
形像 **xíngxiàng** image, form [C]
情形 **qíngxíng** circumstances, situation [B]

| 升 982 4 strokes | 一 | 二 | 千 |
| | 升 | | |

SHĒNG, to ascend, to raise; Chinese dry quart (31.6 cubic inches); quart box [B]
升学 **shēngxué** be promoted to a higher grade in school [D]
升平 **shēngpíng** be peaceful, peace
一升米 **yìshēngmǐ** quart of rice

低 983 7 strokes	丿	亻	亻
	仁	任	低
	低		

DĪ, be low, to lower [A]
减低 **jiǎndī** to reduce [D]
低下 **dīxià** be low (status, standard of living) [D]
低头 **dītóu** to bow the head
低声下气 **dīshēngxiàqì** be meek (literally, "lower your voice and keep down your energy")
低三下四 **dīsānxiàsì** be humble, servile

降 984 8 strokes	阝	阝	阝
	阝	陊	降
	陊	降	

JIÀNG, to descend; to lower, to demote [B]; XIÁNG, to surrender; to control
降低 **jiàngdī** to drop, to lower [B]
下降 **xiàjiàng** to descend; to drop, fall
降价 **jiàngjià** to reduce prices [D]
升降机 **shēngjiàngjī** elevator (literally, an ascend-and-descend machine)

197

照	冂	日	日⁻
	日⁻	昭	昭
985 **13 strokes**	照	照	照

ZHÀO, to reflect; to shine on; according to [A]

照常　zhàocháng　as usual [B]
按照　ànzhào　　according to ... [B]
护照　hùzhào　　passport [B]
照样　zhàoyàng　following a model; in the same old way, as before [C]
照相　zhàoxiàng　take a photograph [A]
照相机 zhàoxiàngjī camera [C]

而	一	一	厂
	厂	而	而
986 **6 strokes**			

ÉR, beard; and, and yet, but. BEARD radical (169) [A]

而 is a picture of a beard. Distinguish it from "face" 面 (675, p. 136).

而且　érqiě　　and moreover [A]
然而　rán'ér　but, moreover [B]
而已　éryǐ　　That's all [C]
而后　érhòu　　after that, then [D]

忽	丿	勹	勺
	勿	勿	忽
987 **8 strokes**	忽	忽	

HŪ, suddenly; to neglect [A]

忽然　hūrán　all of a sudden [A]
忽而... 忽而... huér... huér... do one thing one minute, another thing the next
忽而哭忽而笑 huér kū huér xiào weep one minute and laugh the next

乐	一	匚	千
	乐	乐	
988 **5 strokes**			樂

YUÈ, music; family name [A]; LÈ, happiness; family name [A]

音乐　yīnyuè　music [A]
快乐　kuàilè　be happy, happiness [B]

线	㇇	纟	纟
	纟	纟	线
989 **8 strokes**	线	线	綫

XIÀN, thread, wire; clue [B]

毛线　máoxiàn　knitting wool [C]
线路　xiànlù　(electricity) circuit; (transportation) line, route [C]
视线　shìxiàn　line of sight [D]
线人　xiànrén　stool pigeon; spy, informer
平行线 píngxíngxiàn parallel lines

邮	丨	冂	日	**YÓU, postal [A]** 邮包 **yóubāo**　parcel [C] 邮电 **yóudiàn**　post and telecommun- 　　　　　　ications [D] 邮政 **yóuzhèng** postal service [D] 邮费 **yóufèi**　postage 邮件 **yóujiàn**　mail
	由	由	邮	
990 7 strokes	邮			郵

局	⌐	⊐	尸	**JÚ, office; situation [A]** 局部 **júbù**　part [C] 局面 **júmiàn**　aspect, phase [C] 局势 **júshì**　situation [D] 邮局 **yóujú**　post office [A] 邮局长 **yóujúzhǎng** postmaster [B] 电话局 **diànhuàjú**　telephone office
	月	局	局	
991 7 strokes	局			

空	丶	丷	宀	**KŌNG, be empty; sky, air; for nothing, in vain; KÒNG, be empty, leave empty; empty space; free time** 空气 **kōngqì**　air [B] 空间 **kōngjiān**　space (as "outer ...") [B] 空中 **kōngzhōng**　in the sky; overhead [B] 空前 **kōngqián**　be unprecedented [B] 太空 **tàikōng**　outer space [D] 空话 **kōnghuà**　empty talk, chatter [D] 空心 **kōngxīn**　be hollow [D]
	宀	穴	空	
992 8 strokes	空	空		

色	丿	𠂊	㑒	**SÈ, color; looks; kind; desire [A]; SHǍI, color** 气色 **qìsè**　complexion 好色 **hǎosè**　be lustful 春色 **chūnsè**　spring scenery 色子 **shǎizi**　dice
	各	色	色	
993 6 strokes				

困	丨	冂	冃	**KÙN, difficulty, hardship; to trap; to maroon; to beseige; to be sleepy [A]** 困 shows a tree in a box to suggest the idea of "difficulty," "be in difficulties." 困睡 **kùnshuì** be sleepy, tired [A] 困难 **kùnnán** be difficult, difficulty [A] 围困 **wéikùn** to surround, hem in, beseige
	闲	闲	闲	
994 7 strokes	困			

滿	氵	氵	汁	**MĂN, be full; be contented, satisfied [A]**
	汁	汁	满	满意 **mǎnyì** be satisfied [A]
995	满	满	满	满足 **mǎnzú** to satisfy [B] 充满 **chōngmǎn** be full of, be brimming with, be permeated with [B] 满月 **mǎnyuè** full moon [D] 不满 **bùmǎn** be resentful, discontent
13 strokes				滿

角	ノ	⺈	⺊	**JIĂO, horn; angle; corner; a measure for dimes; role; JUÉ, role. HORN radical (201)**
	刀	角	角	The character is a picture of an animal's horn. 角度 **jiǎodù** angle; point of view; perspective [C]
996	角			直角 **zhíjiǎo** right angle
7 strokes				牛角 **niújiǎo** oxhorn

解	ノ	⺈	勹	**JIĔ, to loosen, to untie [A]**
	角	角	角	解决 **jiějué** to solve; to kill; solution [A] 了解 **liǎojiě** to understand [A] 解放 **jiěfàng** to liberate [B]
997	解	解	解	解答 **jiědá** to answer, explain [B] 解除 **jiěchú** to get rid of [D] 讲解 **jiǎngjiě** to explain [D]
13 strokes				

织	⺃	纟	纟	**ZHĪ, to weave [A]**
	纠	织	织	"Silk" helps with the meaning. 只 **zhǐ** is, of course, there for the sound. 组织 **zǔzhī** to organize; organization [A]
998	织	织		织造 **zhīzào** weaving
8 strokes				织毛衣 **zhīmáoyī** to knit a sweater 織

复	ノ	广	宀	**FÙ, 1) to return; to repeat; to recover; again; to reply; 2) to be complex; to repeat [A]**
	乍	乍	乍	复习 **fùxí** to review (lessons) [A] 重复 **chóngfù** to go over, repeat [B] 复活 **fùhuó** to resuscitate; Resurrection [D]
999	卢	复	复	复原 **fùyuán** to get well again; to restore [D] 复员 **fùyuán** to demobilize 复写纸 **fùxiězhǐ** carbon paper
9 strokes				複 (2nd meanings) 復 (1st meanings)

200

杂	ノ	九	九	**ZÁ, be mixed, be miscellaneous [A]**
	朵	杂	杂	复杂 **fùzá**　be complex [A] 杂文 **záwén**　an essay [C] 杂乱 **záluàn**　be disorderly, jumbled up [D] 杂交 **zájiāo**　to hybridize [D]
1000 6 strokes				雜

典	丨	冂	日	**DIǍN, canon, be canonic; to borrow or lend money on security of land or house [A]**
	由	曲	曲	字典 **zìdiǎn**　dictionary of characters [C] 典礼 **diǎnlǐ**　ceremony, celebration [C] 典故 **diǎngù**　classical allusion; historical background
1001 8 strokes	典	典		

查	一	十	才	**CHÁ, to investigate [A]**
	木	朮	杏	查明 **chámíng** investigate and prove; ascertain [D] 查处 **cháchǔ**　investigate and deal with as appropriate [D] 查点 **chádiǎn** to check a list of goods 查对 **cháduì**　to verify 查字典 **chá zìdiǎn** to look up in the dictionary
1002 9 strokes	杏	杳	查	

限	⻖	阝	阝¬	**XIÀN, limit [B]**
	阝ᅴ	阝ᅴ	阳	限度 **xiàndù**　limit [D] 限于 **xiànyú**　be limited to [D] 局限 **júxiàn**　to limit, be limited; to confine [D] 限定 **xiàndìng** to set a limit 限量 **xiànliàng** limit; to estimate 有限 **yǒuxiàn**　be limited; "Ltd." 无限 **wúxiàn**　be infinite, unlimited
1003 8 strokes	限	限		

提	扌	扣	护	**TÍ, to raise; to lift in the hand; rising stroke (in writing); DĪ in some compounds [A]**
	护	捍	捍	提高 **tígāo**　to raise, enhance [A] 提前 **tíqián**　to change to an earlier date; be beforehand [B] 提包 **tíbāo**　handbag, tote bag [C] 提问 **tíwèn**　to put questions to [C] 提案 **tí'àn**　a motion, proposal [D] 提防 **dīfáng** to guard against
1004 12 strokes	捍	捍	提	

201

肯	丨	﹂	﹂	**KĚN, be willing [B]** 肯定 **kěndìng** to accept; to recognize (e.g., another nation, diplomatically) [B]
	止	广	肯	
1005 **8 strokes**	肯	肯		

冬	ノ	ク	夂	**DŌNG, winter; family name [A]** 冬天 **dōngtiān** winter [A] 冬至 **Dōngzhì** Winter Solstice 冬菜 **dōngcài** preserved, dried cabbage or greens
	冬	冬		
1006 **5 strokes**				

夏	一	一	厂	**XIÀ, summer; family name [A]** 夏天 **xiàtiān** summer [A] 夏至 **Xiàzhì** Summer Solstice 夏收 **xiàshōu** summer harvest
	丆	百	百	
1007 **10 strokes**	夏	夏	夏	

冷	丶	冫	冫	**LĚNG, be cold; family name [A]** 冷淡 **lěngdàn** be cheerless, be desolate; be indifferent [D] 冷清 **lěngqīng** be deserted, be desolate 冷货 **lěnghuò** goods not much in demand 干冷 **gānlěng** be dry and cold (of the weather) 冷漠 **lěngmò** be cold and indifferent
	氵	氵	冷	
1008 **7 strokes**	冷			

谊	丶	讠	讠	**YÌ, friendship [B]** 友谊 **yǒuyi** friendship
	讠	讠	讠	
1009 **10 strokes**	讠	讠	谊	誼

	＇	ｒ′	宀
血	血	血	血

1010
6 strokes

XUÈ, blood. BLOOD radical (181) [B]
Colloquially, 血 may be pronounced **xiě**.
Distinguish from the "dish" radical 皿 (138, p. 28)
血汗 **xuèhàn** blood and sweat; sweat and toil
高血压 **gāoxuèyā** high blood pressure

	＼	＼	氵
温	汩	汩	渭
	渭	渭	温

1011
12 strokes

WĒN, be warm; review; family name [B]
What looks like the "sun" radical here was originally a picture of a man in a box— in prison. "Prisoner" over "dish" suggests "feed a prisoner," whence "be warmhearted, be warm."
温度 **wēndù** temperature [B]
温带 **wēndài** temperate zone [C]
温习 **wēnxí** review, study

	＼	讠	讠
该	讠	讠	讠
	该	该	

1012
8 strokes

GĀI, to owe; to be someone's turn; ought to; the said (aforementioned) ... [A]
应该 **yīnggāi** ought [A]
应当 **gāidāng** to deserve; should [B]
该死 **gāisǐ** (colloquial) damned, accursed (oath of disapproval)
该我 **gāiwǒ** It's my turn!

該

		冂	内
肉	内	肉	肉

1013
6 strokes

RÒU, meat; fruit pulp; be sluggish [A]
肉 is said to be a picture of dried meat.
牛肉 **niúròu** beef

		冂	日
星	日	尸	星
	昆	星	星

1014
9 strokes

XĪNG, star, planet; a bit [A]
星星 **xīngxīng** star [B]
明星 **míngxīng** star as in "movie star," etc. [D]
火星 **huǒxīng** a spark; Mars

假	ノ	亻	𠂆	**JIǍ, to borrow; to be fake, false; JIÀ, vacation [A]**
	伫	伫	作	放假 **fàngjià** to have a vacation [A]
1015 11 strokes	假	假	假	假如 **jiǎrú** if [C] 假使 **jiǎshǐ** if [C] 假期 **jiàqī** vacation time [C] 假牙 **jiǎyá** false tooth, denture 假意 **jiǎyì** with false intent

与	一	与	与	**YǓ, to hand over; with; YÙ, to participate in [B]**
1016 3 strokes				与其 **yǔqí** rather than [B] 与会 **yùhuì** to participate in a conference [D] 与世无争 **yǔ shì wú zhèng** not to fight the world; to disdain the rat race <div align="right">與</div>

举	丶	丷	丷丿	**JǓ, to lift; to begin; behavior; all [A]***
	丷丷	丷丷	兴	选举 **xuǎnjǔ** to elect, election [B] 举行 **jǔxíng** to hold (e.g., a meeting) [B] 举办 **jǔbàn** to conduct [C] 举头望明月，低头思故乡 **jǔ tóu wàng míng yuè, dī tóu sī gù xiāng** (I) raise
1017 9 strokes	兴	兴	举	(my) head and look at the bright moon, Lower (my) head and think of home (李白 *Li Bai*) 舉

叉	𠃌	又	叉	**CHĀ, a fork; to work with a fork; CHǍ, to part so as to make a fork; CHÁ, to jam, block up [B]**
				Distinguish from the second character below.
1018 3 strokes				钢叉 **gāngcha** steel fork 叉鱼 **chāyú** to spear fish

乂	ノ	乂		**No pronunciation; radical (25), "bottom of 义" (see next)**
1019 2 strokes				

*In *Han-Ying Cidian*, 举 is one of 11 "left-over" characters, not classified under a radical.

义 1020 3 strokes	丶	丷	义	**YÌ**, commitment to the common good; justice; be just; meaning [A] Distinguish from the preceding character. See note under 仁 (450, p. 91) on Confucian thought on social order. 义务 **yìwù** duty, obligation; without pay [C] 主义 **zhǔyì** doctrine, -ism [D] 社会主义 **shèhuìzhǔyì** socialism [C] 望文生义 **wàng wén shēng yì** take a text too literally 義

议 1021 5 strokes	丶	讠	讠	**YÌ**, to discuss [B] 提议 **tíyì** to propose
	议	议		議

仪 1022 5 strokes	丿	亻	亻	**YÍ**, appearance, bearing; ceremony, rite [B] 仪表 **yíbiǎo** appearance; meter (measuring apparatus) 仪器 **yíqì** gadget 仪容 **yíróng** appearance
	仪	仪		儀

智 1023 12 strokes	丿	二	午	**ZHÌ**, wisdom [C] See note under 仁 (450, p. 91) on Confucian thought on social order.
	矢	知	知	
	智	智	智	

被 1024 10 strokes	丶	冫	衤	**BÈI**, quilt; by (sign of agent in passive construction); to be . . . (sign of passive construction—see 被告 in the examples) [A] 被子 **bèizi** quilt [B] 被动 **bèidòng** be passive [C] 被告 **bèigào** the accused, defendant [D]
	衤	衤	衤	
	衤	衤	被	

205

利	一	二	千	**LÌ, interest (on money); profit; be sharp; family name [A]**
	禾	禾	利	利用 **lìyòng** to make use of [A] 净利 **jìnglì** net profit 复利 **fùlì** compound interest 吉利 **jílì** be lucky, be auspicious
1025 7 strokes	利			

存	一	丆	亻	**CÚN, to keep, to store; deposit [B]**
	存	存	存	保存 **bǎocún** to preserve [B] 存放 **cúnfàng** to entrust to somebody; to deposit [D] 存在 **cúnzài** to exist, existence [B] 存在主义 **cúnzàizhǔyì** Existentialism
1026 6 strokes				

消	丶	冫	氵	**XIĀO, to consume, to abolish; to be necessary [A]**
	氵	氵	氵	消息 **xiāoxi** news, information [A] 取消 **qǔxiāo** to abolish [B] 消化 **xiāohuà** to digest, digestion [B] 消费 **xiāofèi** to consume [B] 消除 **xiāochú** to eliminate, to clear up [C] 消极 **xiāojí** be negative; be passive [C]
1027 10 strokes	消	消	消	

制	丿	亠	匕	**ZHÌ, to measure, to regulate; institution; system; to make, to manufacture [B]**
	乍	告	告	限制 **xiànzhì** to limit, to restrict [B] 制度 **zhìdù** system [B] 制定 **zhìdìng** to work out (e.g., a plan, a system) [B] 制造 **zhìzào** to make, manufacture [B] 制止 **zhìzhǐ** to stop, put an end to [B] 製 ("to make, to manufacture")
1028 8 strokes	制	制		

考	一	十	土	**KǍO, to test; to be tested; exam [A]**
	耂	老	考	大考 **dàkǎo** final exam 考古 **kǎo gǔ** to practice archaeology; archaeology [D] 考古学 **kǎogǔxué** archaeology
1029 6 strokes				

206

	`	讠	讠	**SHÌ, to try [A]**
试	讠	讠	讠	考试 **kǎoshì** to take or give an exam; exam [A]
1030				口试 **kǒushì** oral exam (C)
8 strokes	试	试		笔试 **bǐshì** written exam (C) 試

	ㄥ	厶	厶	**CĀN, to take part in; to refer; to consult; SHĒN, ginseng [A]**
参	乒	乒	叁	参加 **cānjiā** to take part in [A]
				参观 **cānguān** to sightsee [A]
1031				参考 **cānkǎo** to consult, to consider [C]
8 strokes	参	参		人参 **rénshēn** ginseng [D] 參

	一	厂	下	**BIĀO, long hair. HAIR radical (220)**
髟	匡	手	長	The "streaks" radical stands for the hair; the "long" radical gives the rest of the meaning.
1032				
10 strokes	髟	髟	髟	

	`	㇀	丬	**QIĀNG, bed. BED radical (with the form 爿, = radical (42))**
丬				This radical is a picture of a bed. The student should distinguish it from 片, the "slice" radical ((114), p. 85). "Bed" is now usually written 床, pronounced **chuáng** (Pt. 2, p. 218b).
1033				
3 strokes				

	`	㇀	丬	**JIĀNG, to take hold of; to be about to; just; to nurture; JIÀNG, a general (military officer) [A]**
将	丬	丬	丬	将来 **jiānglái** in the future [A]
				将要 **jiāngyào** be going to, will do... [B]
				将近 **jiāngjīn** be close to, be almost... [D]
1034				将就 **jiāngjiu** to make do with, to
9 strokes	将	将	将	compromise 將

207

奖	丶	丷	爿	**JIǍNG, a prize; to give a prize to, to award [B]**
	爿	丬	兆	奖金 **jiǎngjīn** award of money, bonus [C] 奖学金 **jiǎngxuéjīn** scholarship; exhibition [B]
1035 9 strokes	兆	奖	奖	獎

酱	丬	丬	丬	**JIÀNG, sauce; (food) paste [B]**
	兆	酱	酱	酱油 **jiàngyóu** soy sauce (油: see p. 217b)
1036 13 strokes	酱	酱	酱	醬

浆	丬	丬	丬	**JIĀNG, to starch; thick fluid, starch [C]**
	浆	浆	浆	
1037 10 strokes	浆			漿

属	┐	尸	尸	**SHǓ, to belong to; genus, family; be subordinate [B]**
	戸	戸	屌	属于 **shǔyú** to belong to, be tantamount to [B] 属国 **shǔguó** dependent territories, colonies 属性 **shǔxìng** qualities, attributes
1038 12 strokes	属	属		屬

毕	一	ヒ	ヒ丶	**BÌ, to finish; family name [B]**
	比	毕	毕	Distinguish from 华 (788, p. 158). 毕业 **bìyè** to graduate [B] 毕生 **bìshēng** all one's life
1039 6 strokes				畢

拾	一	丁	扌	**SHÍ, to pick up; to find; ten [A]**
	扌	扒	扲	This is a form of 十 used in accounting (to minimize the possibilty of error or fraud).
1040 9 strokes	拾	拾	拾	拾取 **shíqǔ** to pick up, collect

亢	、	亠	宀	**KÀNG, be high, to go high; be haughty [D]** The student should distinguish this character from 允 **yún** "to consent; be sincere" (971, p. 195) and from 充 **chōng** "to fill up" (972, p. 195).
1041 4 strokes	亢			高亢 **gāokàng** be sonorous, resounding 亢进 **kàngjìn** hyperactive (of a bodily organ—a medical term)

航	'	丿	凢	**HÁNG, to sail, to navigate [B]** 航空 **hángkōng** aviation; air- [B] 航行 **hángxíng** to sail, fly, navigate [C] 航线 **hángxiàn** shipping/flight route [D]
	凢	舟	舟	航运 **hángyùn** shipping [D] 航海 **hánghǎi** navigation [D]
1042 10 strokes	舟	舟	航	航天 **hángtiān** spaceflight [D] 航道 **hángdào** channel, lane [D]

旅	、	亠	亣	**LǙ, to travel; troops, brigade [A]** 旅行 **lǚxíng** to take a trip, to travel [A] 旅馆 **lǚguǎn** hotel [B]
	方	亣	旃	旅客 **lǚkè** traveler, passenger; hotel guest [B]
1043 10 strokes	旃	旅	旅	旅社 **lǚshè** inn 旅长 **lǚzhǎng** brigade commander

急	丿	勹	刍	**JÍ, be hurried; be upset; be urgent [A]** 着急 **zháojí** to worry, feel anxious [A] 急忙 **jímáng** be hassled, busy [B] 急切 **jíqiè** be impatient; in a hurry [D]
	刍	刍	刍	急症 **jízhèng** acute disease 急救 **jíjiù** first aid; emergency treatment
1044 9 strokes	急	急	急	急性子 **jíxìngzi** to be an impatient type; an impatient type

209

寄	、	宀	宀	**JÌ, to mail; to entrust; to dwell [A]** 寄信 **jìxín** to mail a letter 寄存 **jìcún** to deposit; deposits 寄卖 **jìmài** to consign (goods) 寄件人 **jìjiànrén** sender
	宇	宊	宏	
1045 11 strokes	宊	客	寄	

票	一	厂	帀	**PIÀO, ticket, stamp, bank note, check, document; vote [A]** 邮票 **yóupiào** postage stamp [A] 支票 **zhīpiào** check [D] 传票 **chuánpiào** summons (legal) 票房 **piàofáng** a place to buy tickets, booking office, box office
	兩	襾	覀	
1046 11 strokes	票	票	票	

漂	氵	汀	沪	**PIĂO, to float, to drift (usually on water: compare with next item); PIĂO, bleach, rinse; 1st syllable of 漂亮 *piàoliang* be good-looking; be brilliant, outstanding [A]**
	浐	湮	漕	
1047 14 strokes	潭	漂	漂	

飘	帀	襾	覀	**PIĀO, to float (in the air or on the water) [B]** 飘然 **piāorán** to float in the air 飘飘 **piāopiāo** to flutter 飘飘然 **piāopiāorán** be smug
	票	剽	飘	
1048 15 strokes	飘	飘		飄

标	一	十	才	**BIĀO, target; to quote a price; to bid (commercially); sign [B]** 标准 **biǎzhūn** criterion; be standard [B] 标点 **biāodiǎn** punctuation; to punctuate [B] 标语 **biāoyǔ** slogan; poster [C] 标题 **biāotí** heading, headline, caption [D]
	木	杧	杧	
1049 9 strokes	杧	标	标	標

布 1050 5 strokes	一	广	右	**BÙ, cotton cloth; to publish; to spread, lay out; to announce [A]**
	右	布		布告 **bùgào** notice, bulletin [C]
				公布 **gōngbù** to announce, to publish [C]
				布局 **bùjú** layout; composition (of a painting, of a piece of writing); arrangement (of pieces on a chessboard [D]
				幕布 **mùbù** theatre curtain; movie screen

唤 1051 10 strokes	丨	刂	口	**HUÀN, to call out [C]**
	吖	吟	唅	叫唤 **jiàohuan** to call out [D]
	唤			唤起 **huànqǐ** to incite, to stir up

换 1052 10 strokes	一	扌	扌	**HUÀN, to exchange [A]**
	扩	护	抢	换取 **huànqǔ** to get something by exchange, to barter for something [D]
	换	换		换钱 **huànqián** to change money
				改换 **gǎihuàn** to change
				换句话说 **huàn jù huà shuō** in other words

适 1053 9 strokes	一	二	千	**SHÌ, to follow, to chase; be suitable [A]**
	千	舌	舌	合适 **héshì** be appropriate [A]
	活	话	适	适合 **shìhé** to suit, to fit [B]
				适当 **shìdàng** be proper, be suitable [B]
				适应 **shìyìng** to suit, to fit, to match [B]
				适用 **shìyòng** to be applicable, to suit [B]
				适宜 **shìyí** be suitable, to fit [C]
				适时 **shìshí** be timely 适

鞋 1054 15 strokes	艹	艹	苴	**XIÉ, shoe [A]**
	革	革	鞋	布鞋 **bùxié** shoes made of cloth
	鞋	鞋	鞋	皮鞋 **píxié** leather shoes
				鞋底 **xiédǐ** shoe sole
				鞋跟 **xiégēn** heel of a shoe
				(口 53, 土 34)

211

德	彳	彳	彳	**DÉ, virtue; personal energy; 1ˢᵗ syllable of 德国, Germany; family name [B]** Scholars say: The upper righthand part of **dé** is 真 "be real, be true" (404, p. 81), distorted. With "heart" and "step" ("step" for "action"), **dé** combines meanings: "true-heartedness in action," i.e. virtue. 德语 **Déyǔ** the German language [B] (灬 175)
	彳	彳	彳	
1055 **15 strokes**	德	德	德	

颜	亠	立	产	**YÁN, color, face; family name [A]** 颜色 **yánsè** color; countenance [A] 容颜 **róngyán** looks, appearance 颜面 **yánmiàn** face; prestige, respect
	产	产	颜	
1056 **15 strokes**	颜	颜		颜

烟	丶	丷	火	**YĀN, smoke; tobacco, cigarette [B]** 吸烟 **xīyān** to smoke (tobacco) [B] 烟袋 **yāndài** pipe (for tobacco) 烟鬼 **yānguǐ** opium addict; nicotine fiend 烟火 **yānhuǒ** fireworks
	火	灯	炟	
1057 **10 strokes**	炳	烟	烟	

囱	丿	厂	冂	**CŌNG, smoke-hole, chimney, flue [C]** 烟囱 **yāncōng** chimney, stovepipe
	冈	囱	囱	
1058 **7 strokes**	囱			

需	一	宀	雫	**XŪ, to need [A]** 需要 **xūyào** to need, need [A] 必需 **bìxū** be essential, be indispensable [C] 需求 **xūqiú** to require, to demand [D]
	雫	雫	雫	
1059 **14 strokes**	需	需	需	(雨 368)

212

偷	亻	伫	伫	**TŌU, to steal [B]**
	价	偷	偷	偷税 **tōushuì** to evade tax [D]
				偷看 **tōukàn** to steal a look at, to peep, look at surreptitiously
1060	偷			偷闲 **tōuxián** to loaf, to shirk
11 strokes				偷偷的 **tōutōude** stealthily, on the sly [B]

敬	艹	艻	苟	**JÌNG, to revere; family name [B]**
	苟	苟	苟	敬爱 **jìng'ài** to honor [B]
				敬礼 **jìnglǐ** to salute; salutation, formal greeting [B]
1061	苟	敬	敬	敬酒 **jìngjiǔ** to propose a toast, a toast [C]
12 strokes				敬重 **jìngzhòng** to respect a person
				敬而远之 **jìng ér yuǎn zhī** to respect and stay at a respectful distance from [D]

警	艻	苟	苟	**JǏNG, to warn [B]**
	敬	敬	警	**Jǐng** combines meanings: use "words" to induce "reverence, caution" = "to warn." (Karlgren thinks 敬 is phonetic here, or 敬 and 警 stand for cognates. *AD* 396).
1062	警	警	警	警告 **jǐnggào** warning; to warn, caution [C]
19 strokes				火警 **huǒjǐng** fire alarm
				警报 **jǐngbào** alarm, warning, siren

察	宀	夕	夕	**CHÁ, to investigate [B]**
	夘	夘	宨	观察 **guānchá** to observe, to survey [B]
				考察 **kǎochá** to inspect; to observe and study [C]
1063	窔	穼	察	察看 **chákàn** to look into
14 strokes				警察 **jǐngchá** policeman [B]
				警察局 **jǐngchájú** police station

银	⺮	⻐	钅	**YÍN, silver; family name [A]**
	钅┐	钅ヨ	钅ヨ	银行 **yínháng** bank (financial institution) [A]
				银子 **yínzi** silver
1064	钜	银	银	白银 **báiyín** silver
11 strokes				银河 **yínhé** the Milky Way
				銀

				YUĒ, to agree [B]
约	㇛	纟	纟	约会 **yuēhuì** appointment, engagement [B] 条约 **tiáoyuē** treaty [B] 约束 **yuēshù** to restrain, to keep within bounds [D]
	纟	约	约	失约 **shíyuē** to miss an appointment [D]
1065 6 strokes				约定 **yuēdìng** to agree to <div align="right">約</div>

				QIÓNG, be poor, be impoverished [B]
穷	丶	八	宀	穷人 **qióngrén** poor people [C] 穷苦 **qióngkǔ** be poverty-stricken [D] 穷忙 **qióngmáng** be busy without purpose 哭穷 **kūqióng** to complain about being poor; to go about pleading poverty
	宀	空	穷	
1066 7 strokes	穷			贫穷 **pínqióng** be poor, needy <div align="right">窮</div>

				JÌNG, be quiet, be peaceful; family name [A]
静	二	三	主	安静 **ānjìng** be quiet [A] 静电 **jìngdiàn** static electricity 静止 **jìngzhǐ** be motionless, be static
	青	青	青	
1067 14 strokes	静	静	静	(青 249, 争 709)

Remaining Characters of the "A" List,

"B" List, and "C" List

草	**CǍO**, grass [A] 草地 **cǎodì** lawn [B] 草原 **cǎoyuán** prairie [B]	图	**TÚ**, picture, map, diagram [A] 图书馆 **túshūguǎn** library (A) <div align="right">圖</div>
雪	**XUĚ**, snow; family name [A]. Karlgren explains this as "rain which you can take in the hand" (*AD* 844).	彐	**JÌ**, pig's head. PIG'S HEAD radical (70). The forms ⺕ and ⺕ are also classified as radical 70.
鸟	**NIǍO**, bird. BIRD radical (152) [B] 鸟叫 **niǎo jiào** bird cries, bird song <div align="right">鳥</div>	录	**LÙ** , to record, to copy; to tape-record; to employ [A] <div align="right">錄</div>
场	**CHǍNG**, field; a measure for events; **CHÁNG**, a measure for periods [A] <div align="right">場</div>	绿	**LÙ**, be green [A] 绿化 **lǜhuà** to make green – plant flowers, reforest, etc. (D) <div align="right">綠</div>
扬	**YÁNG**, to lift up, throw in the air, winnow, display; publish, praise (verbs) [A] <div align="right">揚</div>	饿	**È**, be hungry; to starve [A] <div align="right">餓</div>
汤	**TĀNG**, soup, hot water; a family name [A] 泡汤 **pào tāng** (colloq) to fall through <div align="right">湯</div>	鹅	**É**, goose [B] 鹅毛 **émáo** goose feathers <div align="right">鵝</div>
烫	**TÀNG**, be scalding hot; to scald, to heat up; to iron; to get a permanent (hair-do) [B] <div align="right">燙</div>	俄	**É**, in foreign words [C] 俄语 **éyǔ** Russian language (spoken) [C] 俄文 **éwén** Russian language (written) [C]
肠	**CHÁNG**, intestine; sausage [B] 肠儿 **chángr** sausage <div align="right">腸</div>	害	**HÀI**, to harm; be harmed by, 'catch' (i.e., a disease); evil, calamity [B] 害怕 **hàipà** get scared [B]
畅	**CHÀNG**, be unimpeded; be uninhibited [C] <div align="right">暢</div>	练	**LIÀN**, to practice; a family name [A] 练习 **liànxí** practice, to practice [A] <div align="right">練</div>

私	**SĪ**, be private; be selfish [B] 私人 **sīrén** be personal [B] 私有 **sīyǒu** be private [C]
科	**KĒ**, category [A] Distinguish from the next character. 科学 **kēxué** science [A]
料	**LIÀO**, material, grain; to expect [B] Distinguish from the preceding character.
痛	**TÒNG**, to ache [A] 痛快 **tòngkuài** happy [A] 痛苦 **tòngkǔ** to weep [B] 痛处 **tòngchù** sore spot
烧	**SHĀO**, to burn [A] 发烧 **fāshāo** be fevered [A] 烧饭 **shāofàn** fix a meal 燒
晓	**XIǍO**, be clear; down; to understand [B] 晓得 **xiǎode** to know [B] 曉
检	**JIǍN**, to look into [A] 检查 **jiǎnchá** look into [A] 检察官 **jiǎncháguān** public prosecutor 檢
药	**YÀO**, medicine; (some) chemicals [A] 药方 **yàofāng** prescription [C] 藥
球	**QIÚ**, ball, orb, sphere [A] 足球 **zúqiú** football [A] 球场 **qiúchǎng** ball field [B]
戏	**XÌ**, (theater) play [B] 京戏 **jīngxì** Beijing Opera [B] 马戏 **mǎxì** circus [D] 戲
拉	**LĀ**, to pull; used for foreign words [A] 拉手 **lāshǒu** shake hands 拉皮条 **lāpítiáo** to act as a pimp, procuror
双	**SHUĀNG**, pair; even (opposite of "odd") [A] 双方 **shuāngfāng** both sides [B] 雙
集	**JÍ**, to get together; family name [A] 集合 **jíhé** assemble [A] 集中 **jízhōng** to focus [B] 集体 **jítǐ** be collective [B]
蛋	**DÀN**, egg [A] 坏蛋 **huàidàn** bad guy 蛋白石 **dànbáishí** opal 咸蛋 **xiándàn** salted egg
诚	**CHÉNG**, be sincere [B] 诚实 **chéngshí** sincere [B] 诚心 **chéngxīn** sincerity 誠
军	**JŪN**, military, army; army corps [A] 军人 **jūnrén** soldier 軍
巛	No pronunciation. RIVER radical (78)
虎	**HǓ**, tiger; family name [B] 骑虎难下 **qíhǔ nánxià**, "Once mount tiger's back, problem to get down" (i.e. a difficult situation)
鬲	**LÌ**, cauldron. CAULDRON radical (219) 鬲
臣	**CHÉN**, bureaucrat. BUREAU-CRAT radical (164)
赤	**CHÌ**, be bright red; be sincere; be bare. RED radical (190) 赤道 **chìdào** equator [C] 赤字 **chìzì** deficit [D]
豸	No pronunciation. SNAKE radical (198)

鹿	**LÙ**, deer. DEER radical (222)	卡	**KǍ**, to put a stop to; used to write foreign words; **QIǍ**, get stuck; a clip; a checkpost [A]
鼠	**SHǓ**, mouse. MOUSE radical (225)	术	**SHÙ**, craft, art, profession; device [A] 技术 **jìshù** technique, technology　術
趣	**QÙ**, be interesting; be pleasant [B] 有趣 **yǒuqù** interesting [B] 趣味 **qùwèi** interest [C] 兴趣 **xìngqù** interest, liking for [C]	团	**TUÁN**, corps, club; a measure for round things [A]　團
耒	**LĚI**, plow. PLOW radical (176) 木 "tree" plus two strokes (for the blades of the plow).	享	**XIǍNG**, to offer a sacrifice; to receive [B] Picture of a dish for offerings of food (lid on)
负	**FÙ**, back; to carry on the back; be negative; turn one's back on [A] 辜负 **gūfù** to disappoint; to let down　負	孰	**SHÚ**, (bookish) be cooked; be done; who? which?
赖	**LÀI**, to hang about (too long); to deny responsibility; family name [D]　賴	熟	**SHÚ**, be cooked, be done; be ripe; be very familiar with (also **SHÓU**) [A]
懒	**LǍN**, be lazy [B] 懒洋洋 **lǎnyángyáng** take your own sweet time; dilly-dally　懶	油	**YÓU**, oil [B] 酱油 **jiàngyóu** soy sauce [B]
鸡	**JĪ**, chicken [A] 鸡蛋 **jīdàn** (chicken's) egg [A] 公鸡 **gōngjī** rooster　雞	香	**XIĀNG**, be fragrant, smell sweet; incense, scent. SCENT radical (215) [A] 香港 **Xiānggǎng** Hong Kong
计	**JÌ**, to calculate, to reckon; stratagem, plan; family name [A] 会计 **kuàijì** accounting [D]　計	齐	**QÍ**, to line up, arrange; be uniform, even; surname. LINE-UP radical (160) [A]　齊
叶	**YÈ**, a leaf; a family name [B] 叶子 **yèzi** leaf [B]　葉	济	**JÌ**, to help out; to complete [A] 经济 **jīngjì** economics　濟
划	**HUÀ**, to mark, to cut, engrave; **HUÁ**, to row (a boat); be profitable; to scratch [A]　劃	壮	**ZHUÀNG**, be strong [C] 状大 **zhuàngdà** get/make stronger, expand [C]　壯

装	**ZHUĀNG**, to load up [A] 装备 **zhuāngbèi** to equip; equipment [C] 装	初	**CHŪ**, the beginning, the first [A]
惯	**GUÀN**, be used to [A] 习惯 **xíguàn** habits 惯性 **guànxìng** inertia 惯	段	**DUÀN**, paragraph, section; passage (of writing); a measure for such passages [A]
轻	**QĪNG**, be light (in weight) [A] 轻重 **qīngzhòng** weight 輕	破	**PÒ**, be broken [A] 破坏 **pòhuài** to wreck; to change drastically [B]
器	**QÌ**, dish, implement [A] 4 口's ＋犬 = "dish"? The logic's unclear.	须	**XŪ**, 1) must; be necessary; 2) whiskers beard [A] 1: 須 2: 鬚
床	**CHUÁNG**, bed [A] 床位 **chuángwèi** bunk	川	**CHUĀN**, river [D] 四川 **Sìchuān** Sichuan (the province—old style "Szechwan")
基	**JĪ**, base, foundation [A] 基本 **jīběn** be basic [A] 基地 **jīdì** base (military) [C]	顺	**SHÙN**, to move with, to agree with; favorable, prosperous [A] 順
落	**LUÒ**, to fall, to come down; to let fall, to drop; **LÀ**, leave out, be left out; to leave behind; to lag. Pronounced **LÀO** in some compounds.	训	**XÙN**, to give advice [B] 训练 **xùnliàn** to drill 訓
志	**ZHÌ**, 1) will, volition; 2) to remember, to record, a record [A] 誌 (2nd meanings only)	烦	**FÁN**, to pester, annoy [A] 煩
联	**LIÁN**, to unite [A] 联系 **liánxì** to contact [A] 联欢 **liánhuān** to throw a party [B] 聯	暖	**NUĂN**, be warm [A] 暖和 **nuǎnhuo** be warm
司	**SĪ**, to control; company [B] 公司 **gōngsī** company, corporation [B]	援	**YUÁN**, to pull along; to give a hand to, to aid [B]
章	**ZHĀNG**, chapter, section, paragraph; a measure for parts of literary or musical works; a surname [A]	缓	**HUĂN**, be slack; to goof off; be late [C] 緩

啦	**LĀ**, imitative; **LA**, sentence particle: 了 + 啊 [A] 哩哩啦啦 **līlīlālā** (vernacular), off and on		读	**DÚ**, to recite; to study [A] 读书 **dúshū** to read, study [B] 读者 **dúzhě** reader [B] 讀
舒	**SHŪ**, to relax, to stretch out [A] 舒展 **shūzhǎn** to fold out; limber up		遇	**YÙ**, to run into [A] 遇到 **yùdào** to encounter [A]
责	**ZÉ**, responsibility [A] 负责 **fùzé** be responsible for; be conscientious [A] 責		例	**LÌ**, line, rank; to line up, to rank [B]
绩	**JÌ**, to join threads; to finish; accomplishment [A] 績		退	**TUÌ**, to back off; to give back; to fade [A] 退步 **tuìbù** to regress [C] 退休 **tuìxiū** to retire [C]
债	**ZHÀI**, to owe money; debt [C] 借债 **jièzhài** borrow money 債		腿	**TUǏ**, leg, thigh [A] 大腿 **dàtuǐ** thigh
确	**QUÈ**, be true, be definite [A] 確		挂	**GUÀ**, to hang [A] 挂号 **guàhào** to register (as, at a hospital; also, a letter) [B] 掛
吹	**CHUĪ**, to blow [A] 吹牛 **chuīniú** to boast		眼	**YǍN**, eye; hole; a measure for glances, wells, and musical beats [A] 眼睛 **yǎnjīng** eye
散	**SÀN**, to scatter, to disperse [A]		指	**ZHǏ**, to point; a finger [A] 指示 **zhǐshì** to point out [B]
继	**JÌ**, to continue, to succeed to [A] 繼		增	**ZĒNG**, to add to [A] 增长 **zēngzhǎng** to increase, to grow [B]
断	**DUÀN**, to break into segments; to stop (doing); to decide a law case [A] 斷		层	**CÉNG**, story (of a building) [A] 層
续	**XÙ**, to add to; to prolong; to follow [A] 继续 **jìxù** to continue [A] 續		妈	**MĀ**, mama, "ma;" woman servant, nurse [A] 媽

码	**MǍ**, to lay in neat piles; yard (of cloth); counter or marker [C] 碼	蓝	**LÁN**, be blue (color); family name [A] 藍
骂	**MÀ**, to scold; to curse [B] 斥骂 **chìmà** reprimand, scold 罵	篮	**LÁN**, basket (usually with a curved handle); "basket" (basketball) [A] 籃
碗	**WǍN**, bowl [A] 饭碗 **fànwǎn** "rice bowl," livelihood	滥	**LÀN**, to overflow, to flood; be excessive, be indiscriminate [C] 濫
况	**KUÀNG**, even more so [A] 景况 **jǐngkuàng** circumstances, situation 况且 **kuàngqiě** furthermore　況	览	**LǍN**, to look at [A] 覽
村	**CŪN**, village [A] 村长 **cūnzhǎng** village chief	播	**BŌ**, to spread, to scatter [A] 播送 **bōsòng** to broadcast, to transmit [C]
输	**SHŪ**, to lose (as in gambling) [A] 輸	翻	**FĀN**, to flip; to translate; search through; change one's attitude; to reprint; go over (a hill) [A]
物	**WÙ**, thing, object [A] 动物 **dòngwù** animal [A] 植物 **zhíwù** plants; flora [A]	译	**YÌ**, to explain, to interpret, to translate [A] 翻译 **fānyì** to translate [B] 譯
讨	**TǍO**, to ask for; to marry (be a groom); to discuss [A] 討	择	**ZÉ, ZHÁI**, to pick out [B] 擇
胜	**SHÈNG**, victory [A] 胜利 **shènglì** victory; to win, to vanquish [A] 勝	释	**SHÌ**, to loosen up, to explain [B] 釋
盐	**YÁN**, salt [B] 盐水 **yánshuǐ** brine 鹽	泽	**ZÉ**, marsh; to dampen; to enrich; to favor [C] 澤
监	**JIĀN**, to supervise; prison [C] 監	农	**NÓNG**, farming [A] 农业 **nóngyè** agriculture [A] 農

浓	**NÓNG**, be heavy, be thick; be strong in flavor; be intense (as, an interest) [B]
扁	**BIĂN**, door-plaque; sign-board; be flat [B] For 扁 as phonetic, see the next five characters.
遍	**BIÀN**, go around; be ubiquitous; a turn, a time [A]
篇	**PIĀN**, article, essay; a measure for articles and essays [A]
编	**BIĀN**, to weave, to braid; to classify; to compile [B]
偏	**PIĀN**, to lean to one side; be partial; on the side, secondary [B]
骗	**PIÀN**, to fool, to cheat [B] 骗人 **piànrén** Nonsense! 欺骗 **qīpiàn** to dupe 騙
芇	No pronunciation. Radical (134). "Top of 劳" (see next character).
劳	**LÁO**, hard work [A] 勞
捞	**LĀO**, to drag for, to fish for; to make money improperly [B] 撈
荣	**RÓNG**, to flourish, be glorious [B] 榮

营	**YÍNG**, camp; battalion; to manage [B] 營
验	**YÀN**, to try out; to examine [A] 验证 **yànzhèng** to verify 驗
签	**QIĀN**, to sign (formally); lots (as in "draw lots"); label [B] 簽
福	**FÚ**, good luck [A] 福利 **fúlì** prosperity; material benefits
富	**FÙ**, be rich, abundant; family name [A]
副	**FÙ**, assistant [B] 副手 **fùshǒu** assistant
幅	**FÚ**, a width of cloth; size; a measure for cloth, silk, wool, paintings, drawings, etc. [B]
碰	**PÈNG**, to touch; to run into [A] 碰头 **pèngtóu** to talk over
舞	**WǓ**, dance [A] 舞动 **wǔdòng** to brandish; wave
顾	**GÙ**, look after, take care of; take into consideration [A] 顧
之	**ZHǏ**, a particle similar to 的; (noun/pronoun) 's; him, her, it, them [A] ...之间 **zhījiān** between [A]

221

乏	**FÁ**, be exhausted; be feeble in ability; low (said of a fire) [B] 贫乏 **pínfá** poor, inadequate [D]	荒	**HUĀNG**, be deserted, be desolate; be reckless; excessive; famine... [C]
娘	**NIÁNG**, mother; young woman [A] 新娘 **xīnniáng** bride [D] <div align="right">孃</div>	慌	**HUĀNG**, be nervous [B] 慌忙 **huāngmáng** be in a big hurry [C]
渴	**KĚ**, be thirsty [A] 渴望 **kěwàng** to yearn for [C]	周	**ZHŌU**, circle, revolution, to go around; be ubiquitous; everywhere; all; a week; surname [A] <div align="right">週</div>
态	**TÀI**, attitude [A] 态度 **tàidu** attitude [A] <div align="right">態</div>	调	**DIÀO**, tune; to transfer; **TIÁO**, to harmonize; to incite... [B] <div align="right">調</div>
游	**YÓU**, to swim; to travel; to saunter; section of a river; to travel around [A] <div align="right">遊</div>	族	**ZÚ**, race, tribe [A] 族长 **zúzhǎng** clan head
育	**YÙ**, give birth to; bring up, nourish [A]	始	**SHĬ**, to begin [A] 开始 **kāishǐ** to begin [A]
批	**PĪ**, to comment on; annotation; to mark (exam); batch; wholesale [A]	导	**DǍO**, to lead [A] 领导 **lǐngdǎo** to lead; leader [A] <div align="right">導</div>
屁	**PÌ**, gas (in the bowels); fart; (figuratively, of speech) be stupid [C] 放屁 **fàngpì** to fart; talk rubbish	排	**PÁI**, to arrange; a row; to shove, get rid of [A] 排除 **páichú** get rid of [A] 排斥 **páichì** to reject [B]
势	**SHÌ**, power; momentum; tendency; outward appearance; gesture [B] <div align="right">勢</div>	悲	**BĒI**, be sad, grieved [B] 悲痛 **bēitòng** grieved [B] 悲观 **bēiguān** be pessimistic [C]
范	**FÀN**, pattern, rule; family name [B] 范围 **fànwéi** scope [B] <div align="right">範</div>	辈	**BÈI**, a generation; kind or class; life-time [C] <div align="right">輩</div>
流	**LIÚ**, to flow; go astray; be prevalent; a current; a measure for (a person's) social class; class, ilk [A]	拍	**PĀI**, to pat, to clap; to bounce; take (a picture); send (a telegram); fawn on; a beat in music [A]

伯	**BÓ**, father's elder brother; earl, count [B] 伯母 **bómǔ** wife of father's elder brother, aunt [B]
迫	**PÒ**, to oppress, to persecute; be in difficulties [B] 迫切 **pòqiè** be urgent [B]
乘	**CHÉNG**, to ride; to take advantage of, make use of (e.g., an opportunity) [B] 乘客 **chéngkè** passenger [C]
剩	**SHÈNG**, to have left, be left over; a remnant [A] 剩余 **shèngyú** remainder [C]
寅	**YÍN**, to respect; the third "earthly branch" 寅时 **yínshí** 3-5 a.m.
演	**YǍN**, to act (in a play); to put on a show [A] 演出 **yǎnchū** perform [A] 演员 **yǎnyuán** actor, actress [B]
康	**KĀNG**, good health; family name [A] 健康 **jiànkāng** health, be healthy [A]
哈	**HĀ**, ha! ha! to blow [A] 哈欠 **hāqiàn** a yawn
师	**SHĪ**, specialist; teacher; (army) division [A] 师傅 **shīfu** journeyman [A] 師
丰	**FĒNG**, 1) be pretty, graceful, elegant; 2) be abundant, fruitful, luxuriant 豐 (2nd meanings)
奉	**FÈNG**, to give respectfully; receive orders; to revere; to believe in; to wait on [D]

逢	**FÉNG**, to meet with; to happen; whenever [B] 逢迎 **féngyíng** to fawn on; curry favor with
蜂	**FĒNG**, bees, hornets, wasps [B] 蠭
缝	**FÉNG**, to stitch or sew; **FÈNG**, seam; a crack [C]
峰	**FĒNG**, peak, summit; (camel's) hump [C] 峯
棒	**BÀNG**, bat, nightstick; be terrific — be totally cool (Beijing slang) [C]
捧	**PĚNG**, hold something in cupped hands; measure for two handfuls; praise; to support (as patron) [B]
祝	**ZHÙ**, to wish; to pray; family name [A]
节	**JIÉ**, joint; tempo; festival; section; to restrain; restraint; to economize [A] 節
汉	**HÀN**, the Han (Chinese) race; man [A] 好汉 **hǎohàn** honest man; hero 漢
脏	**ZÀNG**, viscera, entrails; **ZĀNG**, dirty [A] 心脏 **xīnzàng** heart [B] 臟
深	**SHĒN**, be deep [A] 深入 **shēnrù** to penetrate; be thoroughgoing [B]

223

探	**TÀN**, to lean out; to search out [B] 探听 **tàntīng** to ask around	燥	**ZÀO**, be dry (as, weather) [B] 燥热 **zàorè** be hot and dry
做	**ZUÒ**, to make; to be; to act as [A] 做梦 **zuòmèng** have a dream/pipe dream; dream [B]	躁	**ZÀO**, be rash, reckless [C] 性子躁 **xìngzi zào** be quick-tempered
克	**KÈ**, to conquer; gram [A]	宿	**SÙ**, to lodge; be old, be in the past; **XIǓ**, a measure for nights; night [A]
误	**WÙ**, be late; be too late for; mistake, by mistake; to lead astray [A] 誤	缩	**SUŌ**, to coil up; to bind fast; to draw in, to shorten, to shrink [B]
庭	**TÍNG**, hall, courtyard; family [A]	奶	**NǍI**, breasts; milk; to suckle [A] 奶头 **nǎitóu** (colloquial) nipple, tit 奶奶 **nǎinai** grandmother [B]
挺	**TǏNG** be straight and stiff; to hold onto; fairly; a measure for machine guns [A]	刮	**GUĀ**, to scrape; to pare; take advantage of, exploit [A] 刮脸 **guāliǎn** to shave
词	**CÍ**, word, term; statement; a *ci* (*tz'u*) poem [A] 词典 **cídiǎn** dictionary [A] 詞	室	**SHÌ**, a room [A]
桥	**QIÁO**, bridge [A] 旱桥 **hànqiáo** overpass, flyover 橋	突	**TŪ**, to stick out; to break through [A] 突出 **tūchū** breakthrough; to highlight, give prominence [A] 突然 **tūrán** suddenly, abruptly [A]
骄	**JIĀO**, a high-spirited horse; "get on your high horse," be arrogant [B] 驕	咱	**ZÁN**, I [A] 咱们 **zánmen** we (including the person spoken to) [A]
澡	**ZǍO**, to bathe [A] 洗澡 **xǐzǎo** to bathe [A]	疼	**TÉNG**, to ache; to dote on [A] 疼痛 **téngtòng** to ache [D]
操	**CĀO**, take hold of, take charge of [A] 操场 **cāochǎng** sports ground, drill field [A]	哪	**NǍ**, **NĚI**, which one? whichever; **NA**, a sentence-final particle: 啊 or 呢 + 啊 [A]

坚 堅	**JIĀN**, be firm, be strong [A] 坚定 **jiāndìng** be firm, steadfast; to strengthen [A]
脱	**TUŌ**, to take off clothes; to shed skin; to escape from [A] 脱离 **tuōlí** separate from [B]
脚	**JIǍO**, foot; kick [A] 脚步 **jiǎobù** pace, step [C]
寒	**HÁN**, be cold, wintry [A] 胆寒 **dǎnhán** be terrified (lit., have your gall-bladder chilled)
愉	**YÚ**, be happy [A] 愉快 **yúkuài** be happy [A] Distinguish from the next character and note: 忄 + 俞 is *not* = 心 + 俞.
愈	**YÙ**, to heal; to be better; the more... the more, as: 愈多愈好 **yùduō yù hǎo** the more the better [C]
握	**WÒ**, to hold fast [A] 握手 **wòshǒu** shake hands
喂	**WÈI**, to feed (child or animal); "hello!" (on the phone) [A]
炼 煉, 鍊	**LIÀN**, to melt down; to refine, to purify [A] 炼铁 **liàntiě** iron-smelting
酸	**SUĀN**, acid; to taste sour; be pedantic; be grieved
谅 諒	**LIÀNG**, to suppose; to forgive; to sympathize with
概	**GÀI**, in general [A] 概念 **gàiniàn** concept [B]
踢	**TĪ**, to kick [A] 踢皮球 **tī píqiú** kick a ball; pass the buck
嘴	**ZUǏ**, mouth, bill, spout [A] 闭嘴 **bìzuǐ** shut up!
赛 賽	**SÀI**, to compete, to rival [A] 赛马 **sàimǎ** horse race
擦	**CĀ**, to rub, wipe, brush, scrape [A] 擦澡 **cāzǎo** take a sponge bath
挤 擠	**JǏ**, to crowd, be crowded; to squeeze (e.g., a pimple) [A]
袜 襪	**WÀ**, stocking, sock [A] 袜子 **wàzi** stocking, socks [A]
骑 騎	**QÍ**, to sit astride, to ride (e.g., an animal or bicycle) [A]
础 礎	**CHǓ**, plinth [A] 础石 **chǔshí** stone base of a column
锻 鍛	**DUÀN**, forge [A] 锻炼 **duànliàn** get some exercise; to temper, toughen [C]
啡	**FĒI**, used in writing foreign words, like 咖啡 **kā-fēi** coffee [A] 吗啡 **mǎ-fēi** morphine

辅	**FǓ**, to assist; to supplement [A] 辅导 **fǔdǎo** to guide, coach [A] 輔	摩	**MÓ**, to rub; to touch; to mull over, to study [C]
践	**JIÀN**, to trample; to carry out [A] 踐	嗯	Used for exclamations: ŃG!, Ń? (doubt); Ňg, Ň (surprise); Ǹg, Ǹ, like English "Hm" [A]
焦	**JIĀO**, be scorched, burnt; be worried; a family name [C] 焦急 **jiāojí** be worried [C]	啤	**PÍ**, see below [A] 啤酒 **píjiǔ** beer [A]
蕉	**JIĀO**, name of several broadleaf plants [A] 香蕉 **xiāngjiāo** banana [A]	宴	**YÀN**, to entertain with a banquet; a banquet [A] 宴会 **yànhuì** banquet [A] 宴请 **yànqǐng** entertain [D]
瞧	**QIÁO**, (colloquial) to look, see [B] 瞧病 **qiáobìng** to consult/ examine (patient/doctor)	赢	**YÍNG**, to win; winnings, profit [A] 赢得 **yíngdé** to win [D] 贏
矛	**MÁO**, spear. SPEAR radical (155) Distinguish from 予 (775, p.156). 矛头 **máotóu** spearhead	泳	**YǑNG**, to swim [A] 游泳 **yóuyǒng** to swim [A]
橘	**JÚ**, tangerine [A] 橘子 **júzi** tangerine	窗	**CHUĀNG**, window [A] 窗户 **chuānghu** a window
林	**LÍN**, forest; a family name [B] 树林 **shùlín** woods [B]	持	**CHÍ**, to support; to grasp; to hold; to manage; to restrain [A] 坚持 **jiānchí** to persist in 持久 **chíjiǔ** enduring, lasting
麻	**MÁ**, hemp [A]. HEMP radical (221) 麻烦 **máfan** be troublesome; to pester [A]	般	**BĀN**, to transport; to distribute, to classify, classification, category [A]
嘛	**MA**, sentence-final particle indicating obvious logic, obviousness [A]	搬	**BĀN**, to lift (a heavy object) palms up (not above the head); to transport [A]
磨	**MÓ**, to rub; to grind; to wear down; to pester; to get obliterated; to dawdle [B]	顿	**DÙN**, to pause; to prepare; suddenly; a measure for actions and for dishes (food items) [A] 頓

互	HÙ, mutually; each other [A] 互相 hùxiāng on each other [A]
抽	CHŌU, to draw out; to smoke (tobacco); to levy; to whip; to shrink; a conscript [A]
掉	DIÀO, to fall, to let fall; to lose; to fade; to remove (a stain); verb-suffix: "away, out" [A]
罢 (罷)	BÀ, to cease, to quit; BĀ, a sentence-final particle (= 吧, 303, p. 61) [C]
摆 (擺)	BǍI, to swing; pendulum; to display; to put in order; to put [A]
杯 (盃)	BĒI, cup, glass, goblet or other small vessel to drink from; a measure for these [A]
磁	CÍ, be magnetic; porcelain, china [A] 磁带 cídài magnetic tape [A] 磁铁 cítiě magnet
迟 (遲)	CHÍ, be late [A] 迟到 chídào arrive late 迟早 chízǎo sooner or later
卓	No pronunciation. Radical (203) "Side of 朝 cháo" (see next character)
朝	CHÁO, dynasty; imperial; reign; to face; visit a superior [A]. ZHĀO, morning
潮	CHÁO, tide; be damp [C] 低潮 dīcháo low tide

繁	FÁN, be complicated, be numerous [B] 繁荣 fánróng be prosperous; make prosperous [B]
骨	GǓ, bone. BONE radical (214) [B] 骨干 gǔgàn backbone (lit. and figuratively) [C]
刃	RÈN, knife edge, blade [D] Note the "knife" in 刃。 刀刃 dāorèn knife-blade; crucial point [D]
忍	RĚN, to bear, endure [B] 忍受 rěnshòu to endure [C] 忍不住 rěnbuzhù be unable to bear [C]
坡	PŌ, slope, bank [B] 坡度 pōdù gradient
波	BŌ, a wave; to flow [C] 波动 bōdòng to undulate [D]
婆	PÓ, old woman; mother-in-law; step-mother [C]
疲	PÍ, be worn out [B] 疲劳 píláo be worn out [B]
绝 (絕)	JUÉ, to break off; (before a negative) very [B]
积 (積)	JĪ, to accumulate [B] 积极 jījí be positive; be energetic [B] 积累 jīlěi to accumulate [B]
似	SÌ, to resemble (also pronounced shì in some combinations) [B]

227

野	**YĚ**, be wild, uncivilized [B] 野心 **yěxīn** be overly ambitious [D]	盯	**DĪNG**, to stare at [C]
印	**YÌN**, to print; to tally, agree; family name [B] 印象 **yìnxiàng** impression [B]	列	**LIÈ**, line, rank, to line up, to rank; each; a measure for trains [B]
功	**GŌNG**, achievement; effectiveness; hard work [B]	烈	**LIÈ**, to blaze; be brilliant or famous [B] 烈士 **lièshì** a martyr; a fighter for the Good Cause [C]
攻	**GŌNG**, to attack [B] 攻破 **gōngpò** to break through 攻击 **gōngjī** to attack; to villify [C] 攻克 **gōngkè** to capture [C]	裂	**LIÈ**, to split [C] 分裂 **fēnliè** to split
贡	**GÒNG**, tax; to tax; contribution; to announce [B] 貢	阵	**ZHÈN**, a measure for wind-storms or rain-storms [B] 陣
项	**XIÀNG**, nape of the neck; a measure for articles in documents, or items [B] 項	秘	**MÌ**, be secret, be private [B] 秘书 **mìshū** secretary [C]
致	**ZHÌ**, to send; to cause [B] 致意 **zhìyì** to pay respects to	密	**MÌ**, be secluded; be deep, secret, mysterious, still [B] 秘密 **mìmì** be secret, clandestine, confidential [B]
订	**DÌNG**, to investigate; to decide; to revise for publication [B]	蜜	**MÌ**, honey [B] 蜜蜂 **mìfēng** honeybee [B] 蜜月 **mìyuè** honeymoon
顶	**DĬNG**, top of the head; to carry on the head; be lofty; to oppose; very [B] 頂	泌	**MÌ**, to secrete [C]
厅	**TĪNG**, hall, room; department of a provincial government [B] 廳	待	**DÀI**, to deal with; to wait for [B] 待遇 **dàiyù** treatment; remuneration [C]
钉	**DĪNG**, nail [C] 钉帽 **dīngmào** head of a nail 钉子 **dīngzi** nail; snag 釘	班	**BĀN**, a measure for classes (students), squads, and trips (flights, trains); shift, troupe [B]

228

添	**TIĀN**, to add on [B] 增添 **zēngtiān** to add (D)
惊	**JĪNG**, to scare [B] 惊人 **jīngrén** be amazing, shocking 驚
猜	**CĀI**, to guess [B] 猜想 **cāixiǎng** to suppose, guess
材	**CÁI**, material; ability; "genius;" coffin [B] Distinguish from 村 (p. 220a)
财	**CÁI**, wealth [C] 财产 **cáichǎn** property [C] 財
暗	**ÀN**, be dark [B] 暗暗 **àn'àn** secretly, to yourself [C] 暗淡 **àndàn** be dim, gloomy [D]
拔	**BÁ**, to pull up, to pull out [B] 拔除 **báchú** to remove
灭	**MIÈ**, to extinguish, to go out (a fire, lights); to wipe out [B] 滅
挥	**HUĪ**, to wave around; to wipe off; to command (e.g., an army); to disperse [B] 揮
败	**BÀI**, defeat [B] 腐败 **fǔbài** be putrid, to rot; to corrupt
厌	**YÀN**, to detest, be fed up with [B] 讨厌 **tǎoyàn** repugnant; troublesome [B] 厭

则	**ZÉ**, and then ... [B] 则 helps with the sound in several characters. See below. 則
测	**CÈ**, to estimate, to guess [B] 测量 **cèliáng** to survey [C] 測
厕	**CÈ**, toilet [B] 厕所 **cèsuǒ** toilet [B] 廁
侧	**CÈ**, side; to lean aside; to side with someone; secondary [C] 侧面 **cèmiàn** side, flank; aspect [D] 側
伤	**SHĀNG**, wound, to wound [B] 悲伤 **bēishāng** be sorrowful [D] 傷
述	**SHÙ**, to tell a story; to transmit [B]
束	**CÌ**, THORN radical (167) Distinguish from 束 "bundle" (745, p. 150).
刺	**CÌ**, thorn, splinter, fish-bone; to stab, to pierce; to murder; be "thorny," unpleasant [B]
策	**CÈ**, plan, policy; whip [B] 策动 **cèdòng** to instigate; to rouse
兵	**BĪNG**, soldier; weapons [B] 兵法 **bīngfǎ** art of war
乒	**PĪNG**, bang! (onomatopoetic); see 兵 (next character) [B]

乒	**PĀNG**, in 乒乓 **pīngpāng**, ping-pong [B] 乒乓球 **pīngpāngqiú** ping-pong [B]	捕	**BŬ**, to seize, to arrest [B] 捕获 **bǔhuò** to capture
抄	**CHĀO**, to copy; to confiscate; to parboil [B]. 少 (380, p. 77) gives the sound in several characters (below).	补	**BŬ**, to mend, patch up; to fill in [B] 添补 **tiānbǔ** to replenish 補
吵	**CHǍO**, to quarrel; to make noise, disturb with noise [B] 吵闹 **chǎonào** to wrangle [D]	薄	**BÓ, BÁO**, be thin, be weak [B]
炒	**CHǍO**, to fry [C] 炒冷饭 **chǎo lěngfàn** to rehash	博	**BÓ**, be broad or comprehensive (in knowledge); of all kinds; to win, to gain [C]
钞	**CHĀO**, paper money; collected writings [C] 钞票 **chāopiào** banknote [C]	宝	**BǍO**, be precious; "your" (polite) [B] 宝贵 **bǎoguì** be valuable; regard as valuable [B] 寶
沙	**SHĀ**, sand, gravel; to sound hoarse, be hoarse; a family name [B]	陪	**PÉI**, to keep someone company; with [B] 陪同 **péitóng** to accompany
妙	**MIÀO**, be slender, be beautiful, be graceful; be marvelous; be clever [C]	赔	**PÉI**, to pay damages; to lose money (in business) [B] 賠
秒	**MIǍO**, beard of grain; smallest part; a measure for seconds (of time or angles) [C]	币	**BÌ**, currency, coin; silk; gifts [B] 外币 **wàibì** foreign money 幣
藏	**ZÀNG**, stash, treasure; Tibet; **CÁNG**, to hide, to store [B]	泼	**PŌ**, to throw liquid out of a container; to spill; be shrewish [B] 潑
夺	**DUÓ**, take by force [B] The old form: a bird escaping a snatching hand. 奪	拨	**BŌ**, to move (as with a fingertip); to set, adjust, transfer [C] 撥
奋	**FÈN**, to exert yourself; to lift up [B]. Karlgren says "fly away over the fields" (*AD* 380). 奮	废	**FÈI**, to abolish, discard; be crippled, useless [C] 废除 **fèichú** to abolish, annul [C] 廢

挨	**ĀI**, to crowd against; in sequence; **ÁI**, to delay; to suffer [B]	逼	**BĪ**, to press, crowd, annoy [B] 逼迫 **bīpò** to compel [D]
唉	**ĀI**, Yes? Right!; (as a response): **ĀI**, **ÀI**, Alas! That's too bad! [C]	插	**CHĀ**, to stick in, to insert, to interrupt [B]
册	**CÈ**, booklet, album; a measure for copies (of a book) [B] 小册子 **xiǎo cèzi** booklet	傲	**ÀO**, be arrogant [B] 傲慢 **àomàn** be haughty
冰	**BĪNG**, ice [B]	碑	**BĒI**, a memorial tablet, monument, gravestone [B]
折	**ZHÉ**, to snap off; discount; **SHÉ**, be broken; lose money; **ZHĒ**, to spill [B]. Distinguish from the next two characters.	鼻	**BÍ**, nose. BIG NOSE radical (226). Called "big nose" to distinguish it from 619, p. 124 [B]
拆	**CHĀI**, to take apart [B] Distinguish from preceding and following characters. 拆除 **chāichú** to demolish	仓	**CĀNG**, granary 仓 helps with the sound (with the rhyme) in several characters (below). 倉
析	**XĪ**, to split wood; to divide up; to analyze [B] Compare with preceding characters. 析义 **xīyì** analyze the meaning	枪	**QIĀNG**, spear, pistol, rifle [B] Distinguish from the next character. 槍
晰	**XĪ**, be clear, be distinct [C]	抢	**QIǍNG**, to rob, snatch [B] Distinguish from the preceding character. 搶
柴	**CHÁI**, firewood; family name [B] 柴草 **cháicǎo** firewood	创	**CHUÀNG**, to begin; **CHUĀNG**, to wound [B] 創
闭	**BÌ**, to close, to stop up [B] 闭合 **bìhé** to close 闭幕 **bìmù** the curtain falls; to end, conclude [D] 閉	苍	**CĀNG**, sky; be sky blue; be pale; be gray; lush vegetation [C] 蒼
笨	**BÈN**, be stupid, be clumsy [B] 笨蛋 **bèndàn** a fool [D]	舱	**CĀNG**, cabin; (space flight) module [C] 客舱 **kècāng** passenger cabin 艙

养	**YǍNG**, to support (one's dependents); to nourish [B] 抱养 **bàoyǎng** adopt a child 養	竟	**JÌNG**, to end; in the end, after all [B] Distinguish from the preceding character. Note use as phonetic (below). 究竟 **jiūjìng** outcome
强	**QIÁNG**, be strong; strength; **QIǍNG**, to force or to compel; **JIÀNG**, be stubborn [B]	境	**JÌNG**, a field's edge; borders; region; circmstances [B] 土 "earth" for meaning.
盗	**DÀO**, to rob, robber [B] 盗用 **dàoyòng** to embezzle	镜	**JÌNG**, mirror, lens [B] 镜子 **jìngzi** mirror; (colloquial) eyeglasses [B] 镜头 **jìngtóu** lens [D] 鏡
狗	**GǑU**, dog [B] 走狗 **zǒugǒu** "running dog," stooge, toady [D]	显	**XIǍN**, be visible; to show; be noteworthy [B] 顯
脑	**NǍO**, brain [B] Distinguish from 胸 (p. 246a). 头脑 **tóunǎo** brain [C] 电脑 **diànǎo** computer [C] 腦	湿	**SHĪ**, be wet [B] 湿潮 **shīcháo** be damp [C] 湿气 **shīqì** dampness, moisture 濕
弄	**NÒNG**, to do; to handle; to make; to play with, fool with [B]	泥	**NÍ**, mud; **NÌ**, to daub with mud or plaster [B]
碎	**SUÌ**, be smashed, be in bits and pieces [B]	关	**JUǍN**, roll, rolled rice dumpling. ROLL radical (158) Note 关 in the next characters.
醉	**ZUÌ**, be drunk [C] 傅奕,青山白云人也。以醉死。呜呼! **Fú Yì qīngshān báiyún rén yě.Yǐzuì sǐ. Wūhū!***	卷	**JUÀN**, roll; scroll; section or chapter; **JUǍN**, to roll up [B] (JUǍN "to roll up") 捲
醒	**XǏNG**, to wake up [B] 醒酒 **xǐngjiǔ** to sober up	圈	**QUĀN**, circle; to encircle; **JUǍN**, to imprison; **JUÀN**, pen, fold (e.g., of sheep) [B]
牌	**PÁI**, placard [B] 路牌 **lùpái** signpost, road sign	倦	**JUÀN**, be tired, be weak [C] 疲倦 **píjuàn** be tired, be weak [C]
竞	**JÌNG**, to quarrel [B] 竞争 **jìngzhēng** to compete; competition 競	拳	**QUÁN**, fist; to tuck in; a measure for punches (with the fist) [C] 握拳 **wòquán** make a fist

*Fu Yi loved the blue mountains and white clouds. He died drunk, alas! (Fu's epitaph, written by Fu himself (555-639 A.D.))

腾	**TÉNG**, to make room for; to ride up on; **TĒNG**, Thump! (onomatopoetic) 騰	丽	**LÌ**, be beautiful [B] 麗
梦	**MÈNG**, dream [B] 梦想 **mèngxiǎng** to dream of; fantasize [D] 夢	庙	**MIÀO**, temple [B] 廟
贺	**HÈ**, to send a present with congratulations; to congratulate [B] 賀	辟	**PÌ**, to open up (e.g., territory); be incisive; to refute [B] Compare with the next 3 characters.
伞	**SǍN**, umbrella [B] 雨伞 **yǔsǎn** umbrella 傘	壁	**BÌ**, wall, screen [B]
诗	**SHĪ**, poem, a **shi** poem; poetry [B] 詩	避	**BÌ**, to flee from [B]
渐	**JIÀN**, gradually [B] 渐显 **jiànxiǎn** fade in (movie term) 漸	譬	**PÌ**, example; analogy [C] 譬如 **pìrú** for example [C]
途	**TÚ**, road, trip; career [B] 途中 **túzhōng** en route	招	**ZHĀO**, to beckon to; to invite; to recruit; to tease; to pass a disease to; to confess [B]
弱	**RUÒ**, be weak, [B] 薄弱 **bóruò** be frail [C]	超	**CHĀO**, to catch up to, to surpass [B] 超级市场 **chāojí-shìchǎng** supermarket
妻	**QĪ**, wife [B]	针	**ZHĒN**, needle, pin [B] 针对 **zhēnduì** be aimed at [B] 針
引	**YǏN**, to lead, to draw out [B] 引起 **yǐnqǐ** to give rise to [B]	季	**JÌ**, season (of the year); family name [B] Distinguish from first and fifth characters following.
赞	**ZÀN**, to approve; to praise, eulogize [B] 赞美 **zànměi** to praise, eulogize 讚	秀	**XIÙ**, grain in the ear; flourish; be elegant; family name [B] Compare with the preceding character and fourth character below.

233

绣	**XIÙ**, to embroider [C] "Silk" for meaning. 绣花 **xiùhuā** to embroider 繡	依	**YĪ**, to agree with; to forgive; according to [B]
透	**TÒU**, to go through [B] 辶 (90, p. 19) for meaning. 湿透 **shītòu** to get drenched	益	**YÌ**, profit [B]
锈	**XIÙ**, rust; to rust [C] "Gold" (metals) for meaning. 銹	众	**ZHÒNG**, crowd [B] "Three's a crowd" may be a mnemonic for English. 眾
委	**WĚI**, to appoint; to abandon; really [B] Distinguish from fourth and fifth characters above.	品	**PĬN**, good; quality, rank; personality; to judge the quality, to sample [B]
盘	**PÁN**, plate, dish; to coil up; to move; to sell; price; a measure for games [B] 键盘 **jiànpán** keyboard 盤	区	**QŪ**, to be small; to distinguish between; region, district [B] 區
职	**ZHÍ**, oversee; job, duty [B] 述职 **shùzhí** to report on your work 職	缶	**FǑU**, crock. CROCK radical (175)
环	**HUÁN**, to encircle; ring, bracelet [B] 環	罐	**GUÀN**, jar, can [B] 罐头 **guàntóu** tin can [B]
质	**ZHÌ**, disposition; substance; to question; (bookish), to pawn, pledge [B] 質	灌	**GUÀN**, to sprinkle; to irrigate; to record (on tape or disc); to assemble [C]
群	**QÚN**, herd, crowd [B]. This character may appear in the form 羣.	尾	**WĚI**, tail [B] 尾巴 **wěiba** tail [B]
尽	**JÌN**, to exhaust; **JǏN**, as much as possible; to put first [B] 盡	皇	**HUÁNG**, emperor, be imperial [B]
达	**DÁ**, to reach [B] 达到 **dádào** to achieve, reach [B] 达成 **dáchéng** to reach (as, an agreement) [C] 達	帝	**DÌ**, emperor; supreme ruler [B] 皇帝 **huángdì** emperor [B]

蹄	**TÍ**, hoof [C] 足 "foot" gives the meaning; **dì** 帝 (above) the sound.	却	**QUÈ**, but, however; step back, cause to step back, i.e., drive back [B]
敌	**DÍ**, enemy [B] 敌人 **dírén** enemy [B] <div align="right">敵</div>	网	**WǍNG**, net, to net [B] 网球 **wǎngqiú** tennis [B] <div align="right">網</div>
滴	**DĪ**, drop, to drip [B] 滴答 **dīdā** tick-tock (in some dialects (e.g., Cantonese) = "*dik-dâp*")	胃	**WÈI**, stomach [B] 胃口 **wèikǒu** appetite
摘	**ZHĀI**, to pick (flowers, fruit); to criticize [B]	谓	**WÈI**, to talk about; to call; to say [B] <div align="right">謂</div>
压	**YĀ**, to push down [B] 压力 **yālì** pressure [C] <div align="right">壓</div>	资	**ZĪ**, fee, capital, resources; talent; to aid [B] <div align="right">資</div>
勇	**YǑNG**, be brave [B] 勇敢 **yǒnggǎn** be brave [B]	姿	**ZĪ**, posture, carriage [C]
守	**SHǑU**, to guard [B] 守备 **shǒubèi** do guard duty	格	**GÉ**, ruled line or space (on paper); category; compartment [B]
抗	**KÀNG**, to resist, oppose [B] 抗争 **kàngzhēng** to resist	堆	**DUĪ**, to pile; pile; crowd [B] 土 "earth" for meaning.
坑	**KĒNG**, pit, shallow hole; to cheat somebody [C]	维	**WÉI**, to maintain, to hold together [B] <div align="right">維</div>
独	**DÚ**, alone [B] 独立 **dúlì** be independent <div align="right">獨</div>	某	**MǑU**, certain, some [B] 某些 **mǒuxiē** certain, some [C]
烛	**ZHÚ**, candle; to illuminate [C] 烛心 **zhúxīn** candle wick <div align="right">燭</div>	煤	**MÉI**, coal [B] 煤气 **méiqì** coal gas [B] 煤油 **méiyóu** coal oil, kerosene

谋	**MÓU**, to find (a job); to plot, a plot [B] 谋	律	**LÙ**, law [B] 法律 **fǎlù** law [B]
矿	**KUÀNG**, mine (for minerals) [B] 礦	序	**XÙ**, introduction (to a book); order, sequence [B]
鼓	**GǓ**, drum, to drum. DRUM radical (224) [B]	际	**JÌ**, boundary; occasion; at the time that … [B] 際
损	**SǓN**, be cruel; be sarcastic; to damage [B] 損	弹	**DÀN**, a bullet; **TÁN**, to hurl; to pluck (a musical instrument) [B] 彈
队	**DUÌ**, squadron; team; file (of people); a measure for formations [B] 隊	仅	**JǏN**, barely [B] 仅仅 **jǐnjǐn** barely, merely [B] 僅
粮	**LIÁNG**, provisions (food) [B] 粮食 **liángshí** grain [B] 糧	扩	**KUÒ**, to expand [B] 扩大 **kuòdà** to enlarge, expand [B] 擴
丈	**ZHÀNG**, ten Chinese feet (= 144 inches); wife's parents; husband [B]	亚	**YÀ**, be inferior; used to write foreign words. INFERIOR radical (168) [C] 亞
仗	**ZHÀNG**, (bookish), weapons; to hold a weapon; to rely on; war [C] 打仗 **dàzhàng** go to war [C]	严	**YÁN**, be airtight, be strict; family name [B] 嚴
悔	**HUǏ**, to repent; to turn away [B] 后悔 **hòuhuǐ** to regret; to feel remorse [B]	恶	**È**, be evil; be fierce; **WÙ**, consider evil, hateful [C] 好恶 **hàowù** likes and dislikes 惡
匀	**YÚN**, be evenly distributed; to spare (space, time, money) [C]	壶	**HÚ**, kettle, jug [B] 茶壶 **cháhú** teapot 壺
均	**JŪN**, be equal, be fair [B] 平均 **píngjūn** average; on average; equally [B]	侵	**QĪN**, to move in on, encroach [B] 侵入 **qīnrù** to invade 侵害 **qīnhài** to encroach [D]

浸	JÌN, to soak, to immerse [C]
扫	SÀO, broom; SǍO, to sweep [B] 扫除 sǎochú to wipe out [D] 掃
妇	FÙ (woman with broom); wife; woman [B] 夫妇 fūfù husband and wife 婦
略	LÜÈ, to omit; be simple, be rough; sketch, plan [B] 侵略 qīnlüè aggression [B]
缺	QUĒ, to lack [B] 缺课 quēkè to cut class; to play truant 缺点 quēdiǎn weak point, defect [B]
宣	XUĀN, proclaim; family name [B] 宣传 xuānchuán to propagandize (for) [B]
终	ZHŌNG, end; to the end of [B] 终究 zhōngjiū after all [D] 終
混	HÙN, to mix up; to fool around; HÚN, see below [B] 混蛋 húndàn scoundrel
棍	GÙN, stick, club; bad guy [C]
阶	JIĒ, step (on a stairway); rank, class [B] 階
恨	HÈN, to hate, to regret [B] 恨不得 hènbudé to want badly to [C]

获	HUÒ, to grab [B] 获得 huòdé to obtain [B] 獲
源	YUÁN, spring (of water) [B]
秩	ZHÌ, order, arrangement [B] 秩序 zhìxù order, sequence [B]
灾	ZĀI, disaster [B] 旱灾 hànzāi drought [D] 災
肥	FÉI, be fat; be fertile (soil); be loose, be baggy; fertilizer [B]
朱	ZHŪ, bright red; a family name [C supplement] 朱红 zhūhóng be vermilion; bright red
珠	ZHŪ, pearl, bead [B] 算盘珠 suànpanzhū abacus beads
括	KUÒ, to embrace, to include [B]
梁	LIÁNG, horizontal beam, bridge, top-handle, ridge; a family name [B]. Distinguish from the next character below.
粱	LIÁNG, (bookish) millet; birdseed; good food [C] Distinguish from the previous cha- racter. Here, lower part of character = rice, not tree.
袖	XIÙ, sleeve [B] 袖口 xiùkǒu cuff (of sleeve)

237

岛	**DǍO**, island [B] 半岛 **bàndǎo** peninsula [C] 島	遥	**YÁO**, be far off; be long [C] 遥远 **yáoyuǎn** be far away [C]
弯	**WĀN**, to bend, a bend [B] 弯曲 **wānqū** be meandering, winding 彎	尊	**ZŪN**, respect; "your" (polite); measure for Buddhist statues and for cannon (artillery) [B]
孔	**KǑNG**, small hole; Confucius; a family name [B] 钻孔 **zuànkǒng** to drill a hole	遵	**ZŪN**, to obey, to comply with [B]
灰	**HUĪ**, ashes, dust; be ash-colored, gray [B] 灰心 **huīxīn** lose heart [C]	冲	**CHŌNG**, to crash through; thoroughfare; **CHÒNG**, to face; strong; tactless [B] 衝
恢	**HUĪ**, to extend, be great [B] 恢复 **huīfù** to restore [B]	肿	**ZHǑNG**, to swell up [C] 腫
斯	**SĪ**, (bookish) this; used to write foreign words; family name [C]	配	**PÈI**, to match up, go well with; to mate (said of animals) [B]
撕	**SĪ**, to tear up [B]	献	**XIÀN**, to give [B] 献计 **xiànjì** to give advice 獻
犯	**FÀN**, to commit an offense; have a recurrence of or revert to; a criminal [B]	耐	**NÀI**, to endure, to bear [B] 耐心 **nàixīn** be patient [B]
刷	**SHUĀ**, a brush, to brush, to give someone the brush-off; to cut class [B]	巨	**JÙ**, chief, large, great [B]. Picture of a carpenter's square, with handle. The radical = 匚 (15)
摇	**YÁO**, to shake, to rock, to swing to and fro [B]	拒	**JÙ**, to refuse, resist [B] 拒绝 **jùjué** to reject [B]
谣	**YÁO**, folk-song, ballad; rumor [C] 民谣 **mínyáo** folk-song 謠	距	**JÙ**, be separated from, be distant from; distance [B] 距离 **jùlí** distance; be away from [B]

矩	**JŬ**, carpenter's square; standard, rule, custom [C] This is 巨, above, reclarified with 矢 "arrow" (82, p. 17).
兼	**JIĀN**, to put together [C] A hand grasps and pulls things together. 兼职 **jiānzhí** hold two jobs
歉	**QIÀN**, apology; crop failure, bad harvest [B]. The 欠 radical (244, p. 49) connotes deficiency. 抱歉 **bàoqiàn** apologetic; be sorry [B]
嫌	**XIÁN**, to dislike; to suspect [C] 嫌恶 **xiánwù** to loathe
赚	**ZHUÀN**, to make money; profit [C] To put cowries together. 賺
具	**JÙ**, tool; to write out; (bookish) a measure for dead bodies and machines [B]
俱	**JÙ**, be complete; every [B] 俱乐部 **jùlèbù** club (social group) [B]
趁	**CHÈN**, to chase; to turn to one's own use; according to [B]
珍	**ZHĒN**, precious object; be precious [C]
诊	**ZHĚN**, to examine medically [C] 診
亩	**MŬ**, Chinese acre ("mou"): 733½ square yards [B] 畝

款	**KUĂN**, sum of money; article (in treaty, contract); inscription; to entertain [B]
承	**CHÉNG**, to inherit; to manage; to admit [B] 承认 **chéngrèn** to recognize, acknowledge [B]
姻	**YĪN**, bride; marriage connections [B]
托	**TUŌ**, to carry on the palm; to rely on; to ask a favor; to entrust [B] 託 (last two meanings)
疑	**YÍ**, to mistrust [B] 疑心 **yíxīn** suspicion [C]
移	**YÍ**, to shift [B] 移动 **yídòng** to shift [B]
黾	**MǏN**, toad. TOAD radical (207) 黽
绳	**SHÉNG**, string [B] 繩
蝇	**YÍNG**, fly (insect) [C] 蠅
庄	**ZHUĀNG**, be serene; hamlet; store; dealer (cards); family name [B] 莊
稳	**WĚN**, be steady; definite, "You can depend on it." [B] 穩

239

隐 隱	**YǏN**, to hide [C] 隐约 **yǐnyuē** be indistinct, dim [C] 隐藏 **yǐncáng** to hide [D]	伴	**BÀN**, to keep someone company, companion [C] 陪伴 **péibàn** to keep company
含	**HÁN**, to hold something in your mouth; to contain [B] 含义 **hányì** implication [D]	畔	**PÀN**, bank (e.g., of a river); edge [C]
肃 肅	**SÙ**, to command respect, to respect [B]	喷 噴	**PĒN**, to spurt, to puff, to spray; **PÈN**, puff [B]
优 優	**YŌU**, to excel; actor [B]	愤 憤	**FÈN**, zeal, ardor; be exasperated with; be very angry [B]
扰 擾	**RǍO**, to annoy [B] 打扰 **dǎrǎo** to annoy [B]	浮	**FÚ**, to float; be flighty, be insubstantial; excess; **FÙ**, to swim [B]
苗	**MIÁO**, sprout; jet of flame; vein of ore; progeny; Miao people; vaccine; family name [C]	搭	**DĀ**, to lay across; to build (for temporary use); to travel by; to add, "plus" [B]
描	**MIÁO**, to trace over [B] 描画 **miáohuà** to depict 描写 **miáoxiě** to describe [B]	塔	**TǍ**, pagoda, tower [B]
猫 貓	**MĀO**, cat [B] 猫叫 **māojiào** purring	端	**DUĀN**, to hold/carry with both hands; be upright; reason; beginning; tip (end)* [B]
巧	**QIǍO**, be ingenious; be timely, opportune [B]	喘	**CHUǍN**, to gasp for breath, breathe heavily; asthma [C] 喘气 **chuǎnqì** to pant [C]
墨	**MÒ**, ink; be inky; family name [B] "黑" + "土" = "墨" 墨水 **mòshuǐ** ink; learning [B]	毯	**TǍN**, rug [B] 地毯 **dìtǎn** carpet [C]
胖	**PÀNG**, be fat (obese) [B] 胖子 **pàngzi** fatso [D]	梯	**TĪ**, ladder, stairs [B] 电梯 **diàntī** elevator [B]

* 四端: the four beginning points of social order in Confucianism, according to Mencius: 仁 (450), 义 (1020), 礼 (591), and 智 (1023).

吐	**TǓ, TÙ**, to spit out, to vomit [B] "口" for meaning, 土 **tǔ** for sound.	构	**GÒU**, see below; sometimes pronounced **JŬ** [B] 构造 **gòuzào** structure; tectonic [B] 構
肚	**DÙ**, belly; **DǓ**, tripe [B] 月 "meat" for meaning. 一肚气 **yídù qì** be very angry (= a belly of fire)	钩	**GŌU**, a hook; to hook; a check mark to crochet [C]
狼	**LÁNG**, wolf [B] 狼狗 **lánggǒu** wolfhound	夸	**KUĀ**, to praise, to boast [C] 夸张 **kuāzhāng** exaggerate 誇
浪	**LÀNG**, waves, breakers; be undisciplined, be reckless [B]	跨	**KUÀ**, a step; to straddle; to extend through; to carry something hanging at your side [B]
龙	**LÓNG**, dragon. DRAGON radical (137) 龍	垮	**KUǍ**, to collapse [C] 累垮了 **lèikuǎ le** be exhausted from overwork
虑	**LÙ**, be anxious;to plan [B] "虍" over "心" = "虑" (be anxious) 慮	恳	**KĚN**, to beseech; earnestly [B] 恳求 **kěnqiú** to implore [D] 懇
拦	**LÁN**, to stop someone from doing something; to enclose; to separate [B] 攔	猴	**HÓU**, monkey [B]
烂	**LÀN**, be tender (from cooking); soggy; be rotten or infected; to glisten [B] 爛	喉	**HÓU**, throat [C] 喉结 **hóujié** Adam's apple
勾	**GŌU**, hook; to involve another person in wrong-doing; to cancel (as, a debt); to remind [C]	稼	**JIÀ**, husbandry; grain; to sow [B]
购	**GÒU**, to buy [B] 购买 **gòumǎi** to buy [C] 購	嫁	**JIÀ**, get married (be a bride); give (a daughter) in marriage [C]
沟	**GŌU**, gutter, ditch; to connect [C] 溝	劲	**JÌN**, strength, energy, spirit; **JÌNG**, be strong [B] 用劲 **yòngjìn** to work hard 勁

夾	**JIĀ**, to press (between two things, like chopsticks, tongs), to squeeze [B] 夾	霜	**SHUĀNG**, frost [C] 霜害 **shuānghài** frostbite
峽	**XIÁ**, gorge [C] "Mountain" for meaning. 海峡 **hǎixiá** strait [C] 峽	微	**WĒI**, be tiny, be small, be slight [B] 稍微 **shāowēi** a tiny bit, a trifle [B]
械	**XIÈ**, tool; weapon; (bookish) shackles, fetters [B] 机械 **jīxiè** machine, mechanism [B]	填	**TIÁN**, to fill, to stuff full [B] 填写 **tiánxiě** to fill in, write [D]
绕	**RÀO**, wind a thing around another; go around; detour; sometimes **RǍO** [B] 繞	慎	**SHÈN**, be attentive, be careful [C]
饶	**RÁO**, let somebody get away with something; to give away [C] 饒	镇	**ZHÈN**, rural market town; to press down; to be calm; to cool [C] 鎮
浇	**JIĀO**, to sprinkle; to wet down; to trickle; to insinuate yourself [C] 澆	彻	**CHÈ**, to penetrate; be thorough [B] 彻底 **chèdǐ** be thorough [B] 徹
稍	**SHĀO**, soldier's ration; a little bit [B] 稍许 **shāoxǔ** a little bit	撒	**SĂ**, scatter; **SĀ**, to release [B] Distinguish from the next character (look at the middle-top).
欣	**XĪN**, be happy [C] 欣赏 **xīnshǎng** to appreciate [C] 欢欣 **huānxīn** be happy	撤	**CHÈ**, to take away [C] 撤除 **chèchú** to take away Distinguish from the preceding character (look at the middle-top).
掀	**XIĀN**, to lift to one side; to raise up; to open; to whisk away [B]	臭	**CHÒU**, to stink; be conceited [B]
型	**XÍNG**, earthen mold for casting; model, pattern [B]	牲	**SHĒNG**, cattle; sacrificial animal [B] "牛" for meaning, 生 **shēng** for sound.
箱	**XIĀNG**, box, case [B] 冰箱 **bīngxiāng** icebox	率	**LÜ**; a suffix: "rate;" [B]. **SHUÀI**, to lead, be led; generally

摔	**SHUĀI**, to throw down; to lose your balance and fall; to plunge [B]	仍	**RÉNG**, as before, still [B] 仍然 **réngrán** still, yet [B] 仍旧 **réngjiù** to remain the same; still [C]
甩	**SHUĂI**, to swing; to throw; to leave behind, escape from (as, pursuers) [B]	瓜	**GUĀ**, melon. MELON radical (151) [B] 西瓜 **xīguā** watermelon [B]
糟	**ZĀO**, be pickled; be rotten, ready to fall apart [B] 糟心 **zāoxīn** be vexed	污	**WŪ**, filth; stagnant water; be foul; to befoul [B] 污水 **wūshuǐ** polluted water [C]
遭	**ZĀO**, to revolve; turn or revolution; to meet with; chance [B]	池	**CHÍ**, pool; space with raised sides; family name [B] 电池 **diànchí** battery
瘦	**SHÒU**, be emaciated; be tight; be poor (as, soil) [B] 枯瘦 **kūshòu** be skinny	扣	**KÒU**, to detain; to deduct; to invert (cup, bowl, etc.); to latch; a measure for a ten percent discount [B]
嫂	**SĂO**, older brother's wife; polite address for a married woman about your own age [B]	尖	**JIĀN**, be sharp [B] 尖利 **jiānlì** be sharp 尖子 **jiānzi** the greatest, the cream of the crop [C]
搜	**SŌU**, to investigate [C] 搜集 **sōují** to gather [C]	劣	**LIÈ**, be vile [C] 粗劣 **cūliè** be shoddy
艘	**SŌU**, a measure for boats and ships [C] 三艘汽船 **sānsōu qìchuán** three steamships	企	**QĬ**, to stand on tiptoe; to expect [B] 企求 **qǐqiú** to hanker after
映	**YÌNG**, be bright; to reflect [B] 映照 **yìngzhào** shine on	朵	**DUŎ**, flower; a measure for flowers and clouds [B] 朵儿 **duǒr** a flower
秧	**YĀNG**, rice shoot, sprout; the young (of animals) [C]	躲	**DUŎ**, to dodge; to hide from, to hide [B] 躲避 **duǒbì** to dodge, hide yourself [D]
扔	**RĒNG**, to throw; to throw away [B] 扔下 **rēngxià** to abandon; to leave behind	伙	**HUŎ**, 1) mess (food); 2) partner-(ship); to join; measure for groups [B] 夥 (for 2nd meanings)

243

伍	**WǓ**, five (used in documents for 五); file of five; company; family name [B]	吊	**DIÀO**, to hang; to raise or lower on a rope; to condole with; to revoke; a crane (machine) [B]
沉	**CHÉN**, be heavy; sink [B]. Sometimes printed as 沈. 沉醉 **chénzuì** get "high" (on experience or alcohol)	皂	**ZÀO**, be black; soap; yamen runner [B] 肥皂 **féizào** soap [C]
址	**ZHǏ**, site [B] 地址 **dìzhǐ** address [B]	肩	**JIĀN**, the shoulder [B] 肩负 **jiānfù** to shoulder
抖	**DǑU**, to tremble, to shiver [B] 抖动 **dǒudòng** to vibrate; to shake	衫	**SHĀN**, shirt, garment for upper part of body [B] 汗衫 **hànshān** undershirt, T-shirt
扶	**FÚ**, to support with your hand; straighten; to help [B] 扶持 **fúchí** to support	武	**WǓ**, military, martial [B] 武器 **wǔqì** weapons of war [B]
丑	**CHǑU**, clown; the second "earthly branch;" be ugly [C] 醜 (for "ugly" meaning)	松	**SŌNG**, 1) pine tree; family name; 2) loosen up; be light (of cakes) [B] 鬆 (2nd meanings)
扭	**NIǓ**, to twist, to wring; to swing the hips when walking [B]	叔	**SHŪ**, father's younger brother; husband's younger brother [B]
投	**TÓU**, to drop; to move to; to surrender; to project; to fit in with [B]	乎	**HŪ**, (bookish) after sentences: indicates question or conjecture; to..., than...; very...; ..., indeed! [B]
抓	**ZHUĀ**, to scratch; to grab; to arrest; to draft someone [B]	呼	**HŪ**, to exhale; to call out; to snore [B] 呼吸 **hūxī** to breathe
否	**FǑU**, not; to deny [B] 否认 **fǒurèn** to repudiate; to deny	兔	**TÙ**, rabbit (distinguish from 免 (564, p. 113)) [B] 野兔 **yětù** wild rabbit
即	**JÍ**, at once; precisely; very soon; even [B]	延	**YÁN**, to delay, protract; lengthen; to invite [B] 延长 **yáncháng** to lengthen, prolong [B] 延期 **yánqī** to postpone

纠	**JIŪ**, to collect; confederacy; to investigate; to correct [B] 纠
染	**RǍN**, dye; form bad habits; to catch (a disease) [B] 污染 **wūrán** to pollute, pollution [B]
迹	**JÌ**, footprint; trace of; to search out or run down, to track [B]
森	**SĒN**, forest; be forest-like (dark; close-set) [B] 森林 **sēnlín** forest [B]
施	**SHĪ**, to spread, to spray; to give as charity; to effect (as, laws) [B]. Distinguish from the next character—note lower right.
旋	**XUÁN**, to revolve; thereupon [C]. Distinguish from the preceding character—note lower right.
挖	**WĀ**, to dig [B] 挖根 **wāgēn** to uproot, deracinate; to expunge from the source/root
砍	**KǍN**, to chop, slash; hit with a thrown object [B] 砍刀 **kǎndào** a chopper
肺	**FÈI**, lungs [B] 肺炎 **fèiyán** pneumonia
促	**CÙ**, to rush, be rushed; to urge [B] 促进 **cùjìn** push forward [B]
追	**ZHUĪ**, to chase; to investigate; to remember [B] 追查 **zhuīchá** to investigate [D]

姨	**YÍ**, mother's sister; wife's sister [B]
哇	**WA**, for 啊 (108, p. 22) when the preceding word ends in –u or –ao; **WĀ**, sound of crying [B]
娃	**WÁ**, baby, child; pretty girl [C] 娃娃 **wáwa** baby, child; doll (term for pretty girl) [C]
蛙	**WĀ**, frog [C]
悟	**WÙ**, to wake up; to notice [B] 悟性 **wùxìng** ability to understand
冻	**DÒNG**, to freeze; be cold, be freezing; jelly [B] 冻冰 **dòngbīng** to freeze 凍
讯	**XÙN**, to admonish someone; to make a judicial investigation 訊
扇	**SHÀN**, a fan; a measure for windows [B] 电扇 **diànshàn** electric fan
素	**SÙ**, be white; be elemental, plain; element [B] Distinguish from the next character. 素食 **sùshí** be vegetarian
索	**SUǑ**, rope; to tie up; to demand; rule [B] Distinguish from the preceding character. 索引 **suǒyǐn** index
埋	**MÁI**, to bury [B]

245

速	**SÙ**, speed [B] 快速 **kuàisù** be fast [D]	软	**RUǍN**, be soft, be pliable [B] 疲软 **píruǎn** be tired, weak 軟
逐	**ZHÚ**, to chase; one by one [B] 逐步 **zhúbù** step by step [B]	授	**SHÒU**, to give, to teach [B] 授意 **shòuyì** give somebody an 　　idea, inspire
捉	**ZHUŌ**, to catch, to capture [B] 捕捉 **bǔzhuō** to catch (as, an 　　insect, an opportunity) [D]	蔬	**SHŪ**, pulse, legumes [B] 蔬菜 **shūcài** vegetables [B]
套	**TÀO**, to wrap in; to harness or hitch up; covering; measure for sets, suits of clothes [B]	梳	**SHŪ**, comb, to comb [C]
闪	**SHǍN**, to flash, dodge; to twist, sprain; lightning [B] 闪光 **shǎnguāng** flash of 　　light, gleam　　閃	桶	**TǑNG**, a (six-pint) bucket; tub, cask [B]
胸	**XIŌNG**, thorax, chest [B] Distinguish from 脑 (p. 232a) 胸部 **xiōngbù** chest	麦	**MÀI**, wheat. WHEAT radical (188) [B] A picture of the wheat plant.　　麥
液	**YÈ**, juices, sap [B] 胃液 **wèiyè** gastric juice	虚	**XŪ**, emptiness; be empty; be timid; be humble; be false; guiding princi- ples; be virtual [C]　　虛
泪	**LÈI**, tears, to weep [B] A meaning-meaning compound 　　　　　淚	蛇	**SHÉ**, snake [B] 画蛇添足 **huá shé tiān zú** overdo 　　and spoil a job (literally, adding 　　feet to a snake)
毫	**HÁO**, a fine hair; one thousandth part; 毫不 intensifies the negation [B] Distinguish from 豪 (p. 266b).	钓	**DIÀO**, to go fishing, to catch with hook and line [B]
启	**QǏ**, to begin; to announce [B] 启事 **qǐshì** announcement [D] 　　　　　啓，啟	斜	**XIÉ**, to slant, to cause to slant [B] 斜坡 **xiépō** slope
粒	**LÌ**, grain, tiny piece [B] 每服五粒 **měifú wǔlì** dose: 5 pills 　　each time	叙	**XÙ**, to chat, to chat about; rank, to rank [C]　　敘

甜	**TIÁN**, sweet [B] 甜美 **tiánměi** be delicious	紫	**ZǏ**, be purple, purple color [B]
梨	**LÍ**, pear [B]	菌	**JÙN**, mushroom; **JŪN**, mildew; bacteria [B] 菌苗 **jūnmiáo** vaccine
渡	**DÙ**, to ferry across; to spend (some time) [B] 渡船 **dùchuán** ferryboat [D]	跌	**DIĒ**, to stumble and fall; to drop (in price) [B] "Foot" + "to lose" = "stumble and fall."
割	**GĒ**, to cut [B] 割断 **gēduàn** to sever	程	**CHÉNG**, a regulation; procedure; journey, stage of a journey; distance; family name [B]
弃	**QÌ**, to throw away [B] 棄	贸	**MÀO**, to barter [B] 贸易 **màoyì** trade, commerce [B] 貿
善	**SHÀN**, be good, be good at [B] 善于 **shànyú** be good at [B] 善心 **shànxīn** benevolence	滑	**HUÁ**, be slippery; be cunning, "slippery;" to slide [B] 滑行 **huáxíng** to slide
拣	**JIǍN**, to choose [B] 拣选 **jiǎnxuǎn** to choose 揀	猾	**HUÁ**, be cunning, sly [C]
棉	**MIÁN**, cotton-padded; cotton, kapok [B] 棉花 **miánhuā** cotton [B]	涂	**TÚ**, to daub; to erase; make a mess of; family name [B] 塗
硬	**YÌNG**, be hard, be stiff; be stubborn; be capable [B] 硬挺 **yìngtǐng** to resist stubbornly	禁	**JÌN**, prohibit; **JĪN**, endure; control oneself [B] 紫禁城 **Zǐjìnchéng** the Forbidden City (in Beijing)
雄	**XIÓNG**, male (animals); be imposing, powerful [B] 雄猫 **xióngmāo** tomcat	叠	**DIÉ**, to pile up; to repeat [B] 叠次 **diécì** repeatedly 疊
寻	**XÚN**, to look for [B] 寻找 **xúnzhǎo** to look for [B] 寻常 **xúncháng** be common 尋	隔	**GÉ**, partition; to partition; be separated from; every other [B]

247

睁	**ZHĒNG**, to open your eyes [B]
歇	**XIĒ**, to rest, to stop [B] 歇工 **xiēgōng** to stop work
爷 爺	**YÉ**, grandfather; father; "sir" [B] 爷爷 **yéye** paternal grandfather; "sir" [B]
筷	**KUÀI**, chopsticks [B] 筷子 **kuàizi** chopsticks [B]
愁	**CHÓU**, be worried; be depressed; to worry about [B] 愁苦 **chóukǔ** anxiety
腰	**YĀO**, waist; small of the back; pocket [B] 弯腰 **wānyāo** to stoop
催	**CUĪ**, to urge, to press [B] 催促 **cuīcù** to urge
滚	**GǓN**, to roll; to boil [B] 滚蛋 **gǔndàn** (rude) Get lost!
涨 漲	**ZHǍNG**, rise (a river, a price); **ZHÀNG**, to swell, to rise [B]
漏	**LÒU**, to leak [B] 漏洞 **lòudòng** a leak, to leak
盖 蓋	**GÀI**, lid, cover; bug's or turtle's shell; put a lid on; build; to mark; family name [B]
厨 廚	**CHÚ**, kitchen [B] 厨房 **chúfáng** kitchen [B]
庆 慶	**QÌNG**, congratulate; celebration; family name [B] 庆祝 **qìngzhù** celebrate [B]
裤 褲	**KÙ**, trousers [B] 裤子 **kùzi** trousers, pants
轮 輪	**LÚN**, wheel; revolve; take turns; round thing [B] 轮船 **lúnchuán** steamship [B] 轮班 **lúnbān** in shifts
醋	**CÙ**, vinegar [B] 吃醋 **chīcù** be jealous
撞	**ZHUÀNG**, to hit; to collide with; to meet by chance [B] 撞击 **zhuàngjī** to ram
扑 撲	**PŪ**, pounce on; to flap [B] 卜 **bǔ** gives the sound. 扑打 **pūdǎ** to swat, to pat
慰	**WÈI**, console, soothe [B] 慰问 **wèiwèn** to console [C]
肤 膚	**FŪ**, skin [B]
阅 閱	**YUÈ**, to examine; to read carefully; to pass through [B]
锐 銳	**RUÌ**, be sharp [B] 尖锐 **jiānruì** be penetrating [B]

稻	**DÀO**, rice plant; paddy [B] 稻田 **dàotián** rice paddy	洒	**SĂ**, to sprinkle, to spill [B] 洒泪 **sălèi** to weep 灑
激	**JĪ**, to force out under pressure (as, water); to spray; to stir up [B]	恋	**LIÀN**, to love [B] 恋爱 **liàn'ài** to love [B] 戀
糕	**GĀO**, cake [B] 糕点 **gāodiăn** cake	露	**LÙ**, dew, juice; to expose to view [B] 露面 **lùmiàn** show your face; make an appearance [B]
燃	**RÁN**, to burn, set on fire [B] 燃烧 **ránshāo** to burn, set on fire [B]	灵	**LÍNG**, be effective; be alert; spirit, soul; remains (of the dead) [B] 靈
拥	**YŎNG**, to hug; to crowd; to rally to the support of [B] 擁	晒	**SHÀI**, to sun a thing; be sunny and hot [B] 晒被子 **shài bèizi** sun a quilt 曬
挡	**DĂNG**, to block [B] 阻挡 **zŭdăng** to resist [D] 倒挡 **dăodăng** reverse gear 擋	判	**PÀN**, to separate, to judge [B] "刂" for meaning, 半 **bàn** for sound.
临	**LÍN**, be near; to copy (a painting or calligraphy) [B] 臨	状	**ZHUÀNG**, shape, appearance; condition; document [B] Distinguish from 壮 (p. 217b). 狀
颗	**KĒ**, a measure for seeds, grains, bullets, stars, jewels [B] 顆	席	**XÍ**, mat; banquet; measure for banquets; family name [B]
阔	**KUÒ**, be wealthy; be broad [B] 闊	牺	**XĪ**, used mainly in 牺牲 **xīshēng**, sacrifice [B] 犧
吓	**XIÀ**, to scare; **HÈ**, to threaten [B] 吓坏了 **xàihuàile** be scared silly	沿	**YÁN**, border, edge; to follow; fringe; along [B] 沿海 **yánhăi** along the coast [C]
鲜	**XIĀN**, be fresh; to taste delicious: **XIĂN**, be rare [B] 鮮	卫	**WÈI**, to defend; a defender, guard; a family name [B] 衛

哎	**ĀI**, an exclamation to express surprise or disaproval or to get attention [B]
宾	**BĪN**, guest [B] 宾馆 **bīnguǎn** hotel, inn [B]　賓
玻	**BŌ**, first syllable of 玻璃—see next character [B] 玻利维亚 **Bōlìwéiyà** Bolivia
璃	**LÍ**, second syllable of 玻璃 **bōli** [B] 玻璃 **bōli** glass; (colloquial) plastic [B]
脖	**BÓ**, neck [B] 脖子 **bózi** neck [B]
膊	**BÓ**, arm [B] 赤膊 **chìbó** be shirtless
餐	**CĀN**, to eat; food [B] 餐厅 **cāntīng**, dining room; restaurant [B] 餐车 **cānchē** dining car [C]
尝	**CHÁNG**, to taste; ever, once [B] 尝试 **chángshì** to try [D]　嘗
衬	**CHÈN**, to line; lining [B] 衬衫 **chènshān** shirt [B] 衬衣 **chènyī** underwear [B]　襯
翅	**CHÌ**, wing; shark's fin [B]
崇	**CHÓNG**, be high, sublime; to esteem; a family name [B] 崇高 **chónggāo** be lofty [B]
触	**CHÙ**, to touch; to hit; to move (emotionally) [B]　觸
闯	**CHUǍNG**, to rush, charge; to get tempered through struggle [B]　闖
脆	**CUÌ**, be fragile; be brittle; be clear (voice) [B] 脆弱 **cuìruò** be frail [D]
措	**CUÒ**, to arrange; to make plans [B] 措施 **cuòshī** an action, a step toward some goal [B]
递	**DÌ**, to give; in succession; in good order [B] 递交 **dìjiāo** to submit, hand over [D]　遞
逗	**DÒU**, to play with; to amuse; to stay, stop; a pause in reading [B] 逗号 **dòuhào** a comma
吨	**DŪN**, a ton [B] A word borrowed from English. 口 suggests "read for the sound."　噸
蹲	**DŪN**, to squat (on your heels); to stay [B]
泛	**FÀN**, (bookish) to float; to flood, be flooded; be extensive; be general [B] 泛滥 **fànlàn** to flood [D]
搁	**GĒ**, to put; put away; **GÉ**, to endure, bear [B] 搁置 **gēzhì** to set aside　擱
胳	**GĒ**, see below [B] 胳膊 **gēbo** arm

250

巩	GǑNG, to consolidate; a family name [B] 巩固 **gǒnggù** to consolidate; be consolidated [B] 鞏	圾	JĪ, first syllable of 垃圾 **lājī**—see next character [B]
锅	GUŌ, pot, pan, boiler; bowl (as, of a pipe) [B] 鍋	垃	LĀ, see below [B] 垃圾 **lājī** garbage [B] 垃圾堆 **lājīduī** garbage dump
拐	GUǍI, to turn; to limp; a crutch; to abduct; to abscond (with) [B] 拐弯 **guǎiwān** to turn [C]	捡	JIǍN, to pick up, to gather [B] 撿
冠	GUĀN, hat, crown, crest; GUÀN, be preceded by; the best [B]	届	JIÈ, to fall due; a measure, as for formal meetings, sessions, academic years [B]
逛	GUÀNG, to walk around, stroll, roam [B]	绢	JUÀN, thin, strong silk [B] 絹
跪	GUÌ, to kneel [B]	扛	KÁNG, carry on your shoulder; GĀNG, lift with both hands; (dialect) carry between two people [B]
盒	HÉ, box, case [B]	烤	KǍO, to bake, to roast; be very hot (as, a stove) [B]
嘿	HĒI, Hey! (at the beginning of a statement to get attention or express surprise or satisfaction) [B]	控	KÒNG, to accuse; to control; to empty a container by turning it upside down [B]
哼	HĒNG, to groan, snort, hum, croon; HNG, before a statement to express dissatisfaction or doubt [B]	捆	KǓN, to tie, to make a bundle of [B]
糊	HŪ, plaster; HÚ, paste; to paste; be burnt (of food); HÙ, (food) paste [B]	郎	LÁNG, boy, young man; "dear" (a woman to her man); surname; old official title [B]
辉	HUĪ, splendor; to shine [B]	朗	LǍNG, be bright; be loud and clear [B] 朗读 **lǎngdú** to read aloud [B]

251

励	**LÌ**, to encourage [B] 勵
聊	**LIÁO**, merely; slightly [B] 聊天儿 **liáo tiānr** to chat [B]
萝	**LUÓ**, trailing plants, vines [B] 萝卜 **luóbo** radish [B] 蘿
迈	**MÀI**, to step, to stride; to be old (of a person) [B] 邁
脉	**MÀI**, artery, vein; pulse [B] 脈
馒	**MÁN**, see below [B] 馒头 **mántou** steamed bun, steamed bread [B] 饅
貌	**MÀO**, looks, appearance [B] 貌似 **màosi** seemingly
默	**MÒ**, be silent; to write from memory [B] 默默 **mòmò** silently [B]
披	**PĪ**, drape over your shoulders; spread out; to split [B]
脾	**PÍ**, spleen [B] 脾气 **píqi** temperament; temper [B]
朴	**PŬ**, be plain; **PIÁO**, a family name 朴素 **pǔsù** be plain [B] 樸

戚	**QĪ**, a relative; sorrow; a family name [B]
牵	**QIĀN**, to lead (by the hand; by a halter, etc.) to involve, be involved in [B] 牽
悄	**QIĂO**, be quiet; (bookish) be grieved; **QIĀO**: 悄悄, quietly [B]
渠	**QÚ**, canal; ditch [B] 渠道 **qúdào** irrigation ditch; channel of communication [C]
裙	**QÚN**, skirt [B] 裙子 **qúnzi** skirt [B]
嚷	**RĂNG**, to shout, yell; **RĀNG**, see below [B] 嚷嚷 **rāngrāng** to yell; to make widely known
惹	**RĚ**, to ask for (e.g., trouble); to provoke; to cause [B]
嗓	**SĂNG**, throat, larynx; voice [B] 嗓子 **sǎngzi** throat, larynx, voice [B]
傻	**SHĂ**, be stupid; think or do mechanically [B] 傻瓜 **shǎguā** a fool 傻子 **shǎzi** a fool [D]
狮	**SHĪ**, lion [B] 狮子 **shīzi** lion [B] 獅
柿	**SHÌ**, persimmon [B]

殊	**SHŪ**, be different; be outstanding; extremely [B]		仰	**YǍNG**, face upward; look up to; rely on [B]
塑	**SÙ**, model; mold [B] 塑料 **sùliào** plastics [B]		邀	**YĀO**, to invite; to seek; to intercept [B] 邀请 **yāoqǐng** to invite [B]
掏	**TĀO**, to pull out; to hollow out; to steal from somebody's pocket [B]		悠	**YŌU**, be protracted; be remote (time or space); (colloquial) to swing [B] 悠久 **yōujiǔ** be age-old [B]
歪	**WĀI**, be awry, askew, slanting; be crooked, devious, "dirty" [B] 不 "not" + 正 "straight" = 歪 "crooked"		跃	**YUÈ**, to jump [B] 跃进 **yuèjìn** to leap forward [C] 躍
雾	**WÙ**, fog; fine spray [B] 霧		扎	**ZHÁ**, to prick; (dialect) to plunge into; **ZHĀ**, to pitch (as, a tent); **ZĀ**, to tie up (one's hair) [B]
悉	**XĪ**, all; to know, to learn about [B]		哲	**ZHÉ**, be wise; a sage [B] 哲学 **zhéxué** philosophy [B]
纤	**XIĀN**, be fine (small, minute); **QIÀN**, a tow line [B] 纖		仔	**ZǍI**, (dialect) son; young animal; **ZǏ**, young (domestic animals or fowls) [B]
羡	**XIÀN**, to envy; to admire [B] 羡慕 **xiànmù** to envy; to admire [B]		综	**ZŌNG**, to sum up [B] 综合 **zōnghé** to synthesize; be composite [B] 綜
熊	**XIÓNG**, a bear; (dialect) to scold; family name [B] 白熊 **báixióng** polar bear 熊猫 **xióngmāo** panda [B]		筑	**ZHÙ**, to build; **ZHÚ**, Guiyang (贵阳, a place name) [B]
迅	**XÙN**, be fast [B] 迅速 **xùnsù** be speedy, prompt [B]		哀	**ĀI**, grief; mourning; pity [C] 哀求 **āiqiú** to implore [D]
咽	**YÀN**, to swallow; **YĀN**, pharynx [B] 咽喉 **yānhóu** pharynx and larynx: throat		癌	**ÁI**, cancer [C]

碍	ÀI, to get in the way [C] 妨碍 **fáng'ài** to obstruct [C]
熬	ÁO, to boil; to endure [C]
奥	ÀO, be profound; be hard to understand [C]
扒	BĀ, hold onto; to rake; to push aside; to take off [C]
叭	BĀ, sometimes used for 吧 **bā** (303, p. 61) [C]
坝	BÀ, a dam; a dyke [C] 壩
柏	BĂI, cypress-tree [C]
瓣	BÀN, petal; fragment; segment (as, of a tangerine, of a clove of garlic) [C]
辩	BIÀN, to argue [C] 辯
暴	BÀO, be violent, be fierce; stick out, lay out [C] 暴力 **bàolì** violence
爆	BÀO, to explode; to fry quickly in hot oil [C] 爆炸 **bàozhà** to explode [C]

剥	BĀO, to peel, to shell; BŌ, see 剥削, under 削, p. 270b [C]
奔	BĒN, to run; to rush; to flee; BÈN, to head for; to approach [C]
甭	BÉNG, (dialect), don't; need not [C] 不 "not" + 用 "use" = 甭 "don't, need not."
柄	BĬNG, a handle; stem of a plant; (bookish) authority [C] 木 for meaning.
菠	BŌ, see below [C] 菠菜 **bōcài** spinach [C] 菠萝 **bōluó** pineapple
勃	BÓ, suddenly [C] 勃发 **bófā** to thrive 勃然 **bórán** excitedly; vigorously
怖	BÙ, to be afraid of [C] 可怖 **kěbù** be frightful; be terrified
惭	CÁN, to be ashamed [C] 大言不惭 **dàyán bùcán** to boast shamelessly
灿	CÀN, see below [C] 灿烂 **cànlàn** be bright; be magnificent [C]
铲	CHĂN, a shovel; to shovel [C] 铲车 **chǎnchē** a forklift 鏟
颤	CHÀN, to quiver, vibrate; ZHÀN, to shiver, shudder [C] 顫

偿	**CHÁNG**, to repay; to meet, fulfill [C] 偿还 **chánghuán** to pay back [D]	患	**HUÀN**, trouble; disaster; worry; to suffer from [C] Distinguish from 忠 (next character). 患者 **huànzhě** a patient [D]
扯	**CHĚ**, to pull; to tear; to buy; to gossip [C]	忠	**ZHŌNG**, be loyal [C] Distinguish from the preceding character. 忠诚 **zhōngchéng** loyal [C] 忠实 **zhōngshí** faithful [C]
撑	**CHĒNG**, to prop up; to move with a pole; to keep up, keep on; to open up; to fill to bursting [C]	酬	**CHÓU**, a toast; to propose a toast; a reward; to fulfill [C]
匙	**CHÍ**, spoon; **SHI**, see 钥匙 **yàoshi** under 钥 **yào**, p. 271a [C] 匙子 **chízi** spoon	仇	**CHÓU**, enemy; enmity; **QIÚ**, a family name [C] 仇恨 **chóuhèn** hostility [C]
蠢	**CHǓN**, be stupid, clumsy; (bookish) to wriggle [C]	搓	**CUŌ**, rub with hands [C] 搓手顿脚 **cuōshǒu dùnjiǎo** rub hands, stamp feet: get impatient, anxious
瓷	**CÍ**, porcelain [C] 瓦 "tile" for meaning; 次 **cì** for sound.	挫	**CUÒ**, to defeat; to frustrate; to subdue [C] 挫折 **cuòzhé** setback [C]
匆	**CŌNG**, hastily [C] 匆忙 **cōngmáng** hastily [C] 匆匆 **cōngcōng** hastily [D]	逮	**DǍI**, to capture; **DÀI**, (bookish) to reach [C] 逮捕 **dàibǔ** to arrest (as, a criminal)
丛	**CÓNG**, to crowd together; thicket; crowd 叢	耽	**DĀN**, to delay; (bookish) to give oneself over to, to indulge in [C]
辞	**CÍ**, phrase, phraseology; take leave of 修辞 **xiūcí** rhetoric 辭	诞	**DÀN**, birth; birthday; be absurd [C] 誕
串	**CHUÀN**, to string together [C] A pictogram—things strung on the downstroke	档	**DÀNG**, to ward off; to block out; a blind; (automobile) gear [C]
窜	**CUÀN**, to scurry; to kick out; to alter (e.g., the wording of a text) [C]	蹈	**DǍO**, (bookish) to step on; to skip (i.e., movement—not omission) [C] 舞蹈 **wǔdǎo** to dance [C]

255

蹬	**DĒNG**, to tread on; to press down with the foot; a pedal, to pedal [C] Compare with 登 (798, p. 160).	沸	**FÈI**, to boil [C]
瞪	**DÈNG**, to look bug-eyed at; to stare; to glare at [C]	坟	**FÉN**, grave, tomb [C] 坟墓 **fénmù** grave, tomb [D] 坟地 **féndì** graveyard
惦	**DIÀN**, to remember and worry about; be concerned about [C] 惦记 **diànjì** worry over; keep thinking of [C]	疯	**FĒNG**, be insane [C] 疯子 **fēngzi** madman [D] 疯人院 **fēngrényuàn** lunatic asylum 瘋
奠	**DIÀN**, to settle; to make offerings (to spirits of the dead) [C] 奠定 **diàndìng** to establish [C]	讽	**FĚNG**, to satirize; (bookish) to chant [C] 諷
殿	**DIÀN**, palace; hall; to be at the rear [C] 殿后 **diànhòu** to bring up the rear	袱	**FÚ**, see below [C] 包袱 **bāofu** cloth used as a wrapper; bundle in cloth wrapper; burden [C]
雕	**DIĀO**, to carve, to engrave [C] 雕刻 **diāokè** to carve, to engrave; a carving [C]	缚	**FÙ**, to tie up [C] 縛
蝶	**DIÉ**, butterfly: see 蝴蝶 under 蝴 (p. 257a) [C]	溉	**GÀI**, see below [C] 灌溉 **guàngài** to irrigate [C]
陡	**DǑU**, be steep; abruptly [C]	鸽	**GĒ**, pigeon, dove [C] 鴿
督	**DŪ**, to supervise, direct [C]	股	**GǓ**, measure for puffs, whiffs, skeins, bands, gangs, surges, and shares of stock [C]
哆	**DUŌ**, in 哆嗦 **duōsuo**, p. 262b [C]	乖	**GUĀI**, be well-behaved (of a child); be clever [C]
番	**FĀN**, a measure for kinds (种), times (回), or positions in a sequence (次) [C]	柜	**GUÌ**, cabinet; cupboard [C] 柜台 **guìtái** counter, bar [C] 柜子 **guìzi** cabinet, cupboard [C]

裹	**GUǑ**, to bind, to wrap [C]
憾	**HÀN**, regret [C]
焊	**HÀN**, to weld, to solder [C] 火 "fire" for meaning, 旱 **hàn** for sound.
呵	**HĒ**, to puff (blow out air); to scold [C] 呵斥 **hēchì** to berate 呵呵 **hēhē** laughing sound
核	**HÉ**, pit, fruitstone; nucleus ; to check up on [C] 核武器 **héwǔqì** nuclear weapon [D]
阂	**HÉ**, be cut off from; not be communicating with [C] 閡
狠	**HĚN**, be ruthless; suppress your feelings; be resolute [C]
痕	**HÉN**, mark, trace, scar [C] 痕迹 **hénjì** trace, vestige [C]
衡	**HÉNG**, a scale (weighing device); to weigh [C]
宏	**HÓNG**, be great, be magnificent [C] 宏伟 **hóngwěi** be magnificent [C]
蝴	**HÚ**, see below [C] 蝴蝶 **húdié** butterfly [C]

幻	**HUÀN**, be illusory; be magical, changeable [C] 幻想 **huànxiǎng** illusion [C]
煌	**HUÁNG**, be brilliant, shine brightly [C] 辉煌 **huīhuáng** be brilliant, be glorious [C]
晃	**HUÀNG**, to bedazzle; to flash past; **HUǍNG** to shake, to sway [C]
慧	**HUÌ**, be intelligent [C]
浑	**HÚN**, be muddy; be a little stupid; be unsophisticated; whole, entire [C] 渾
肌	**JĪ**, muscle; flesh [C] 肌肉 **jīròu** muscle [C] 肌体 **jītǐ** human body; organism
辑	**JÍ**, to edit; to compile; volume; part (e.g., of a book or film) [C] 輯
籍	**JÍ**, a record; registry; native place [C]
疾	**JÍ**, sickness; suffering; to hate; be fast [C]
寂	**JÌ**, be quiet, be lonely [C] 寂寞 **jìmò** be lonely, quiet, deserted [C]
佳	**JIĀ**, be beautiful, be excellent [C]

257

歼	JIĀN, to wipe out [C] 殲	竭	JIÉ, to use up [C] 竭力 **jiélì** to do your best
碱	JIǍN, alkali; soda; to be alkaline [C] "Rock" (for "minerals") + "be salty" = alkaline.	捷	JIÉ, victory; be nimble, be quick [C]
荐	JIÀN, to recommend; (bookish) straw, straw mat [C] 薦	洁	JIÉ, be clean [C] 洁白 **jiébái** be pure white [C] 潔
鉴	JIÀN, old-time mirror (of bronze); to reflect; warning; to look over [C] 鑒, 鑑	谨	JǏN, be circumspect; sincerely [C] 谨慎 **jǐnshèn** be prudent [C] 謹
舰	JIÀN, man-of-war [C] 舰长 **jiànzhǎng** captain of a warship 艦	鲸	JĪNG, whale [C] 鲸鱼 **jīngyú** whale [C] 鲸仔 **jīngzǎi** whale calf 鯨
溅	JIÀN, to splash; to splatter [C] 濺	径	JÌNG, path; means; without delay; diameter [C] 捷径 **jiéjìng** "quick path," i.e., shortcut 徑, 逕
僵	JIĀNG, be stiff; be numb; be dead- locked [C] 殭 ("be stiff")	揪	JIŪ, to hold tight; to tug [C]
疆	JIĀNG, boundary [C]	灸	JIǓ, moxibustion (Chinese medical term) [C]
椒	JIĀO, hot pepper [C] 胡椒 **hújiāo** pepper	壳	KÉ, shell (e.g., egg, nut); (engineer- ing) housing; QIÀO, shell [C] 殼
搅	JIǍO, to stir; to disturb [C] 攪	窟	KŪ, hole, cave, den [C]
揭	JIĒ, to tear off; to uncover; (bookish) to hoist [C] 揭露 **jiēlù** to expose [C]	酷	KÙ, be cruel; very [C] 酷寒 **kùhán** be very cold 酷似 **kùsì** be just like 酷爱 **kù'ài** love ardently

库	**KÙ**, storehouse [C] 库存 **kùcún** reserve (D) 库房 **kùfáng** storehouse (D) 庫	黎	**LÍ**, multitude; family name [C]
亏	**KUĪ**, to lose (e.g., money); be deficient; to treat unfairly; luckily [C] 虧	隶	**LÌ**, be subordinate to; servant, slave [C] 隸
愧	**KUÌ**, be ashamed [C] 惭愧 **cánkuì** ashamed [C] 愧恨 **kuìhèn** shamed and remorseful	帘	**LIÁN**, flag hung out to identify a shop; curtain [C]
昆	**KŪN**, older brother; (bookish) progeny [C] 昆虫 **kūnchóng** insect [C]	僚	**LIÁO**, bureaucrat; colleague [C]
廓	**KUÒ**, be extensive; an outline [C]	疗	**LIÁO**, to treat; to cure [C] 療
喇	**LĂ**, see below [C] 喇叭 **lăba** brass, brasses (category of musical instrument); loudspeaker [C]	猎	**LIÈ**, to hunt; hunting [C] 獵
蜡	**LÀ**, wax; candle; polish [C] 蜡烛 **làzhú** candle [C] 蠟	陵	**LÍNG**, hill; imperial tomb [C]
兰	**LÁN**, orchid [C] 蘭	咙	**LÓNG**, see below [C] 喉咙 **hóulóng** throat [C] 嚨
廊	**LÁNG**, corridor; veranda [C]	笼	**LÓNG**, basket; cage; steamer for food [C] 籠
姥	**LĂO**, see below [C] 姥姥 **lăolao** maternal grandmother	垄	**LŎNG**, ridge in a field; raised path in a field [C] 壟,壠
愣	**LÈNG**, be distracted, be stupefied; (colloquial) be reckless [C]	拢	**LŎNG**, to arrive at; to sum up; to hold together; to comb your hair [C] 攏

窿	**LÓNG**, (dialect) gallery (in a mine) [C] 窟窿 **kūlòng** cavity; deficit, debt [C]	盲	**MÁNG**, be blind [C] 盲目 **mángmù** blind; blindly [C]
驴 驢	**LÜ**, donkey [C]	氓	**MÁNG**, see below; **MÉNG**, common folk [C] 流氓 **liúmáng** hoodlum; hooliganism [C]
铝 鋁	**LǙ**, aluminium [C]	茅	**MÁO**, (botany) a kind of grass; a family name [C] 茅台酒 **máotáijiǔ** Maotai (Chinese *aquavita*) [C]
掠	**LÜÈ**, to pillage; to sweep past [C] 掠夺 **lüèduó** to pillage [C]	霉	**MÉI**, mildew, mould [C]
罗 羅	**LUÓ**, a bird-net; to catch birds; silk gauze; collect; display; surname [D]	眠	**MIÁN**, to sleep [C] 冬眠 **dōngmián** to hibernate [C]
逻 邏	**LUÓ**, to patrol [C] 逻辑 **luóji** logic [C]	蔑 衊	**MIÈ**, 1) to disrespect; to denigrate; 2) paltry; nothing (1st meaning only)
锣 鑼	**LUÓ**, gong [C] 锣鼓 **luógǔ** gongs and drums; percussion band [C]	敏	**MǏN**, be quick, agile [C] 敏捷 **mǐnjié** be agile [C]
搂 摟	**LŌU**, to rake together; to tuck up; to extort money; **LǑU**, to hug [C]	陌	**MÒ**, path between fields; road [C]
喽 嘍	**LOU**, "as soon as (I've done this, I'll do that…);" "Look, now,…" [C]*	凝	**NÍNG**, to congeal, coagulate [C] 凝思 **níngsī** get lost in thought
瞒 瞞	**MÁN**, to hide the truth from somebody [C]	拧 擰	**NÍNG**, to twist; to pinch or tweak [C]
漫	**MÀN**, to overflow; to be everywhere [C] 漫长 **màncháng** be endless [C]	噢	**Ō**, Oh (exclamation indicating understanding, comprehension) [C]

*喽, pronounced **lóu**, may be seen in 喽罗 **lóuluo** "lackey; low-ranking member of a gang."

260

哦	Ó, Is that right?; Really? (= surprise, disbelief); Ò, oh! (= enlightenment, comprehension) [C]	侨	QIÁO, to live abroad; a person living abroad [C] 华侨 **huáqiáo** overseas Chinese [C] 僑
趴	PĀ, to lie prone; to bend over; to lean on [C]	翘	QIÁO, raise your head; be warped; QIÀO, to stick up, hold up, bend upwards [C] 翹
攀	PĀN, to climb; seek connections in high places; to accuse others, implicate [C]	俏	QIÀO, be pretty, be smart; to sell well [C]
培	PÉI, to bank up with earth; to train [C]	顷	QǏNG, a unit of area (6.67 hectacres); (bookish) just now; (bookish) a little while [C] 頃
佩	PÈI, to wear at your waist; to admire [C]	倾	QĪNG, to lean; to bend; to be deviant; to collapse; to turn over and empty; put your all into a thing [C] 傾
蓬	PÉNG, be dishevelled, be fluffy; a bitter plant; a measure for clumps (as, of bamboo) [C]	丘	QIŪ, a hillock; a family name [C] 丘陵 **qiūlíng** hills [C]
棚	PÉNG, a canopy of reed mats; a shed or hut [C]	权	QUÁN, power, authority; right (to...) [C] 权力 **quánlì** power, authority [C] 權
膨	PÉNG, to expand, to dilate [C] 膨大 **péngdà** to expand	壤	RǍNG, soil, earth; area, region [C]
剖	PŌU, to cut apart; to analyze [C]	溶	RÓNG, to dissolve, be dissolved [C] 溶液 **róngyè** (chemistry) solution [C]
葡	PÚ, 1st syllable of 葡萄 **pútáo** grapes [C] 萄: p. 262b, below.	柔	RÓU, be soft, to soften; be gentle or mild [C] 柔软 **róuruǎn** be soft, be lithe [C]
谦	QIĀN, be modest [C] 謙	揉	RÓU, to rub, to knead

261

骚	**SĀO**, to upset; literary writing; be coquettish [C] 离骚 **Lí Sāo** famous poem by 屈原 **Qū Yuán** 騷	诵	**SÒNG**, to read aloud; to recite, to chant [C] 诵读 **sòngdú** read aloud 誦
删	**SHĀN**, to delete [C] 删节 **shānjié** to abridge 删改 **shān'gǎi** to revise	嗦	**SUŌ**, see below [C] 哆嗦 **duōsuo** tremble; shiver 罗嗦 **luōsuo** be long-winded [D]
哨	**SHÀO**, guardpost; (birds) to warble, to chirp; a whistle [C] 哨兵 **shàobīng** sentry [C]	塌	**TĀ**, to collapse; to droop; to calm down [C] 塌实 **tāshi** be dependable; be calm, relieved [C]
摄	**SHÈ**, to absorb; to take a photo; to take care of your health; to serve as acting officer [C] 攝	滩	**TĀN**, beach; shoal [C] 灘
圣	**SHÈNG**, sage; saint; be holy, be sacred [C] 圣诞节 **Shèngdànjié** Christmas [C] 聖	萄	**TÁO**, grapes [C] 葡萄 **pútáo** grapes [C] 葡萄酒 **pútáojiǔ** grape wine
驶	**SHǏ**, to sail, to drive; speed [C] 駛	惕	**TÌ**, be cautious, be alert, watchful 警惕 **jǐngtì** be vigilant [C]
逝	**SHÌ**, to pass; to die [C]	驮	**TUÓ**, carry on the back; **DUÒ**, a load carried by a pack animal; a measure for such loads [C] 馱
烁	**SHUÒ**, to shine, be bright [C] 烁烁 **shuò shuò** to glitter [C] 爍	驼	**TUÓ**, camel; hunchback [C] 驼背 **tuóbèi** hunchback 駝
伺	**SÌ**, to watch, watch for; **CÌ**, in 伺候 to serve [C]	骆	**LUÒ**, horse; a family name [C] 骆驼 **luòtuo** a camel [C] 駱
饲	**SÌ**, to rear, to raise [C[饲养 **sìyǎng** to rear, to raise [C] 飼	吻	**WĚN**, lips; to kiss; animal's mouth [C] 吻合 **wěnhé** be identical
颂	**SÒNG**, to praise; a song, a paean [C] 颂扬 **sòngyáng** to extol 頌	诬	**WŪ**, accuse falsely [C] 诬蔑 **wūmiè** to slander, villify [C] 誣

侮	WǓ, to bully, to insult [C] 外侮 **wàiwǔ** foreign aggression	循	XÚN, to follow, abide by [C]
袭	XÍ, make a surprise attack on; to continue (as, a tradition) [C] 袭击 **xíjī** to raid [C]　　襲	旬	XÚN, a period of ten days; (in an older person's life) a period of ten years [C]
宪	XIÀN, statute; constitution [C] 宪法 **xiànfǎ** constitution [C]　　憲	询	XÚN, to enquire [C] 询问 **xúnwèn** to enquire [C]　　詢
陷	XIÀN, pitfall; to get bogged down; to frame for a crime; to fall to the enemy; defect(ive) [C]	押	YĀ, to pawn; to arrest; to escort; to sign or mark [C]
厢	XIĀNG, wing of a house; railroad carriage; area outside a city-gate; side [C]	崖	YÁ, cliff, precipice [C]
宵	XIĀO, night [C] 通宵 **tōngxiāo** all night 宵禁 **xiāojìn** curfew	淹	YĀN, to flood; to tingle from sweat; (bookish) be broad (as, knowledge) [C]
淆	XIÁO, to mix up, to confuse, to make a mess with	掩	YǍN, to cover over, to hide; to close; attack by surprise; (dialect) get pinched closing a door [C]
胁	XIÉ, upper side of the body (human); to coerce　　脅	艳	YÀN, be very beautiful, be amorous; (bookish) to admire or envy [C]　　艷
朽	XIǓ, be rotten, be decayed; be senile [C] 朽木 **xiǔmù** rotten wood; worthless person	燕	YĀN, northern Hebei (province); a family name; YÀN, swallow (the bird) [C]
墟	XŪ, ruins [C]　　墟	焰	YÀN, to blaze [C] 焰火 **yànhuǒ** (dialect) fireworks
悬	XUÁN, to hang; be unresolved; feel anxious; to imagine; be far apart [C]　　懸	氧	YǍNG, oxygen [C] 羊 **yáng** gives the sound. 氧气 **yǎngqì** oxygen [C] 氧化 **yǎnghuà** oxidize [C]

窑	**YÁO**, kiln; coal pit; cave dwelling [C] The "cave" radical 穴 gives the meaning. 窯	愚	**YÚ**, be stupid; make/be made a fool of [C] 愚 has "monkey" over "heart-mind."
耀	**YÀO**, to shine; to dazzle; to praise highly [C] 耀眼 **yàoyǎn** to be dazzling (D)	渔	**YÚ**, fishing; to take unfairly or illegally [C] 渔民 **yúmín** fisherfolk [C] 漁
冶	**YĚ**, to smelt (metal); to dress sexily [C] 冶金 **yějīn** metallurgy [C]	屿	**YǓ**, islet [C] 嶼
伊	**YĪ**, he, she; family name [C] 伊斯兰教 **Yīsīlánjiào** Islam [C]	宇	**YǓ**, eaves, a house; space; manner, bearing; a family name [C] See 宇宙 (p. 265a).
倚	**YǏ**, to lean on, rely on; (bookish) be biased [C] 倚靠 **yǐkào** to lean on	御	**YÙ**, to drive (a carriage); be imperial; to resist [C] 禦 ("to resist" only)
抑	**YÌ**, to restrain; (bookish) or [C]	狱	**YÙ**, jail; lawsuit [C] 入狱 **rùyù** go to jail 獄
毅	**YÌ**, be resolute [C] 毅力 **yìlì** willpower; stamina [C]	裕	**YÙ**, be plentiful; (bookish) make rich (e.g., a country or a people) [C]
婴	**YĪNG**, baby [C] 婴儿 **yīng'ér** baby [C] 嬰	豫	**YÙ**, (bookish) be pleased; comfort; Henan (province) [C]
哟	**YŌ**, Oh! or Ouch! (mild surprise). **YO** (exhortation, encouragement, at the end of a sentence)	猿	**YUÁN**, an ape [C] 猿人 **yuánrén** ape-man [C]
踊	**YǑNG**, to jump up [C] 踊跃 **yǒngyuè** to jump; to compete [C] 踴	悦	**YUÈ**, be happy; to make happy, to please [C] The "side-heart" 忄 helps with the meaning.
涌	**YǑNG**, to gush up; to emerge [C] 涌现 **yǒngxiàn** to emerge in profusion (D)	砸	**ZÁ**, to pound, tamp down; to smash; get bungled [C] The "rock" radical 石 is here for meaning.

凿	**ZÁO**, to cut a hole; to chisel; **ZUÒ** to mortise; (bookish) irrefutable [C] 鑿	嘱	**ZHŬ**, to urge, to exhort [C] 囑
宅	**ZHÁI**, residence, house [C]	幢	**ZHUÀNG**, a measure for houses [C]; **CHUÁNG**, streamer; stone pillar with Buddhist carvings.
盏	**ZHǍN**, a small cup; a measure for lamps [C] 盞	彼	**BǏ**, that; the other [C] 彼此 **bǐcǐ** each other [C] 彼此彼此 **bǐcǐbǐcǐ** You, too!
崭	**ZHǍN**, (bookish) to tower over; (dialect) be excellent [C] 嶄	裁	**CÁI**, to cut out; to reduce; to dismiss; to judge [C] Distinguish from 栽, 载, 截 below.
障	**ZHÀNG**, to obstruct; an obstruction [C] 障碍 **zhàng'ài** to obstruct; an obstruction [C]	栽	**ZĀI**, to plant, to grow; to insert; impose; to fall [C] Distinguish from 裁, above; 载 and 截, below.
挣	**ZHÈNG**, to struggle to be free; to earn [C]	载	**ZǍI**, a year; to record [C]; **ZÀI**, be loaded with. Compare with 裁, 栽 above; 截, below. 載
帜	**ZHÌ**, (bookish) flag, banner [C]	截	**JIÉ**, to cut, sever; measure for sections, chunks, lengths; stop, check; up to [C] Distinguish from the preceding three characters.
稚	**ZHÌ**, be young, be childish [C] 稚气 **zhìqì** childishness	蚕	**CÁN**, silkworm [C] 蚕丝 **cánsī** natural silk 蚕子 **cánzǐ** silkworm egg 蠶
衷	**ZHŌNG**, inner feelings; heart [C] 衷心 **zhōngxīn** be heart-felt, be wholehearted [C]	残	**CÁN**, be deficient; remnant [C] 残酷 **cánkù** be cruel [C] 殘
宙	**ZHÒU**, time [C] 宇宙 **yǔzhòu** [space + time =] the cosmos, the universe [C]	惨	**CǍN**, be pitiful; be savage; disastrously [C] 惨杀 **cǎnshā** massacre 慘
骤	**ZHÒU**, (of a horse) to trot; be abrupt, sudden [C] 驟	尘	**CHÉN**, dust; the world [C] "Small"+ "earth" = "dust." 尘土 **chéntǔ** dust [C] 塵

陈	**CHÉN**, to display; to explain; be stale; surname [C] 陈列 **chénliè** set out [C] 陳	罚	**FÁ**, to punish [C] 罚款 **fákuǎn** to fine; a fine (D) 罰
纯	**CHÚN**, be pure; be simple; be skilled [C] 纯洁 **chúnjié** be pure, be honest [C] 純	粪	**FÈN**, shit, dung [C] 朽木粪土 **xiǔmùfèntǔ** rotten wood, dung, dirt—worthless stuff 糞
凑	**CÒU**, to collect; to happen by chance; to press against [C] 凑巧 **còuqiǎo** luckily [D] 湊	缸	**GĀNG**, crock, vat [C] 茶缸子 **chá gāngzi** tea mug
摧	**CUĪ**, to break [C] 摧残 **cuīcán** to devastate	耕	**GĒNG**, to plow, farm [C] 耕地 **gēngdì** to plow; cultivated land [C] 耕牛 **gēngniú** farm cattle
单	**DĀN**, unlined (clothes); be single; be odd (not even); sheet; list [C] 單	宫	**GŌNG**, palace, temple, hall; a family name [C] 宫殿 **gōngdiàn** palace [C] 子宫 **zǐgōng** womb
凳	**DÈNG**, stool, bench [C] Distinguish from 登 (798, p. 160). 长凳 **chángdèng** bench 板凳 **bǎndèng** wooden chair or stool	孤	**GŪ**, be orphaned; be alone, solitary [C] 孤立 **gūlì** be isolated [C] 孤单 **gūdān** be alone
堤	**DĪ**, dyke [C] 堤岸 **dī'àn** embankment 堤防 **dīfáng** dyke, embankment	雇	**GÙ**, to hire [C] 雇员 **gùyuán** employee [C] 雇主 **gùzhǔ** employer 僱
抵	**DǏ**, to prop up; to withstand; to compensate for; mortgage; be equal to [C] 抵抗 **dǐkàng** to fight back	寡	**GUǍ**, be few; be tasteless; be widowed [C] 寡妇 **guǎfu** widow [C]
垫	**DIÀN**, to shim; to pad, to cushion; to pay for a person, expecting repayment [C] 墊	归	**GUĪ**, to return (home, or where you belong); give back; a family name [C] 歸
爹	**DIĒ**, (colloquial) Dad [C] 爹爹 **diēdie** Daddy	轨	**GUǏ**, rail (as in "railroad"), path [C] 轨道 **guǐdào** track [C] 軌
额	**É**, forehead; horizontal tablet; a definite amount [C] 額	豪	**HÁO**, a very talented person; be unrestrained, bold [C] Distinguish from 毫 (p. 232a)

耗	**HÀO**, to use up; to waste time; bad news [C] 耗费 **hàofèi** to use up (D)	筐	**KUĀNG**, basket [C] 筐子 **kuāngzi** small basket
吼	**HǑU**, to roar [C]	狂	**KUÁNG**, be insane, violent, wild, arrogant [C] 疯狂 **fēngkuáng** insane [C] 狂风 **kuángfēng** gale [C]
怀 懷	**HUÁI**, to hug; bosom; heart; cherish; conceive (a child) [C]	辣	**LÀ**, be hot (spicy); to sting (as, antiseptic); be ruthless [C] 辣椒 **làjiāo** hot pepper [C]
毁	**HUǏ**, to break apart; to destroy [C] 摧毁 **cuīhuǐ** to smash [C] 撕毁 **sīhuǐ** to rip to shreds	牢	**LÁO**, pen, fold (for animals); jail; sacrifice [C] 牢固 **láogù** be firm [C] 牢骚 **láosāo** grievance [C]
汇 匯	**HUÌ**, 1) to converge; to collect; a collection; 2) to remit [C]	淋	**LÍN**, to pour, to drench [C]; **LÌN**, to filter 淋淋 **línlín** be dripping
魂	**HÚN**, soul; mood [C] 神魂 **shénhún** state of mind; mind	溜	**LIŪ**, to slide; be smooth; sneak off [C]. **LIÙ**, rain runoff; rain gutter; row; fast current; neighborhood
饥 饑	**JĪ**, be hungry; famine [C] 饥饿 **jī'è** starvation [C]	柳	**LIǓ**, willow; a family name [C] 柳树 **liǔshù** willow tree [C]
甲	**JIǍ**, fingernail; carapace; armor; 1st of heavenly stems; "A," first of a series [C]	炉 爐	**LÚ**, stove, furnace [C] 炉子 **lúzi** oven, stove, furnace [C]
筋	**JĪN**, muscle; (colloquial) tendon, sinew, prominent vein; tendon-like thing [C]	卵	**LUǍN**, egg, ovum [C]* 卵白 **luǎnbái** egg white 卵黄 **luǎnhuáng** egg yolk
舅	**JIÙ**, uncle (mother's brother); wife's brother [C] 舅舅 **jiùjiu** uncle (mother's brother) [C]	络 絡	**LUÒ**, net-like thing; hold with a net; string; to wind [C]
聚	**JÙ**, to get together [C] 聚集 **jùjí** to gather [C] 聚精会神 **jùjīnghuìshén** to concentrate on [C]	梅	**MÉI**, plum; family name [C] 梅花 **méihuā** plum blossom [C]

*In *Han-Ying Cidian*, 卵 is one of eleven "leftover" characters that have no radical. See below, p. 272b.

眉	**MÉI**, eyebrow; margin at the top of a page [C] 眉毛 **méimáo** eyebrow [C] 眉头 **méitóu** brows [C]
闷	**MĒN**, be tightly closed; be stuffy; be muffled [C]; **MÈN**, be tightly closed; be depressed 悶
蒙	**MĒNG**, to dupe; guess wildly; be unconscious [C]; **MÉNG**, to cover; to meet; **MĚNG**, Mongol
盟	**MÉNG**, alliance; league; (sworn) brothers [C]
猛	**MĚNG**, be fierce; be energetic; abruptly [C] 猛烈 **měngliè** be fierce [C] 猛然 **měngrán** abruptly [C]
勉	**MIǍN**, strive; exhort [C] 勉强 **miǎnqiǎng** do with difficulty; reluctantly; force to do; inadequate [C]
鸣	**MÍNG**, birdsong; bugs' or animals' sounds; to ring [C] 鳴
抹	**MǑ**, to apply, smear on; to wipe; to cross out, erase [C] 抹杀 **mǒshā** obliterate (D)
牧	**MÙ**, to herd [C] 牛 "cow" is for meaning. 牧场 **mùchǎng** pasture [C] 牧民 **mùmín** herdsman [C]
奈	**NÀI**, see 奈何, below [C] 奈何 **nàihé** how can it be that... (it can't, of course)
嫩	**NÈN**, be delicate; be light (in color); be inexperienced [C] 女 seems to be for meaning here.
捏	**NIĒ**, to hold between your fingers; to knead; to fake (e.g., a report) [C] 捏造 **niēzào** trump up [C]
宁	**NÍNG**, be tranquil [C]; **NÌNG**, rather; could there be...?; a family name 寧, 甯
偶	**ǑU**, image, idol; be even (not odd); be in pairs; spouse; by accident, occasionally [C]
抛	**PĀO**, to throw; to discard [C] 抛弃 **pāoqì** throw away (D) 拋
凭	**PÍNG**, to lean on, to depend on; proof [C] 憑
漆	**QĪ**, lacquer; to paint with lacquer; a family name [C]
恰	**QIÀ**, be proper; exactly [C] 恰当 **qiàdàng** be proper [C] 恰好 **qiàhǎo** just right [C] 恰恰 **qiàqià** exactly [C]
腔	**QIĀNG**, cavity; tune; accent; speech [C] 腔调 **qiāngdiào** tune, accent
琴	**QÍN**, a traditional musical instrument ("Ch'in") [C] 钢琴 **gāngqín** piano (D) 小提琴 **xiǎotíqín** violin
勤	**QÍN**, be hardworking; frequently; attendance [C] 勤劳 **qínláo** be hardworking [C]
曲	**QŪ**, to be bent; a bend; be wronged; a family name; **QǓ**, verse for singing ("Ch'ü"); tune; music [C]

屈 **QŪ**, a bend; to subdue, to be subdued; an injustice; be in the wrong; a family name [C]

娶 **QǓ**, to take a wife, to get married [C]
娶亲 **qǔqīn** (of a man) to get married

辱 **RǓ**, dishonor; bring dishonor to, insult [C]
侮辱 **wǔrǔ** force indignities on, humiliate [C]

润 **RÙN**, be sleek, be moist; to moisten; to embellish; profit [C] 潤

若 **RUÒ**, be like; seem [C]
若干 **ruògān** a certain number or amount; how many? how much? [C]

塞 **SĀI**, to stuff in; a stopper; **SÀI**, strategic place [C]
塞外 **sàiwài** north of the Great Wall

丧 **SĀNG**, funeral; mourning; **SÀNG**, to lose [C]
丧礼 **sānglǐ** funeral service 喪

纱 **SHĀ**, yarn; gauze; be sheer [C]
纱布 **shābù** gauze 紗

涉 **SHÈ**, to ford; to wade/go through; to involve [C]
涉及 **shèjí** to involve (D)

甚 **SHÈN**, very; more than... **SHÉN**, in 甚么 (= 什么) [C]
...日甚一日 **...rì shèn yírì** ... more so every day

盛 **SHÈNG**, to flourish; to be vigorous; be grand; popular; surname; **CHÉNG**, to fill; to contain [C]

蚀 **SHÍ**, to lose; to erode [C]
日蚀 **rìshí** solar eclipse
月蚀 **yuèshí** lunar eclipse (also 日食, 月食) 蝕

饰 **SHÌ**, decorations, adornment; put decorations on, dress up [C] 飾

寿 **SHÒU**, long life; age; a family name [C]
寿命 **shòumìng** lifespan [C] 壽

售 **SHÒU**, to sell; (bookish) to carry out, pull off [C]
售货 **shòuhuò** to sell goods [C]

兽 **SHÒU**, animal; beastly [C]
人面兽心 **rénmiànshòuxīn** be a beast in human form 獸

耍 **SHUǍ**, to play; to wave around; to play tricks [C]
耍滑 **shuǎhuá** "play slippery," i.e., dodge work

衰 **SHUĀI**, to decline, to get weak [C]
衰弱 **shuāiruò** be weak [C]
衰退 **shuāituì** to decline

拴 **SHUĀN**, plug, cork [C]
枪拴 **qiāngshuān** rifle bolt
栓塞 **shuānsè** embolism

孙 **SŪN**, grandson; family name [C]
孙女 **sūnnǚ** granddaughter [C] 孫

锁 **SUǑ**, lock; to lock up [C] 鎖

踏 **TÀ**, to step on; to go make an on-the-spot inspection; **TĀ**, see below [C]
踏实 **tāshí** = 塌实 (p. 262b) [C]

摊 攤	**TĀN**, to spread out; vendor's booth; fry in a thin layer; a measure for puddles, pools, etc. [C]	蚊	**WÉN**, mosquito [C] 蚊子 **wénzi** mosquito [C] 蚊香 **wénxiāng** mosquito-repellent incense
坦	**TĂN**, be flat, level; be calm; be candid [C] 坦克 **tǎnkè** tank (armored military vehicle) [C]	纹 紋	**WÉN**, veins (as in marble); grain (as of wood) [C]
叹 嘆	**TÀN**, to sigh; to exclaim in admiration; praise [C]	翁	**WĒNG**, old man; father; father-in-law; a family name [C]
桃	**TÁO**, peach [C] 桃花 **táohuā** peach blossoms [D]	卧	**WÒ**, to lie down; (of animals) to crouch [C] 卧室 **wòshì** bedroom (D) 卧车 **wòchē** sleeping car
徒	**TÚ**, disciple; apprentice; bloke, guy; be on foot; be empty; be in vain; merely; prison sentence [C]	锡 錫	**XĪ**, tin [C] 锡纸 **xīzhǐ** tinfoil
吞	**TŪN**, to swallow; take possession of [C] 吞吞吐吐 **tūntūntǔtǔ** to hem and haw, to babble	稀	**XĪ**, be rare; be sparse; be thin [C]
妥	**TUŎ**, be appropriate, be proper; (after a verb) settled, done [C] 妥当 **tuǒdàng** be proper [C]	惜	**XĪ**, to cherish; to stint; to feel sorry for [C] 爱惜 **aìxī** to cherish [D]
顽 頑	**WÁN**, be stupid; be stubborn; be poorly behaved [C]	媳	**XÍ**, daughter-in-law [C] 媳妇 **xífù** son's wife; daughter-in-law [C]
挽	**WĂN**, to pull; roll up [C] 挽救 **wǎnjiù** to save [C] 挽回 **wǎnhuí** to retrieve, redeem	瞎	**XIĀ**, be blind; to no purpose [C] 瞎话 **xiāhuà** a lie 瞎子 **xiāzi** blind person
枉	**WĂNG**, to bend, be bent; to wrong a person; in vain [C] 枉然 **wǎngrán** be futile	虾 蝦	**XIĀ**, shrimp [C] 对虾 **duìxiā** prawn 龙虾 **lóngxiā** lobster
威	**WĒI**, awesome strength; by force [C] 威胁 **wēixié** to threaten [C] 威尼斯 **Wēinísī** Venice	削	**XIĀO**, to pare; **XUĒ**, to pare, whittle [C] 剥削 **bōxuē** to "peel and pare," i.e., to exploit [C]

协	**XIÉ**, be joint; to assist [C] 协作 **xiézuò** cooperate [C] 协助 **xiézhù** to help [C] 協
卸	**XIÈ**, to unload; to remove; to shirk [C] 卸货 **xièhuò** unload cargo 卸任 **xièrén** get fired
鸭	**YĀ**, duck [C] 鸭子 **yāzi** duck [C] 母鸭 **mǔyā** female duck 公鸭 **gōngyā** drake 鴨
岩	**YÁN**, rock; cliff [C] 岩石 **yánshí** rock [C] 岩洞 **yándòng** grotto
钥	**YÀO**, see 钥匙 below; **YUÈ**, key [C] 钥匙 **yàoshi** key [C] 鑰
遗	**YÍ**, to lose; a lost thing; to omit; to bequeath [C] 遗留 **yíliú** hand down [C] 遺
饮	**YǏN**, to drink; to nurse (a grievance); **YÌN**, give (an animal) to drink [C] 飲
犹	**YÓU**, be just like; still [C] 犹豫 **yóuyù** to hesitate [C] 犹豫犹豫 **yóuyùyóuyù** dither 猶
幼	**YÒU**, be young; children [C] 幼稚 **yòuzhì** be childish [C]
娱	**YÚ**, to amuse; amusement, pleasure [C] 娱乐 **yúlè** entertainment, recreation [C]
域	**YÙ**, territory, region [C]
浴	**YÙ**, to bathe; bath [C] 浴室 **yùshì** bathroom [C] 淋浴 **línyù** shower (bath)
寓	**YÙ**, to reside; residence; to contain [C] 寓言 **yùyán** allegory, parable [C]
冤	**YUĀN**, injustice; resentment, grievance; loss [C] 冤枉 **yuānwang** to wrong; to be not worthwhile [C]
缘	**YUÁN**, reason; fringe; along [C] 缘故 **yuángù** cause [C] 緣
怨	**YUÀN**, resentment; to blame [C] 怨恨 **yuànhèn** to hate; enmity
晕	**YŪN**, be dizzy; to faint; **YÙN**, be dizzy; halo [C] 晕车 **yùnchē** carsickness 暈
赠	**ZÈNG**, to give as a present [C] 赠送 **zèngsòng** to give as a present [C] 贈
渣	**ZHĀ**, dregs; sediment; broken bits (as, crumbs) [C]
帐	**ZHÀNG**, curtain, canopy; account, account book [C] 帳
胀	**ZHÀNG**, to expand; bloated [C] 膨胀 **péngzhàng** to swell up, distend [C] 脹
罩	**ZHÀO**, to cover; a cover; a bamboo fish-trap [C]

REMAINING CHARACTERS

遮	**ZHĒ**, to cover, hide from view; to obstruct; to keep out [C] 遮瞒 **zhēmán** to conceal, hide [C]	刘	**LIÚ**, a family name [C supplement] 劉
枕	**ZHĚN**, a pillow; to rest one's head on; (engineering) block [C]	吴	**WÚ**, family name; (historical) name of an ancient kingdom in China [C supplement] 吳
蒸	**ZHĒNG**, to evaporate; to steam [C]	陕	**SHǍN**, Shaanxi Province (陕西... **Shǎnxī**) [C supplement] 陝
粥	**ZHŌU**, congee; gruel (of rice, millet, etc.) [C]	宋	**SÒNG**, family name; name of one major (960–1279) dynasty and one minor (420–479) dynasty [C supplement]
皱	**ZHÒU**, wrinkles [C] 皺	孟	**MÈNG**, family name; first month (of a season); elder (brother) [C supplement] 孟子 **Mèngzi** Mencius
株	**ZHŪ**, tree trunk; plant stem; tree, plant; a measure for trees [C]	欧	**ŌU**, family name; short for Europe [C supplement] 歐
铸	**ZHÙ**, casting [C] 鑄	葛	**GÉ**, (botany) *kudzu*; **GĚ**, family name [C supplement]
桩	**ZHUĀNG**, stake; a measure for matters [C] 樁	沈	**SHĚN**, a family name; short for Shenyang Province (沈阳 **Shěnyáng**) [C supplement]
纵	**ZÒNG**, be vertical; north to south; to set free; let yourself go; jump into the air [C] 縱	浙	**ZHÈ**, short for Zhejiang Province (浙江... **Zhéjiāng** [C supplement] 淛
罪	**ZUÌ**, crime; guilt; fault; suffering; to blame [C]		**yúlèi** 余类, the 227th category in *Han-Ying Cidian*, "leftovers:" following characters.
赵	**ZHÀO**, a family name [C supplement] 趙	○	**LÍNG**, zero. (Same as 零; usually used for numerals.) 五○九号 **wǔlíngjiǔhaò** No. 509

屯	TÚN, to collect; to station (troops); village [D]	叛	PÀN, to rebel [D]* 叛卖 **pànmài** to betray
凸	TŪ, to protrude, stick up [D] 凸面 **tūmiàn** be convex	末	MÒ, last part; end; dust 末尾 **mòwěi** the end
凹	ĀO, be concave [D] 凹凸不平 **āotūbùpíng** be full of holes and bumps		

*Also in the *Han-Ying Cidian* category of 余类 **yúlèi**, "leftovers," are five characters which the student has already learned: 东 **dōng** "east" (210), 巴 **bā** "the open hand" (302), 乡 **xiāng** "country" (462), 民 **mín** "folk" (715), and 举 **jǔ** "to lift" (1017).

Alphabetical Index

The alphabetical index includes all of the characters presented in this book and includes elements or parts of characters which are listed with a pronunciation. All of the radicals, including radicals which do not function as independent characters and have no pronunciation, are listed in the chart of 226 radicals (front endpapers). Indexed characters are listed according to their pronunciation in the Hanyu Pinyin system of romanization. A character with two or more pronunciations will be listed under each pronunciation (except where the only difference is a difference of tone). If a character is in Part 1 of the book, that character's series number (1-1,067) is given in roman type. If a character is also a radical, its number in the sequence of 226 radicals is given in superscript. Reference to characters in Part 2 of the book is by page number (pp. 215–73) set in italic type, followed by the letter a or b to indicate whether the character appears on the left (a) or right (b) side of the page.

A

ā	阿	107
ā	啊	108
āi	哎	p250a
āi	哀	p253b
āi/ái	挨	p231a
āi/ài	唉	p231a
ái	癌	p253b
ǎi	矮	84
ài	爱	449
ài	碍	p254a
ān	安	834
àn	岸	230
àn	按	835
àn	案	836
àn	暗	p229a
āo	凹	p273a
áo	熬	p254a
ào	傲	p231b

B

bā	八	124²⁴
bā	巴	302
bā	叭	p254a
bā	扒	p254a
bá	拔	p229a
bǎ/bà	把	304
bà	坝	p254a
bà	爸	305

bà	罢	p227a
ba/bā	吧	303
bái	白	282¹⁵⁰
bǎi	百	575
bǎi	柏	p254a
bǎi	摆	p227a
bài	败	p229a
bài	拜	592
bān	班	p228b
bān	般	p226b
bān	搬	p226b
bǎn	板	421
bǎn	版	423
bàn	办	648
bàn	半	378
bàn	扮	142
bàn	伴	p240b
bàn	瓣	p254a
bāng	邦	632
bāng	帮	633
bǎng	绑	634
bǎng	榜	877
bǎng	膀	878
bàng	傍	876
bàng	棒	p223b
bàng	磅	879
bāo	勹	283²⁶
bāo	包	286
bāo	胞	289
bāo	剥	p254b

báo	薄	p230b
bǎo	饱	294
bǎo	宝	p230b
bǎo	保	884
bào	报	113
bào	抱	288
bào	暴	p254a
bào	爆	p254b
bēi	杯	p227a
bēi	悲	p222b
bēi	碑	p231b
běi	北	666
bèi	贝	140¹⁰⁶
bèi	备	777
bèi/bēi	背	667
bèi	倍	845
bèi	被	1024
bèi	辈	p222b
bēn/bèn	奔	p254b
běn	本	308
bèn	笨	p231a
béng	甭	p254b
bī	逼	p231b
bí	鼻	p231b²²⁶
bǐ	匕	41³⁹
bǐ	比	660¹²³
bǐ	彼	p265b
bǐ	笔	115
bì	币	p230b
bì	必	607

274

guǎn	馆	533	hǎo/hào	好	45	hǔ	虎	p216b
guǎn	管	832	hào	号	773	hù	户	504[86]
guàn	惯	p218a	hào	耗	p267a	hù	互	p227a
guàn	灌	p234b	hē	呵	p257a	hù	护	938
guàn	罐	p234b	hē/hè	喝	501	huā	花	787
guāng	光	839	hé	禾	81[149]	huá/huà	华	788
guǎng	广	363[44]	hé	合	219	huá/huā	哗	789
guàng	逛	p251a	hé	何	913	huá	滑	p247b
guī	归	p266b	hé	河	652	huá	猾	p247b
guī	圭	544.	hé	和	785	huà	化	786
guī	规	889	hé	曷	500	huà/huá	划	p217a
guǐ	轨	p266b	hé	阂	p257a	huà	画	280
guǐ	鬼	385[216]	hé	核	p257a	huà	话	427
guì	柜	p256b	hé	盒	p251a	huái	怀	p267a
guì	贵	163	hè	吓	p249a	huài	坏	651
guì	跪	p251a	hè	贺	p233a	huān	欢	245
gǔn	滚	p248a	hēi	黑	357[223]	huán	环	p234a
gùn	棍	p237a	hēi	嘿	p251a	huǎn	缓	p218b
guō	锅	p251a	hén	痕	p257a	huàn	幻	p257b
guó	国	155	hěn	很	52	huàn	唤	1051
guǒ	果	690	hěn	狠	p257a	huàn	换	1052
guǒ	裹	p257a	hèn	恨	p237a	huàn	患	p255b
guò	过	618	hēng	哼	p251a	huāng	荒	p222b
			héng	衡	p257a	huāng	慌	p222b
H			hng	哼	p251a	huáng	皇	p234b
hā	哈	p223a	hóng	红	780	huáng	黄	699
hāi	咳	333	hóng	宏	p257a	huáng	煌	p257b
hái/huán	还	568	hóng	洪	391	huàng/huǎng	晃	p257b
hái	孩	332	hóu	喉	p241b	huī	灰	p238a
hǎi	海	697	hóu	猴	p241b	huī	恢	p238a
hài	亥	331	hǒu	吼	p267a	huī	挥	p229a
hài	害	p215b	hòu	后	402	huī	辉	p251a
hán	含	p240a	hòu	厚	849	huí	回	550
hán	寒	p225a	hòu	候	574	huǐ	悔	p236a
hǎn	喊	978	hū	乎	p244b	huǐ	毁	p267a
hàn	汉	p223b	hū	忽	987	huì	汇	p267a
hàn	汗	224	hū	呼	p244b	huì	会	441
hàn	旱	231	hū/hú/hù	糊	p251a	huì	慧	p257b
hàn	焊	p257a	hú	和	785	hūn	昏	865
hàn	憾	p257a	hú	胡	711	hūn	婚	866
háng	行	543	hú	壶	p236b	hún	浑	p257b
háng	航	1042	hú	湖	712	hún/hùn	混	p237a
háo	毫	p246a	hú	蝴	p257a	hún	魂	p267a
háo	豪	p266b	hǔ	唬	772[173]	huó	活	748

jiè	借	887	jiù	救	838	kǎo	考	1029
jīn	巾	464[57]	jiù	就	397	kǎo	烤	p251b
jīn	斤	342[115]	jiù	舅	p267a	kào	靠	932
jīn	今	496	jū	居	754	kē	科	p216a
jīn	钅	117[147]	jú	局	991	kē	棵	692
jīn	金	218[209]	jú	桔	241	kē	颗	p249a
jīn	筋	p267a	jú	橘	p226a	ké	壳	p258b
jǐn	仅	p236b	jǔ	举	1017	ké	咳	333
jǐn	紧	599	jǔ	矩	p239a	kě	可	106
jǐn	谨	p258b	jǔ	巨	p238b	kě	渴	p222a
jìn/jǐn	尽	p234a	jù	句	381	kè	克	p224a
jìn	进	594	jù	拒	p238b	kè	刻	614
jìn	近	677	jù	具	p239a	kè	客	433
jìn	劲	p241b	jù	剧	755	kè	课	691
jìn	浸	p237a	jù	俱	p239a	kěn	肯	1005
jìn/jīn	禁	p247b	jù	据	756	kěn	恳	p241b
jīng	京	395	jù	距	p238b	kēng	坑	p235a
jīng	经	567	jù	聚	p267a	kōng/kòng	空	992
jīng	惊	p229a	juān/juàn	圈	p232b	kǒng	孔	p238a
jīng	睛	254	juǎn	关	p232b[158]	kǒng	恐	769
jīng	精	927	juàn	卷	p232b	kòng	控	p251b
jīng	鲸	p258b	juàn	倦	p232b	kǒu	口	53[58]
jǐng	井	590	juàn	绢	p251b	kòu	扣	p243b
jǐng	景	396	juē	夬	383	kū	枯	321
jǐng	警	1062	jué	决	881	kū	哭	639
jìng	劲	p241b	jué	角	996[201]	kū	窟	p258b
jìng	净	710	jué	觉	649	kǔ	苦	320
jìng	径	p258b	jué	绝	p227b	kù	库	p259a
jìng	竞	p232a	jūn	军	p216b	kù	裤	p248b
jìng	竟	p232b	jūn	均	p236a	kù	酷	p258b
jìng	敬	1061	jùn/jūn	菌	p247b	kuā	夸	p241b
jìng	静	1067				kuǎ	垮	p241b
jìng	境	p232b	**K**			kuà	跨	p241b
jìng	镜	p232b	kā	咖	873	kuài	会	441
jiōng	冂	8[19]	kǎ	卡	p217b	kuài	块	384
jiū	纠	p245a	kāi	开	612	kuài	快	583
jiū	究	857	kān	刊	233	kuài	筷	p248a
jiū	揪	p258b	kǎn	凵	579[38]	kuān	宽	950
jiǔ	九	203	kǎn	砍	p245a	kuǎn	款	p239b
jiǔ	久	721	kàn/kān	看	161	kuāng	筐	p267b
jiǔ	灸	p258b	kāng	康	p223a	kuáng	狂	p267b
jiǔ	酒	475	káng	扛	p251b	kuàng	况	p220a
jiù	旧	468	kàng	亢	1041	kuàng	矿	p236a
jiù	臼	281[179]	kàng	抗	p235a	kuī	亏	p259a

lǔ	旅	1043	máo	毛	114[112]	miào	庙	p233b
lǚ	铝	p260a	máo	矛	p226a[155]	miè	灭	p229a
lù	律	p236b	máo	茅	p260b	miè	蔑	p260b
lù	虑	p241a	mào	冒	465	mín	民	715
lù	绿	p215b	mào	贸	p247b	mǐn	皿	138[146]
lù	率	p242b	mào	帽	466	mǐn	黾	p239b[207]
luǎn	卵	p267b	mào	貌	p252a	mǐn	敏	p260b
luàn	乱	920	me	么	206	míng	名	337
lüè	略	p237a	méi	没	235	míng	明	494
lüè	掠	p260a	méi	眉	p268a	míng	鸣	p268a
lún	轮	p248b	méi	梅	p267b	mìng	命	894
lùn/lún	论	840	méi	煤	p235b	mō	摸	941
luó	罗	p260a	méi	霉	p260b	mó	模	940
luó	萝	p252a	měi	每	684	mó	摩	p226b
luó	逻	p260a	měi	美	157	mó	磨	p226a
luó	锣	p260a	mèi	妹	275	mǒ	抹	p268a
luò	络	p267b	mēn/mèn	闷	p268a	mò	末	p273b
luò	骆	p262b	mén	门	25[46]	mò	没	235
luò	落	p218a	mén	们	26	mò	陌	p260b
			mēng/měng	蒙	p268a	mò	莫	939
M			méng	氓	p260b	mò	寞	943
			méng	盟	p268a	mò	漠	942
mā	妈	p219b	měng	猛	p268a	mò	墨	p240a
má	麻	p226a[221]	mèng	梦	p233a	mò	默	p252a
mǎ	马	55[75]	mèng	孟	p272b	móu	谋	p236a
mǎ	码	p220a	mī	秘	p228b	mǒu	某	p235b
mà	骂	p220a	mī/mí	眯	130	mú	模	940
ma	吗	56	mí	迷	127	mǔ	母	268
ma	嘛	226a	mí	谜	128	mǔ	亩	p239a
mǎi	买	177	mǐ	米	126[159]	mù	木	80[94]
mái	埋	p245b	mì	一	36[18]	mù	目	129[141]
mài	迈	p252a	mì	泌	p228b	mù	牧	p268a
mài	麦	p246b[188]	mì	密	p228b	mù	墓	945
mài	卖	178	mì	蜜	p228b	mù	幕	946
mài	脉	p252a	mián	宀	40[45]	mù	慕	944
mǎn	满	995	mián	眠	p260b			
mán	馒	p252a	mián	棉	p247a	**N**		
mán	瞒	p260a	miǎn	免	564	ń/ň/ǹ	嗯	p226b
màn	慢	584	miǎn	勉	p268a	ná	拿	593
màn	漫	p260a	miàn	面	675	nǎ/na	哪	p224b
máng	忙	86	miáo	苗	p240a	nà	那	217
máng	盲	p260b	miáo	描	p240a	nǎi	奶	p224b
máng	氓	p260b	miǎo	秒	p230a	nài	奈	p268a
māo	猫	p240a	miào	妙	p230a			

285

shù	束	745	sòu	嗽	334	táng	堂	723
shù	述	p229b	sú	俗	820	táng	糖	425
shù	树	746	sù	诉	344	tǎng	倘	481
shù/shǔ	数	681	sù	肃	p240a	tǎng	躺	479
shuā	刷	p238a	sù	素	p245b	tàng	烫	p215a
shuǎ	耍	p269b	sù	速	p246a	tàng	趟	480
shuāi	衰	p269b	sù	宿	p224b	tāo	掏	p253a
shuāi	摔	p243a	sù	塑	p253a	táo	逃	816
shuǎi	甩	p243a	sù	酸	p225a	táo	桃	p270a
shuài	率	p242b	suān	酸	p225a	táo	萄	p262b
shuān	拴	p269b	suàn	算	626	tǎo	讨	p220a
shuāng	双	p216b	suī	虽	732	tào	套	p246a
shuāng	霜	p242b	suí	随	843	tè	特	703
shuǐ	氵	77⁴⁰	suì	岁	609	téng	疼	p224b
shuí	谁	60	suì	碎	p232a	téng/tēng	腾	p233a
shuǐ	水	473¹²⁵	sūn	孙	p269b	tī	梯	p240b
shuì	说	313	sǔn	损	p236a	tī	踢	p225b
shuì	税	312	suō	嗦	p262b	tí/dī	提	1004
shuì	睡	636	suō	缩	p224b	tí	题	822
shùn	顺	p218b	suǒ	所	536	tí	蹄	p235a
shuō	说	313	suǒ	索	p245b	tǐ	体	898
shuò	烁	p262a	suǒ	锁	p269b	tì	惕	p262b
sī	厶	46³⁷				tì	替	896
sī	纟	48⁷⁷				tiān	天	63⁹⁰
sī	丝	750	**T**			tiān	添	p229a
sī	司	p218a	tā	他	24	tián	田	10¹⁴²
sī	私	p216a	tā	它	42	tián	甜	p247a
sī	思	461	tā	她	23	tián	填	p242b
sī	斯	p238a	tā	塌	p262b	tiāo/tiǎo	挑	815
sī	撕	p238a	tǎ	塔	p240b	tiáo	条	656
sǐ	死	821	tà/tā	踏	p269b	tiáo	调	p222b
sì	巳	299	tái	台	955	tiào	跳	814
sì	四	199	tái	抬	956	tiē	贴	366
sì/shì	似	p227b	tài	太	98	tiě	铁	954
sì	伺	p262a	tài	态	p222a	tīng	厅	p228a
sì	饲	p262a	tān	滩	p262b	tīng	听	495
sōng	松	p244b	tān	摊	p270a	tíng	亭	841
sòng	宋	p272b	tán	谈	758	tíng	庭	p224a
sòng	诉	344	tán	弹	p236b	tíng	停	842
sòng	送	595	tǎn	坦	p270a	tǐng	挺	p224a
sòng	诵	p262b	tǎn	毯	p240b	tōng	通	802
sòng	颂	p262a	tàn	叹	p270a	tóng	同	860
sōu	搜	p243a	tàn	探	p224a	tóng	铜	861
sōu	艘	p243a	tāng	汤	p215a	tóng	童	149
			táng	唐	424			

xì	系	951	xiǎo	小	37[79]	xū	须	p218b
xì	细	915	xiǎo	晓	p216a	xū	虚	p246b
xiā	虾	p270b	xiào	孝	498	xū	需	1059
xiā	瞎	p270b	xiào	笑	66	xū	墟	p263a
xiá	峡	p242a	xiào	校	521	xǔ	许	688
xià	下	463	xiào	效	525	xù	序	p236b
xià	吓	p249a	xiē	些	349	xù	叙	p246b
xià	夏	1007	xiē	歇	p248a	xù	绪	188
xiān	先	328	xié	协	p271a	xù	续	p219a
xiān	纤	p253a	xié	胁	p263a	xuān	宣	p237a
xiān	掀	p242a	xié	斜	p246b	xuán	旋	p245a
xiān/xiǎn	鲜	p249a	xié	鞋	1054	xuán	悬	p263a
xián	闲	258	xiě	写	460	xuǎn	选	864
xián	咸	977	xiè	卸	p271a	xuē	削	p270b
xián	嫌	p239a	xiè	械	p242a	xué	穴	454[128]
xiǎn	险	848	xiè	谢	239	xué	学	335
xiǎn	显	p232b	xīn	忄	19[41]	xuě	雪	p215a
xiàn	县	952	xīn	心	87[81]	xuè	血	1010[181]
xiàn	现	410	xīn	辛	70[186]	xún	寻	p247a
xiàn	线	989	xīn	欣	p242a	xún	旬	p263b
xiàn	限	1003	xīn	新	467	xún	询	p263b
xiàn	宪	p263a	xìn	信	597	xún	循	p263b
xiàn	陷	p263a	xīng	星	1014	xùn	训	p218b
xiàn	羡	p253a	xíng	行	543	xùn	讯	p245b
xiàn	献	p238b	xíng	形	981	xùn	迅	p253a
xiāng	乡	462	xíng	型	p242a			
xiāng/xiàng	相	368	xǐng	醒	p232a	**Y**		
xiāng	香	p217b[215]	xìng/xīng	兴	437			
xiāng	厢	p263a	xìng	幸	71	yā	压	p235a
xiāng	箱	p242a	xìng	姓	336	yā/ya	呀	672
xiáng	详	914	xìng	性	882	yā	押	p263b
xiáng	降	984	xiōng	凶	678	yā	鸭	p271a
xiǎng	享	p217b	xiōng	兄	310	yá	牙	671[99]
xiǎng	响	886	xiōng	胸	p246a	yá	芽	674
xiǎng	想	387	xióng	雄	p247a	yá	崖	p263a
xiàng	向	885	xióng	熊	p253a	yà	讶	673
xiàng	巷	392	xiū	休	793	yà	亚	p236b[168]
xiàng	项	p228a	xiū	修	947	yān	烟	1057
xiàng	象	733	xiǔ	朽	p263a	yān	淹	p263b
xiàng	像	734	xiǔ	宿	p224b	yān/yàn	燕	p263b
xiāo	削	p270b	xiù	秀	p233b	yán	讠	58[10]
xiāo	消	1027	xiù	绣	p234a	yán	延	p244b
xiāo	宵	p263a	xiù	袖	p237b	yán	言	57[185]
xiáo	淆	p263a	xiù	锈	p234a	yán	严	p236b

yǔ/yú	予	775	yǔn	允	971	zhān/zhàn	占	358
yǔ	羽	869 [183]	yùn	运	93	zhān	沾	362
yǔ	屿	p264b				zhān	粘	360
yǔ	宇	p264b	**Z**			zhǎn	斩	718
yǔ	雨	368 [204]	zā	扎	p253b	zhǎn	展	895
yǔ	语	958	zá	杂	1000	zhǎn	盏	p265a
yù	玉	74 [131]	zá	砸	p264b	zhǎn	崭	p265a
yù	育	p222a	zāi	灾	p237b	zhàn	战	361
yù	狱	p264b	zái	栽	p265b	zhàn	站	359
yù	预	776	zǎi	仔	p253b	zhāng	张	279
yù	浴	p271b	zǎi/zài	载	p265b	zhāng	章	p218a
yù	域	p271a	zài	在	411	zhǎng	长	278
yù	遇	p219b	zài	再	585	zhǎng/zhàng	涨	p248a
yù	裕	p264b	zán	咱	p224b	zhǎng	掌	484
yù	御	p264b	zàn	暂	719	zhàng	丈	p236a
yù	寓	p271b	zàn	赞	p233a	zhàng	仗	p236a
yù/yú	愈	p225a	zàng/zāng	脏	p223b	zhàng	帐	p271a
yù	豫	p264b	zàng	藏	p230a	zhàng	胀	p271b
yuān	冤	p271b	zāo	遭	p243a	zhàng	障	p265a
yuán	元	89	zāo	糟	p243a	zhāo	招	p233b
yuán	员	825	záo	凿	p265a	zhāo	朝	p227a
yuán	园	96	zǎo	早	563	zháo	着	586
yuán	原	443	zǎo	澡	p224a	zhǎo	爪	306 [116]
yuán	圆	826	zào	皂	p244b	zhǎo	找	32
yuán	援	p218b	zào	造	743	zhào	召	830
yuán	缘	p271b	zào	燥	p224b	zhào	兆	813
yuán	源	p237b	zào	躁	p224b	zhào	赵	p272a
yuán	猿	p264b	zé	则	p229b	zhào	照	985
yuǎn	远	91	zé	责	p219a	zhào	罩	p271b
yuàn	院	95	zé	泽	p220b	zhē	遮	p272a
yuàn	怨	p271b	zé	择	p220b	zhé/zhē	折	p231a
yuàn	愿	444	zěn	怎	548	zhé	哲	p253b
yuē	曰	110 [104]	zēng	曾	439	zhě	者	182
yuē	约	1065	zēng	增	p219b	zhè	这	216
yuè	月	104 [118]	zèng	赠	p271b	zhè	浙	p272b
yuè/lè	乐	988	zhā	渣	p271b	zhe	着	587
yuè	钥	p271a	zhá/zhā	扎	p253b	zhèi	这	216
yuè	阅	p248b	zhà	乍	451	zhēn	针	p233b
yuè	悦	p264b	zhà	炸	453	zhēn	珍	p239a
yuè	跃	p253b	zhāi	摘	p235a	zhēn	真	404
yuè	越	736	zhái	宅	p265a	zhěn	诊	p239a
yūn/yùn	晕	p271b	zhái	择	p220b	zhěn	枕	p272a
yún	云	92	zhǎi	窄	455	zhèn	阵	p228b
yún	匀	p236a	zhài	债	p219a	zhèn	振	853

Stroke Index

This second index of characters is arranged by stroke count (the number of strokes in a character). The student therefore can find, for reference or review, a character in this book whose pronunciation he or she does not know or is unsure of. This index has been organized by stroke count rather than by radicals because mastery of the radical system requires considerable time and is one of the aims of this book, not a skill assumed of its users, whereas the stroke-count system can by used by a student almost immediately.

In order to use the index, you need simply to count the number of strokes in the character and then go to the group of characters in the index having that number of strokes. As you learn new characters and how to write them from the diagrams, the ability to count correctly the number of strokes and to use the little tricks familiar to every first-year student of Chinese will come naturally. (For example, the shape 乙 is counted as one stroke rather than two.) This index begins with characters of one stroke and concludes with a character having twenty-three strokes. Within each group of characters having the same number of strokes, characters are arranged alphabetically by the Hanyu Pinyin romanization of the pronunciation. The system of reference to characters and page numbers is explained in the introduction to the alphabetical index.

圣	shèng	p262a		乐	yuè/lè	988		导	dǎo	p222b

至	zhì	514[171]	词	cí	p224a	何	hé	913
众	zhòng	p234b	囱	cōng	1058	宏	hóng	p257a
舟	zhōu	538[182]	村	cūn	p220a	吼	hǒu	p267a
朱	zhū	p237b	呆	dāi	883	护	hù	938
竹	zhú	65[178]	但	dàn	560	花	huā	787
庄	zhuāng	p239b	岛	dǎo	p238a	怀	huái	p267a
壮	zhuàng	p217b	低	dī	983	坏	huài	651
字	zì	338	弟	dì	272	鸡	jī	p217a
自	zì	619[180]	盯	dīng	p228b	极	jí	662
戈		470[165]	钉	dīng	p228a	即	jí	p244a
			冻	dòng	p245b	技	jì	353

7 strokes

阿	ā	107	豆	dòu	797[191]	际	jì	p236b
把	bǎ/bà	304	抖	dǒu	p244a	坚	jiān	p225a
坝	bà	p254a	肚	dù/dǔ	p241a	歼	jiān	p257b
吧	ba/bā	303	兑	duì	311	间	jiàn/jiān	259
扮	bàn	142	吨	dūn	p250b	角	jiǎo/jué	996[201]
伴	bàn	p240b	返	fǎn	420	进	jìn	594
报	bào	113	泛	fàn	p250b	近	jìn	677
别	bié	261	饭	fàn	419	劲	jìn/jìng	p241b
兵	bīng	p229b	妨	fáng	511	究	jiū	857
伯	bó	p223a	纺	fǎng	508	灸	jiǔ	p258b
步	bù	753	吩	fēn	136	局	jú	991
补	bǔ	p230a	纷	fēn	135	拒	jù	p238b
财	cái	p229a	坟	fén/fèn	p256b	均	jūn	p236a
材	cái	p229a	佛	fó/fú	961	抗	kàng	p235a
灿	càn	p254b	否	fǒu	p244a	壳	ké/qiào	p258b
苍	cāng	p231b	扶	fú	p244a	克	kè	p224a
层	céng	p219b	甫	fǔ	530	坑	kēng	p235a
肠	cháng	p215a	附	fù	905	库	kù	p259a
抄	chāo	p230a	改	gǎi	827	块	kuài	384
吵	chǎo	p230a	肝	gān	225	快	kuài	583
扯	chě	p255a	杆	gān/gǎn	226	狂	kuáng	p267b
彻	chè	p242b	纲	gāng	123	况	kuàng	p220a
陈	chén	p266a	岗	gǎng	122	困	kùn	994
辰	chén	851[187]	告	gào	341	来	lái	555
沉	chén	p244a	更	gèng/gēng	164	劳	láo	p221a
迟	chí	p227a	攻	gōng	p228a	牢	láo	p267b
赤	chì	p216b[190]	贡	gòng	p228a	冷	lěng	1008
初	chū	p218b	沟	gōu	p241a	李	lǐ	330
串	chuàn	p255a	估	gū	318	里	lǐ	145[195]
床	chuáng	p218a	谷	gǔ	489[199]	励	lì	p252a
吹	chuī	p219a	还	hái/huán	568	利	lì	1025
纯	chún	p266a	含	hán	p240a	丽	lì	p233b
			旱	hàn	231	连	lián	701

谅	liàng	p225a	扇	shàn	p245b	效	xiào	525
料	liào	p216a	烧	shāo	p216a	胸	xiōng	p246a
烈	liè	p228b	哨	shào	p262a	绣	xiù	p234a
铃	líng	373	射	shè	238	袖	xiù	p237b
陵	líng	p259b	涉	shè	p269a	鸭	yā	p271a
留	liú	829	谁	shéi/shuí	60	烟	yān	1057
流	liú	p222a	逝	shì	p262a	盐	yán	p220a
旅	lǚ	1043	殊	shū	p253a	验	yàn	p221b
虑	lǜ	p241a	衰	shuāi	p269b	宴	yàn	p226b
埋	mái	p245b	颂	sòng	p262a	艳	yàn	p263b
秘	mī/bì	p228b	素	sù	p245b	秧	yāng	p243a
眠	mián	p260b	速	sù	p246a	氧	yǎng	p263b
莫	mò	939	损	sǔn	p236a	样	yàng	655
拿	ná	593	索	suǒ	p245b	倚	yǐ	p264a
难	nán/nàn	488	谈	tán	758	谊	yì	1009
脑	nǎo	p232a	唐	táng	424	益	yì	p234b
能	néng	438	倘	tǎng	481	涌	yǒng	p264a
娘	niáng	p222a	烫	tàng	p215a	娱	yú	p271a
捏	niē	p268b	桃	táo	p270a	预	yù	776
哦	ó/ò	p261a	套	tào	p246a	浴	yù	p271b
畔	pàn	p240b	特	tè	703	冤	yuān	p271b
旁	páng	875	疼	téng	p224b	原	yuán	443
袍	páo	291	铁	tiě	954	圆	yuán	826
陪	péi	p230b	通	tōng	802	阅	yuè	p248b
配	pèi	p238b	透	tòu	p234a	悦	yuè	p264b
疲	pí	p227b	途	tú	p233a	晕	yūn/yùn	p271b
瓶	píng	740	涂	tú	p247b	砸	zá	p264b
破	pò	p218b	徒	tú	p270a	栽	zái	p265b
剖	pōu	p261a	袜	wà	p225b	载	zǎi/zài	p265b
起	qǐ	557	顽	wán	p270a	脏	zàng/zāng	p223b
铅	qiān	125	挽	wǎn	p270a	造	zào	743
钱	qián	212	蚊	wén	p270b	窄	zhǎi	455
桥	qiáo	p224a	翁	wēng	p270b	债	zhài	p219a
悄	qiǎo/qiāo	p252b	悟	wù	p245b	展	zhǎn	895
倾	qīng	p261b	息	xī	794	盏	zhǎn	p265a
请	qǐng	250	牺	xī	p249b	站	zhàn	359
拳	quán	p232b	席	xí	p249b	涨	zhǎng/zhàng	p248a
缺	quē	p237a	夏	xià	1007	哲	zhé	p253b
热	rè	764	陷	xiàn	p263a	浙	zhè	p272b
容	róng	490	消	xiāo	1027	真	zhēn	404
辱	rǔ	p269a	宵	xiāo	p263a	振	zhèn	853
弱	ruò	p233a	晓	xiǎo	p216a	症	zhèng/zhēng	606
润	rùn	p269a	笑	xiào	66	值	zhí	405
晒	shài	p249b	校	xiào/jiào	521	致	zhì	p228a

The Chart of Traditional Radicals

This chart gives the number of each traditional radical, its independent form, its English name, and the location in the text of its independent form (the first reference number) and any alternate or combining forms treated separately (the second reference number). Numbers in roman type refer to radicals included in the first character group of 1,067 basic characters. Page numbers in italic type refer to radicals in the second character group (pp. 215–273); *a* means "left column," *b* means "right column" on the pages. A dash (–) means that the radical is not represented as a separate item in this edition. A chart of "modern radicals," based on the 漢英詞典, appears as the front endpapers.

		— 1 —		33.	士	knight 35		68.	斗	peck 765
1.	一	one 1		34.	夂	follow 431		69.	斤	axe 342
2.	丨	down 13		35.	夊	slow 431		70.	方	square 505
3.	丶	dot 73		36.	夕	dusk 158		71.	无	lack 69
4.	丿	left 2		37.	大	big 61		72.	日	sun 179
5.	乙	twist 15		38.	女	woman 3		73.	曰	say 110
6.	亅	hook –		39.	子	child 44		74.	月	moon 104
				40.	宀	roof 40		75.	木	tree 80
		— 2 —		41.	寸	thumb 237		76.	欠	yawn 244
7.	二	two 5		42.	小	small 37		77.	止	toe 246
8.	亠	lid 33		43.	尢	lame 68		78.	歹	chip 408
9.	人	man 4, 14		44.	尸	corpse 440		79.	殳	club 234
10.	儿	legs 67		45.	屮	sprout 580		80.	毋	don't 265
11.	入	enter 204		46.	山	mountain 118		81.	比	compare 660
12.	八	eight 124		47.	川	river *p.216b*		82.	毛	fur 114
13.	冂	borders 8		48.	工	work 566		83.	氏	clan 276
14.	冖	crown 36		49.	己	self 297		84.	气	breath 64
15.	冫	ice 657		50.	巾	cloth 464		85.	水	water 473, 77
16.	几	table 541		51.	干	shield 223		86.	火	fire 295, 54
17.	凵	bowl 579		52.	幺	coil 47		87.	爪	claws 306, 447
18.	刀	knife 131		53.	广	lean-to 363		88.	父	father 264
19.	力	strength 11		54.	廴	march 933		89.	爻	crisscross –
20.	勹	wrap 283		55.	廾	clasp 193		90.	爿	bed 1033
21.	匕	ladle 41		56.	弋	dart 29		91.	片	slice 422
22.	匚	basket 197		57.	弓	bow 270		92.	牙	tooth 671
23.	匸	box –		58.	彐	pig's head *p.215b*		93.	牛	cow 340
24.	十	ten 7		59.	彡	streaks 909		94.	犬	dog 183
25.	卜	divine 159		60.	彳	step 50				
26.	卩	seal 112								**— 5 —**
27.	厂	slope 229				**— 4 —**		95.	玄	dark *p.248*
28.	厶	cocoon 46		61.	心	heart 19, 87		96.	玉	jade 74
29.	又	right hand 101		62.	戈	lance 30		97.	瓜	melon *p.243b*
				63.	戶	door 504		98.	瓦	tile 739
		— 3 —		64.	手	hand 27, 28		99.	甘	sweet 195
30.	口	mouth 53		65.	支	branch 351		100.	生	birth 329
31.	囗	surround 9		66.	攴	knock 316		101.	用	use 529
32.	土	earth 34		67.	文	pattern 215		102.	田	field 10